Touring Vermont's Scenic Roads

A Comprehensive Guide

Ken Aiken

Down East Books / Camden, Maine

To my father, for all the day trips of my youth

Copyright © 1999 by Kenneth J. Aiken
ISBN 0-89272-444-7
Design by Faith Hague, Watermark Design
Cover photograph by Alan Graham
Maps by Lynda Mills
Printed at Bookcrafters, Inc.

5 4 3 2 1

Down East Books / Rockport, Maine
Orders: 1-800-766-1670

LIBRARY OF CONGRESS CATALOGING-IN-PUBLICATION DATA

Aiken, Kenneth, 1952–
Touring Vermont's Scenic Roads: a comprehensive guide /
Kenneth Aiken
p. cm.
Includes index.
ISBN 0-89272-444-7 (pbk.)
1. Vermont—Tours. 2. Automobile travel—Vermont—
Guidebooks. 3. Scenic byways—Vermont—Guidebooks. I. Title.
F47.3.A39   1998
917.4304'43—dc21   98-29364
                                                CIP

Contents

Preface

Not that many people want to travel Route 100 from Massachusetts to Canada, or Route 4 from White River Junction across the state to Fair Haven—this isn't the normal travel pattern for tourists or for locals. Some of the routes in this book are broken into sections because they are rarely traveled end to end, but rather used in combination with other roads to go from one region to another. To go from Montpelier to Rutland, a Vermonter might choose I-89 or Route 14 to Route 107; Route 107 to Route 100 to Killington; and finally Route 4 over Mendon Mountain. This book offers the roads of Vermont in a manner that allows you to consider what combination of routes you'd like to take to arrive at your destination or to see particular sites.

Some people tour Vermont as part of a vacation to Canada or New England. For those who don't wish to speed through the state on one of the interstate highways, keep in mind that the roads you choose for the limited number of hours of traveling will be what you remember of Vermont. For others, touring will be limited to day trips from the town in which they are visiting. Different people have dif-

The Cornish bridge in Windsor is the longest double-span covered bridge in the world.

ferent interests. A sport-touring motorcyclist wants twisting roads climbing through gulfs and over mountain ridges; someone in a thirty-foot RV doesn't. One person wants to stop at every antiques shop or tourist attraction in town; another wants to drive through shaded woods and rolling farmland. This book tells you what a map doesn't—what a particular road is like and what's on it.

The numerous guides published about Vermont seem stamped from a similar mold—though some are better than others—assuming what the visitor wants to see and that all visitors want to see the same thing. All of these guides create a sense of destination but not of exploration. The Grafton Inn, for example, is a historical building often photographed for illustrated magazines and guidebooks. A few miles away on Route 121 in Cambridgeport, the stone ruin of a mill conveys as much history about the area as the inn. How often is the old mill passed by because the focus is on arriving in Grafton? How many miss the wonderful photographic possibilities of this stone structure while using up an entire roll of film in the next village? There's much to see in this beautiful state, and many places hold fascinating stories. It's these stories, the histories, the anecdotes that give a sense of what a place *is*. One of the goals of this guide is to convey a sense of Vermont that goes beyond the aesthetic to the essence of what the state is to those who live here.

Introduction

Why People Tour Vermont

Natives and visitors alike agree that the Green Mountain State feels different from her neighbors. Vermont's geological and political history have set this small state apart from the lands surrounding it. Idealized in the American consciousness as a place of great beauty where a person can "do his own thing," Vermont has an extraordinarily high percentage of its population engaged in creative endeavors.

One of the best states to explore, at least for five months of the year, Vermont is filled with twisting roads, beautiful scenery, and minimal traffic. Most highways have plenty of turnoffs, almost no offensive litter, and absolutely no billboards (it's the law). Vermont offers rustic farms, quaint villages, and historic sites; accommodations that range from lean-tos in state parks to world-class inns; and great food, one of its better-kept secrets.

Tourism is Vermont's second largest industry. Some quaint villages, like Grafton and Jamaica, are dependent upon tourists and idealized by public relations specialists. Others, like Stratton, Manchester, and Stowe, are exciting places to visit but don't have much in common with the rest of the state. Riding through Strafford, Montgomery Center, or Rochester, one comes to realize that the idealized Vermont does indeed exist, and it's difficult to imagine living in a more beautiful setting. There are also towns like Middlebury, Montpelier, and Brattleboro, for example, where the mix of native residents and transplants has created diverse and vital communities. Towns with this mix are probably the most interesting to visit and to plan overnight stops around.

Whatever the reason you come to Vermont, even if it's just to escape the hot city pavement and find some cool air, you will leave richer if you know what you've seen and where you've been. And for those of you who plan to spend part of your vacation in the Green Mountains, a little advance planning can make your Vermont trip a memorable experience.

Geology, Flora, Fauna, and Terrain

The geology of this land was determined 350 million years ago when the ancient continent of Africa, moving on its tectonic plate like a colossal bulldozer, pushed the primordial seabed onto the proto-North American continent. Miles high, the Green Mountains were formed the same way the Himalayas are presently forming—a fraction of an inch a year over a span of 100 million years. Still another great cataclysmic event sheared off the top of the southern Green Mountains and moved them miles westward, the vast geological pressure generating so much heat that it cooked thousands of feet of limestone into the marble of western Vermont. The continental plates began to move apart at the end of the great age of dinosaurs. Part of old Africa remained attached, and the resulting stretching of the planet's crust caused molten rock to rise from deep within the earth to form blisters under the skin of the earth's surface near the tear. Vermont's northern highlands, New Hampshire's White Mountains, and the plutons of igneous granite that made first Hardwick and now Barre the Granite Capital of the World are evidence that this event transpired 200 million years ago.

The mountains of Vermont have been worn down by millions of years of wind and water. Four times in recent geological history—the last three million years—ice sheets miles thick have sculpted the contours of the land, each one erasing evidence of its predecessor. The last glaciers of the Ice Age disappeared from the Green Mountains only ten thousand years ago, leaving land scraped to bedrock, deep gouges forming our northern lakes, and vast hills of sand and gravel. But the land was reborn and as recently as eight thousand years ago supported a growing native population.

"Verd mont" means green mountains, which is how Samuel Champlain described the prominent feature of this land in his journal in 1609. The first settlers who came to Vermont in the mid-1700s faced a trackless virgin forest of which it was said that a squirrel could travel from the Connecticut River to Lake Champlain without ever setting foot on the ground. By the 1850s, 75 percent of the state was deforested, and erosion from the denuded hills had fouled the streams and silted the dams upon which the water-powered mills and the economy of Vermont depended. In 1864 the modern environmental movement was born when George Perkins Marsh—a Vermonter, statesman, and U.S. diplomat—published his book *Man and Nature*. Now the reverse is true: 75 percent of the state is forested and its streams run clear again.

Today almost half a million acres, over 12 percent of the land in Vermont, are preserved in national or state forests and parks. Add to this an additional four million acres of privately owned forested land, and it becomes understandable why visitors find Vermont's air so much cleaner, fresher, and cooler than in urban areas. In the fall, when millions of acres of deciduous trees and shrubs transform their greenery into brilliant hues of fluorescent reds, oranges, yellows, mahoganies, russets, and golds, people come from all parts of the world to witness this natural phenomenon. Following the reforestation of Vermont and the establishment of natural habitats, many species of animals have migrated back or have been reintroduced to the state. Touring at dawn or dusk, one must beware of animals crossing the roads. Vermont is filled with creatures, not just dogs and cats and cows, but wild beasts—raccoons, porcupines, woodchucks, rabbits, beavers, foxes, coyotes, bear, deer, and dreaded moose—all of which like to come out of the woods after the sun goes down.

Animals are part of the charm of Vermont, and I've had numerous encounters that have enriched my rides on otherwise familiar highways. Deer, fox, beaver, woodchuck, raccoon, skunk, and rabbit are prevalent almost anywhere in the state, but certain animals are more likely to be found in one type of habitat than in another. In the northeastern part of the state, colloquially known as the Northeast Kingdom, the flat, boggy terrain with dense softwood forests is home to the greatest number of moose, often spotted along Route 2 between Montpelier and Burlington and especially along Route 12 from Montpelier to Morrisville. I've only seen one black bear, on Route 100 just south of Warren, but the black bear population thrives along Route 232 through Groton State Forest, Route 155 near Ludlow, and Routes 100 and 8 south of Wilmington. Peregrine falcons nest on the cliffs in Smugglers Notch on Route 108, in Brandon Gap on Route 73, and on Mount Pisgah on Route 5A. Wood ducks, osprey, and great blue herons are found in great numbers in the Champlain Valley. Of course, if you want to see wildlife, travel the routes that will increase your chances. Highways that go through wildlife management areas, especially those near a town or along a busy highway, will present more viewing opportunities than remote fourth-class gravel roads because the animals are used to traffic.

Most people envision Vermont as rolling farmland, quaint villages, and steep mountains, the popularized tourist image of the state. While this is true, it doesn't convey the great variety of terrain Vermont offers. The lower Champlain valley is flat, lush farmland with the Green Mountains and New York's Adirondacks rising on both sides. Urban, upscale, and beautiful, the Burlington area is very different from the lower Champlain Valley to the south and the Champlain Islands to the north. Flat, sparsely populated, filled with beautiful lakes and dense softwood forests, the Northeast Kingdom doesn't offer the vistas found in the rolling Vermont Piedmont to its south. Vermont's southwestern portion is majestic, with the Valley of Vermont passing between the Taconic and Green Mountain ranges. But it is the rolling hills of the southeastern counties that continually unfold as the photo-perfect images associated with this state. Any and all of these areas offer fantastic touring.

Weather: Everybody Talks About It

One famous Vermont saying goes, "If you don't like the weather, wait five minutes." An exaggeration, of course, but the weather can change dramatically hour by hour. Vermont's weather is exciting for meteorologists: five major storm tracks—the United States and Canada have a total of seven—pass through or affect Vermont. Due to the state's terrain, many localized weather conditions also exist. Dense fog can settle in the river valleys, while the mountain roads above can bring you into sunshine and a flawless blue sky; it might be overcast and raining where you are, while fifty miles away the weather is ideal.

In Vermont the official weather records begin in 1873. Since then the official temperature has risen above 100 degrees only four times—twice during July 1995, several towns tied for the record of 105 degrees, held since 1911 by the southern town of Vernon. I've seen temperatures above this on the digital bank signs in downtown Brattleboro (107 degrees) and Burlington (106 degrees) and although they weren't "official" temperatures, they felt real enough. In this state the portion of the thermometer we're most concerned with is the bottom half. In February 1933 the town of Bloomfield set an official record of 50 degrees below zero; in January 1995 I was motorcycling on another record-breaking day—62 degrees above! One year we had a snowstorm that left twenty inches of snow covering the fall foliage at the beginning of October. Another year I watched it snow on Memorial Day, but it didn't accumulate on the ground. On June 25, 1983, one-quarter inch of snow accumulated near Sharon. On August 1, 1964, the official temperature was 32 degrees—the earliest freeze in modern history—but on August 2, 1975, it was 99 degrees in Chelsea. Basically, if you're planning to tour or camp in Vermont, do so between mid-May and the end of September—but plan for anything weatherwise, just to be safe.

On Lake Champlain in the northwestern portion of the state, Burlington is the second cloudiest city in the United States due to the localized "lake effect." But statistics like this are misleading. The weather may be nasty and raining in central Vermont, yet ten degrees warmer and sunny in Burlington only thirty miles away. On July 8, 1914, Jericho received an amazing 8.5 inches of rain in an hour and a half, yet Burlington, eight miles away, received only .25 inches! You just can't predict. The annual rainfall in the Burlington area is just a fraction over 32 inches a year, but on August 4, 1995,

10.5 inches of rain fell on Mount Mansfield—one-third of the annual rainfall for *Burlington* in just twenty-four hours—and Vermont has the *least* amount of rainfall of all of the New England states! So be prepared, even if you are just on a day tour or a weekend camp-out. My father taught me to carry a spare blanket, a change of clothes, and a coat in the car at all times. When motorcycling, I always take along raingear and, in the spring and fall, an electrically heated vest and chaps.

A Little Bit of History

Vermont is especially rich in history. First "discovered" by Samuel Champlain in 1609, this wilderness became a contested no-man's-land during the French and Indian Wars. At the conclusion of the last of these in 1763, this wilderness, then known as The Grants, became the colonial frontier. Fleeing from the rigid Puritanism of the New England colonies, settlers moved into the area, following the

Once Elijah West's tavern, The Constitution House in Windsor was the gathering place for delegates from all over the state in 1777. After six days of debate, they were interrupted by news that General Burgoyne and his troops were closing in. Fortunately, a severe thunderstorm prevented the delegates from leaving immediately, and they quickly emerged with Vermont's first constitution.

rivers northward. When conflicts arose between New York and New Hampshire over the validity of their land grants—both claimed this territory—the local settlers, claiming a state of natural law, declared their independence of both the colonies and England. From 1777 to 1791 Vermont was an independent republic with its own constitution, coinage, and militia. In 1791 Vermont joined the Union as the fourteenth state.

Vermont played a role in the growth of the United States far out of proportion to its size and population. With abundant resources and water power, it became a leader in the American Industrial Revolution. It's been said that more patents have been issued to Vermonters than to any other group, starting with patent number one. Vermont was, at one time, the leading producer of iron, copper, limestone, marble, lumber, wool, and dairy products. Vermonters invented the steamboat, the internal combustion engine, the cast-iron cookstove, the electric motor, the rotary pump, the turret lathe, the platform scale, the elevator, the circular saw, the carpenter's square, the modern screw, and much more. Two different Vermonters built the first practical locomotive and the first electric one. Also, Vermonters played a major role in the building and managing of the railroads of the West. Vermonters founded and owned America's expanding communication system (the Pony Express, Postal Telegraph, Railway Express, Wells Fargo, and American Express) and established industrial empires (John Deere Co., Winchester Arms, First National Store, and True Temper Company).

Education has always been a priority in the Green Mountain State. Vermont's constitution was the first to provide for a system of public school education. The first normal school for the training of teachers, the first textbook on teaching, the first use of the blackboard, the first educational society, the first private military college, the first college for women, and even the Head Start Program all originated here. Many Vermonters have established colleges across America (Wesley, Emerson, Vassar, Marietta, the University of Wisconsin, and others), and many more have become leaders of this country's universities. Vermont is known for its authors—both native and transplants—but it's often forgotten that Vermonters once managed America's influential newspapers: the *New York World*, the *New York Herald Tribune*, the *New York Times*, the *New York Daily News*, the *Detroit Free Press*, and others were founded by Vermonters.

Only two U.S. presidents have come from Vermont, but Fillmore, Taft, Hayes, Harrison, Garfield, and Theodore Roosevelt had family ties here. When his father was president of the Champlain Transportation Company, Franklin Roosevelt spent many of his boyhood summers on Lake Champlain, boasting that he was one of only two civilians who could maneuver a steamship through the neck of the Gut (a bay on Lake Champlain). Others have served major posts and influenced the course of the nation since George Washington's administration—though Vermont was an independent republic at that time. Vermont was a major political power from the mid-1800s to the 1920s, and many names will be familiar to history buffs.

But Vermont has had its hard times, too. Vagaries of weather, economic upheavals, and political events have often combined to this state's detriment. The financial panics of the mid-1800s, combined with floods, the opening of the West, and the Civil War, caused massive waves of emigration—you can still find place names on Vermont maps where no houses stand. Vermont industry was rebuilt after the devastating flood of 1927, but the floods of 1932 and 1936, in the midst of the Great Depression, destroyed much of the prosperity Vermonters had enjoyed in the preceding decades.

The family farm has been dying for decades. In the aftermath of World War II, the state lost an average of one family farm per day for almost fifteen years! The growth of the ski industry and the building of the interstate highway system transformed Vermont during the 1950s and 1960s, resulting in the abundant lodging, fantastic dining, and major summer events that we enjoy here today.

Vermont's Architectural Heritage

Vermont doesn't have buildings that reach into the sky—the only skyscraper, nine stories high, is a 1930s Art Deco building in downtown Rutland. Nor does it have vast enclosed spaces like Grand Central Station or Government Plaza in Albany. I don't suppose Gutterson Field House at UVM or the massive barn at Shelburne Farms could be considered anything more than just large interiors. What Vermont offers is a constant unfolding of interesting homes, barns, bridges, community buildings, and downtown historic districts interspersed with farmland, forests, lakes, and mountains.

The Vermont Division for Historic Preservation has identified over twenty thousand buildings of architectural or historic importance, over five thousand of which are entered in the National Register of Historic Places. White steepled churches and wooden covered bridges form the picturesque image of New England and, if you take a closer look, you might be able to identify the similarities that define a style and the differences that show the skills of the individual builders. The Old South Congregational Church in Windsor was built by Asher Benjamin, the famous Boston architect who popularized the Federal style. The First Congregational Church of Chelsea, built from 1811 to 1813, is built from plans in Asher Benjamin's *The Architect's*

Companion, the first published book on architecture in America. The great castlelike brick buildings—usually municipal offices, schools, or libraries—are generally Richardsonian Romanesque and are, of course, listed in the National Register of Historic Places. However, there's only one in Vermont that was actually designed by Henry Hobson Richardson—his last, Billings Center on the UVM green. You'll also see Federal, Georgian, Greek Revival, Gothic, neo-Gothic, and Art Deco–style buildings and combinations thereof. Hopefully you'll see unique styles by local craftsmen, such as the schneckled (a Scottish technique that randomly fits together irregular flat stones) stone buildings in the Chester area made by the Clark Brothers. Regardless of architectural classification, many buildings are just plain interesting; round barns, rambling farmhouses, and old railroad depots that have been converted into banks, bed-and-breakfast inns, and restaurants without losing their charm. This great diversity is a feast for eyes dulled by the sameness of modern construction.

Most historic buildings can be placed within an architectural style, but it's the story behind them that we focus upon. Many of them are open to the public and provide us with a lesson in living history. The Chimney Point Tavern, built in 1784 by Benjamin Paine, who operated the ferry to Crown Point, has a restored eighteenth-century taproom and contains exhibits commemorating the contributions made to Vermont by native inhabitants and French Canadians. Hildene is the Georgian Revival mansion built by Robert Todd Lincoln, which remained in the hands of the Lincoln family until 1974. An architectural gem, it is more noted for being completely furnished with the Lincoln family's possessions. The entire village of Plymouth, also known as Calvin Coolidge's birthplace, is a historic site; the rooms above the general store became the summer White House from 1923 to 1929. The oldest log cabin in the United States conveys its own story, as do the Wilson Castle, the Park-McCullough House, and the Dana House Museum.

Some buildings that represent an architectural style and are historic properties also have other notable attributes. The Fairbanks Museum, designed and built by Lambert Packard in 1896 to house Franklin Fairbank's extensive natural history collection, is still Vermont's premier educational museum and even boasts a planetarium. The Athenaeum, designed by John Davis Hatch, III and built by Packard, was presented, stocked with thousands of volumes, to the city of St. Johnsbury as the town library by Horace Fairbanks in 1871. Still the town library, it retains its original Victorian furnishings and houses the oldest unmodified art gallery in the United States. The most popular historical structures that represent an architectural style—our covered bridges—have also retained their notable attributes; not only are they the best way to cross a river, they also provide shelter if you get caught in a sudden summer cloudburst.

So Much To Do, So Little Time

If you should get tired of touring Vermont's roads, there are plenty of other things to see and do while you're here. During the summer there are music, ethnic, and food festivals; art, crafts, and car shows; antiques, flea, and farmers' markets, and numerous sporting events, from World Cup tennis to championship kayaking and local stock car racing. Fall foliage is perhaps the best known Vermont natural spectacle, but the run of lake trout climbing the falls at Brownington is fantastic. And one of the best of all visual treats is the regular evening ferry ride from Burlington to Port Kent just as the sun is sinking behind the ghostly blue shapes of the Adirondack Mountains, followed by a mellow ride back as the lights of Burlington define the darkening shore.

Consider visiting the Shelburne Museum to walk the decks of the steamship *Ticonderoga* and to view the carved circus figures that were the life's work of Roy Arnold of Hardwick. Enjoy the collections in the American Precision Museum, housed in the original factory building where the American tool industry was born. Or try the American Museum of Fly-Fishing, which sits not far from the Battenkill, one of the most famous trout streams in the country. You might wish to tour the reconstructed President Chester A. Arthur birthplace or the original home and summer White House of Calvin Coolidge.The Eureka Schoolhouse in Springfield, the birthplace of the Mormon prophet Joseph in Sharon, and the Hyde Log Cabin on Grand Isle are other interesting places to visit.

A multitude of special events takes place during the summer. In late June, the Green Mountain Chew Chew in Burlington is a three-day event where people eat the outrageous samplings of the area's fine restaurants and caterers while wandering along the reclaimed waterfront. There are hot-air balloon festivals, antique car shows, county fairs, and a wide variety of special-interest offerings around the state. Many visitors come to Vermont just to participate; the acclaimed Bread and Puppet Circus, for example, attracts people from around the world.

I guess there are two ways to approach the plethora of shows, performances, museums, and other offerings. One: Plan your trip carefully by reading this book and obtaining the current listing of Vermont summer offerings or fall-foliage events, then decide when and where you want to do what. Two: Flow with it, stop where you want to stop, and find out what's happening locally by picking up the newspapers, promotional flyers, and event listings that are available throughout the state. You might want to see the annual Working Dogs in Action in Burlington or go to the National Nude Weekend at Lake Willoughby. I prefer the Fourth of July bash in Warren, while some go to local chicken barbecues and others to the Peacham Pond Loon Watch. You may wish to listen to a Mozart concert high upon Mount Mansfield in a meadow at the Trapp Family Lodge, or perhaps you'd rather hear a local band playing in the gazebo on one of many village greens throughout the state. There's something for everyone— it's deciding among them that's difficult.

Tourism

Tourism is Vermont's second largest industry. In the winter months, Vermont ski areas measure the snowfall in millions of dollars per inch; during the peak of fall foliage the population of the state triples; and from May to September, the Green Mountain State plays host to summer residents and tourists. Ski resorts now compete to sponsor world-class events in the summer and special events for foliage season. Stratton Mountain, but one example of the transformation of a ski village into a three-season resort, hosts a few major arts and crafts shows, a series of weekend concerts by top-name groups, ladies' World Cup tennis, and part of the LPGA tour. Just a few miles away, another major resort, Mount Snow, hosts the UCI Mountain Bike World Cup Championship, the Vermont State Chili Cook-off, an Irish music festival, and another for microbrewers, plus farmers' markets and crafts shows. And so it goes with Okemo, Killington-Pico, Sugarbush, and Stowe. Local Chambers of Commerce publish guides to events, lodging, dining, and other things of interest. Most are just folded brochures, some are substantial booklets, and two are four-color glossy magazines—*Stratton Magazine* and *Vermont Magazine.*

People come to Vermont to hike hundreds of miles of trails, including the famous Long Trail and this segment of the twenty-one-hundred-mile Appalachian Trail. They come to fish the glacial lakes and famous trout streams; to attend writers' conferences, summer stock theater, and music academies; and some just come to get away from the frantic cities during the hot summer. The highways of Vermont are a popular destination for bicyclists, vintage-car clubs, and motorcyclists. In fact, the highways of Vermont *are* a tourist attraction, although only the bicycle touring businesses publicly promote this. Whether you come to Vermont to hike, attend a convention, fish, or motorcycle, you need food and lodging, the mainstay of its tourist industry.

Bed-and-breakfast inns have become the elite of the state's lodgings. One of the most beautiful sites in America is Shelburne Farms on the edge of Lake Champlain, where you can spend the night in the largest house and grandest estate in Vermont, the late Victorian "cottage" of Lila Vanderbilt Webb, and enjoy a stupendous view of the Adirondack Mountains. Most of these inns are in beautiful Victorian homes, but some are part of working farms and private residences. Others have special attributes such as period furnishings or a special theme—often the hobby or special interest of the proprietors. Classic tourist cabins, restored strip motels from the 1950s, exquisite resort lodging, and the everpresent motel chains are all to be found here but are not evenly distributed. Rutland seems to have the highest concentration of motel chains, while they are almost completely absent in the Northeast Kingdom. The Manchester area has the greatest number of specialty inns, but Brandon has numerous fine bed and breakfasts. Most of the old-style strip motels are built along Routes 7 and 7A, and most of the convenience motels that cater to truckers and traveling salesmen will be found in Brattleboro or White River Junction. If resort inns are your style, be sure to plan to spend a night in Stowe—possibly at Topnotch. Often the best lodging can be found for fifteen dollars—camping in a log lean-to in one of Vermont's state parks.

Where you eat often depends upon where you stay. Some bed-and-breakfast inns offer free coffee and a continental breakfast, many advertise a full country breakfast, and a few chef-owned inns serve a regal gourmet meal to begin your day.

There are so many wonderful restaurants that listing all the ones I like would create a small book in itself, but I have included some. Don't hesitate to stop and ask someone to suggest a place or to tender a second opinion.

It's an adventure to "wing it," not to have the constraints of a schedule or an exact plan of where you're going. Usually there are plenty of places to stay during the summer, but you might also arrive in an area only to find out that Bob Dylan and The Band are playing there that night, and fifteen thousand people showed up before you did—worse yet, you don't have tickets. Choice weekend accommodations like lean-tos in the most popular state parks are reserved months in advance. *Don't even come to Vermont during fall foliage season unless you have a confirmed reservation!* Write to the Vermont Chamber of Commerce, the area chambers, or the Vermont Department of Tourism for suggestions.

Food: Vermont's Best-Kept Secret

From the first sugar-on-snow parties to the last foliage harvest festival, the people of this state get together and eat. Looking at an events calendar you will discover church fairs, street fairs, and county fairs; strawberry suppers, corn roasts, and barbecues; you'll also find special food events celebrating chocolates, cheeses, and wines. My favorite beers are brewed in-state. My favorite cheeses, breads, ice cream, chocolates, potato chips, and pasta are all Vermont products. Of course, the milk, butter, yogurt, potatoes, onions, garlic, apples, cider, maple syrup, honey, and vegetables (when in season) that are part of our grocery list are all local products. Any food product that earns the official—and coveted—Vermont Seal of Quality will be the best you can buy anywhere.

Ben & Jerry's ice cream is a product tied to the Vermont image. This international company was started by two guys with an old wooden five-gallon ice-cream maker that they ingeniously converted with a motorized crank. But Ben & Jerry's is not the only premium ice cream made in Vermont. Long before their ice-cream parlor opened, Vermonters were enjoying ice cream made by Seward's Dairy, and in the 1970s, B & J's main local competitor was the UVM dairy. Today twelve other companies produce premium ice cream in Vermont but most of them, such as Gelato del Conte in Burlington and The Real Scoop in Brattleboro, are small local parlors. Of course, you can still find Ben & Jerry's in almost any major village in Vermont, whether it's in one of their scoop shops or the ice-cream freezer in most grocery and general stores.

Vermont has been known for its dairy products since the later part of the 1800s. Until fast, reliable, refrigerated transportation became available the milk produced by the dairy herds of the state was made into cheese and butter. Kraft Cracker Barrel Vermont Cheddar, produced by the Agri-Mart conglomerate, is found in grocery stores and gourmet shops throughout the United States. Cabot Creamery produces not only yogurt, butter, and sour cream, but also a variety of cheddar cheeses of international reputation. Cheese, like ice cream, is also made by small producers. I like Brie, and some of the best I've ever eaten came from Blythedale Farm in Springfield. A hundred years ago different local dairies developed special cultures that made their cheeses famous, some of which, Chelsea and Crowley, are still being produced in limited quantities for the gourmet market. The Plymouth Cheese Company, still owned by the Coolidge family, produces the traditional handmade cheeses developed by Calvin Coolidge's father.

Brewing in Vermont doesn't have the long history of cheese making or maple sugaring. Vermont's oldest brewery, The Catamount Brewing Company, was founded in 1986. Located in White River Junction, its brewmaster, Stephen Mason, supervises the production of British-style ales, bock, and porter. Otter Creek Brewing Company in Middlebury is the state's largest brewery, but there are other operations, such as the Franklin County Brewing Company and The Black River Brewing Company that are making a name for themselves. Some of these—the Long Trail Brewing Company in Bridgewater Corners, for example—offer tours, while others may have a pub. Vermont is one of those states where people often transform their passionate interests into small businesses. Ray McNeill brews twenty-four different ales and lagers in his microbrewery on Elliot Street in Brattleboro. You can only purchase these at his pub, but the effort is worth it. He won the gold medal at the 1995 Great American Beer Festival for his altbier, as well as an honorable mention for his porter; in 1994 he won the bronze medal for Big Nose Blond Ale. Consider staying at The Norwich Inn in Norwich, where brewmaster Timothy Wilson produces a limited number of barrels of English-style ales for his clientele each year.

King Arthur Flour is considered to be the best on the market, so it should come as no surprise to find that this is a Vermont company. In the Montpelier area we enjoy Upland Bakers, Manghi's, Il Fornaio, Klingers, and K.C. Bagels, just to name a few. And you'll forget about Godiva chocolates after having a truffle made by Champlain Chocolates or Green Mountain Chocolates. Then there's Miguel's Salsa, Champ's Chips, jams, jellies, mustards, fancy vinegars, and a vast array of other gourmet foods and condiments being made and sold throughout the Green Mountains.

It's easy to take all of this bounty for granted. From late spring through harvesttime, most communities have a weekly farmers' market where the public can buy locally grown or produced vegetables, herbs, baked goods, flowers, honey, organic meats, wool, and even craft items or artworks.

As you travel through the Green Mountain State, expand your experience by eating the foods produced on this land. Stop at a general store or farmers' market and then drive off to the next turnoff or picnic area with a beautiful view—you might find yourself enjoying one of the best meals you've ever eaten.

Acknowledgments

There's a story behind every book, a backdrop of time and circumstance. This one came about as the result of a writers' workshop presented by Jules Older. Actually, I didn't attend this day-long event, my wife did. But it was something that Jules said to them that got my attention: "Write what you know." I had just read a message on an electronic bulletin board in which a motorcyclist was commenting on his cross-country trek. This rider complained of the awful traffic on Routes 7 and 9 in Vermont. My response was that he had picked the two worst highways for his Vermont experience. So it was Jules and this anonymous rider who put the idea for this book in my mind.

Before I could write this book, I had to travel all the state highways and many of the town roads in Vermont. My mother made it financially possible to stay on the motorcycle. Without her this book could not have been written.

Finally, I'm indebted to my partner. My wife's constant support and encouragement kept me working on this manuscript. More important, she is the wordsmith. As a poet, a translator, and a professional editor, she is teaching me how to write. Tami Calliope's name should be listed under mine.

Primary North-South Routes

ROUTE 100N:
Wilmington to Newport

Some of the most exciting touring east of the Rockies can be found on Route 100 as it winds its way through the heart of the Green Mountains from Heartwellville to Newport. It should come as no surprise that the majority of Vermont's famous ski areas are located along this highway and, as a consequence, provide an abundance of fine restaurants and lodging.

Except for several short segments, this road is relatively free of truck traffic; however, auto traffic can get heavy at the various ski areas where numerous world-class sporting, art, and music events are held during the summer. This is also one of the most popular foliage routes from mid-September to mid-October.

Route 100 actually begins a few miles north of the Massachusetts border, but for practical reasons I set my odometer at 0.0 at the traffic light in the center of Wilmington.

0.0 We begin in downtown Wilmington at the only traffic light in this part of Vermont. There's no bypass here, so if you are coming from Bennington, Brattleboro, or Jacksonville you'll find yourself dealing with congested traffic at this intersection. During ski season this bottleneck is a nightmare as people from Boston to New York try to reach the slopes of the ski areas just north of here; during foliage season it's not much better.

Wilmington is the closest village to Haystack, Mount Snow, and

Stratton Mountain ski areas, so you'll find plenty of restaurants in the village and a modest amount of lodging in the area.

As you begin to drive north along the Deerfield Valley, you are 1,580 feet above sea level, over 1,200 feet higher than Brattleboro.

2.5   If you wish to visit the Haystack ski area, turn left (west) and ride up the access road.

Continuing straight on Route 100, you'll pass through southern Vermont's major skiing and recreational area. Approximately five miles north of Wilmington you will drive through a three-mile strip of restaurants, inns, and motels. Within twelve miles of highway are the entrances to Haystack, Mount Snow, and Stratton Mountain ski areas.

8.7   On the left is the Mount Snow ski area. Developed in 1953 on Mount Pisgah (3,605 feet), and named not for the white gold that covers the slopes but rather for Rubin Snow, whose farm was located here, this recreation area is now the largest in Vermont and can be extremely busy on summer weekends due to the many world-class events being held here. For information on summer events in the area, write to the local Chamber of Commerce or pick up a copy of the *Mount Snow Haystack Region Guide* at one of the local restaurants or convenience stores.

This is the north end of the Deerfield Valley. After you pass the ski area, the road becomes narrower as it twists and turns, following Dover Brook to a higher elevation.

13.9   The road to the village of Stratton and the southern access to the Stratton Mountain ski area is on the left. Although you'd never know it without looking at a map, you're in the village of West Wardsboro.

Route 100 continues to follow the narrow valley and Wardsboro Brook. In this area, it seems, a small ski cottage was built on every piece of flat land between the brook and the steep hillsides. There are not many turnoffs along the brook for fishing access, which is unusual for a Vermont road that follows a stream. A fun stretch of road for motorcyclists but not for a fully loaded RV, it snakes through the mountains alongside the brook.

Caution: You'll meet two sets of ninety-degree turns, one just before the village and one in the center of North Wardsboro. The signs say 25 MPH and show a single ninety-degree turn; however, the first is really a double turn with a short, narrow bridge connecting them—be careful of dirt and gravel on this turn! The second ninety-degree turn in the village can be a surprise, as the road dips down just before it. It's a blind turn, often with gravel on the corner, and traffic going south sometimes just cuts across it to get to the store.

Just before Route 100 merges with Route 30W you'll come to a one-lane iron-truss bridge over the West River, locally popular for its white water. Look for kayakers or canoeists in the river below running white water, or if there's a race in progress, park your vehicle and get a grandstand seat on the girders of this bridge.

22.6 Route 100 merges with Route 30 in East Jamaica, but don't look for a village. **Turn left (west) on the combined routes.** *Route 30E (right) goes to downtown Brattleboro. Take this turn if you are just doing a short day trip around southern Vermont.*

You are now in the West River Valley with rolling hills on either side. Jamaica, the quaint, beautiful village often depicted in the glossy magazines, with its antiques shops and art galleries, is the kind of rural village that many people dream of moving to, and have.

30.7 The division of Route 30W and Route 100N is in Rawsonville. **Turn right (north).**

Once a village flourished here, but now all that remains is the name, which is not uncommon in Vermont. The state grew rapidly, then experienced several large waves of emigration during the middle 1800s.

If you look at a three-dimensional relief map of the southern Green Mountains, you'll probably notice that the huge section from Rawsonville to Londonderry is relatively flat and the same size and shape as the Taconic Mountains to the west. A cataclysmic event occurred about 200 million years ago, shearing off the southern peaks of this range and forcing them westward. The Taconic Mountains are the tops of the ancient Green Mountains.

37.8 The intersection of Route 11 is in Londonderry. *Route 11W leads to Manchester while Route 11E goes to Springfield.*

The next village is Weston, one of Vermont's featured tourist towns, touting the Vermont Country Store, fine art galleries, and specialty shops. The oldest professional theater in Vermont, The Weston Playhouse, is located on the green. Another good place to visit is the Farrar-Mansur House & Mill Museum, an eighteenth-century tavern and mill furnished with heirlooms and tools. Weston hosts several fine inns and motels.

Caution: Cars are apt to turn or stop without warning in this congested area.

43.0 On the north side of the village of Weston is a gas station on the left (west) and a glass studio (Vitriesse Glass) on the right. *The road on the right leads over the hill through Andover to Chester.*

46.1   The junction of Route 155N is just north of town. **Turn right (east)** and begin to ascend the shoulder of Terrible Mountain. *Route 155N goes to East Wallingford and Routes 103 and 140.*

You are in the center of the Green Mountains. In the spring or late fall, when there are no leaves on the trees, you'll see mountain peaks rolling away in all directions. After cresting the ridge, you descend into Ludlow.

53.1   Route 100 merges with Route 103 in downtown Ludlow. **Turn left** and continue on combined Routes 100N and 103W.

If you're doing a day tour, or exploring southern Vermont, consider going south on Route 103. Just southeast of Ludlow, Route 131 goes east to Route 106; Route 10 in Gassetts leads to Springfield; Route 35 goes from Chester to Grafton; and finally Route 103 junctions with Route 5 in Rockingham.

Ludlow is home to the Okemo Ski Area and Resort, where you will find many fine restaurants, lodging, and specialty shops. Most of the lodging is on Route 103 in the southern portion of the village, while most restaurants are in the north. In the small cluster of shops on the left at the entrance to Okemo ski area is the Sweet Surrender Bakery, a good place to stop for a fresh cup of coffee and a homemade pastry.

55.0   **At the division of Routes 103W and 100N, turn right.** *Route 103 climbs to the plateau of Mount Holly and continues on to Rutland.*

You're now on the Calvin Coolidge Memorial Highway. Even though this is not a fast-moving road because of the summer camping activity, it's an extremely pleasant drive on a hot summer day. As you continue up the narrow valley you'll see a series of long, narrow mountain lakes on the east (right) side of the highway for the next five miles. Reservoir Pond, Lake Rescue, Echo Lake, and Amherst Lake are all connected by the Black River. Use one of the roadside turnoffs or access areas to stop, rest, have a picnic, or soak your feet in the cool water.

At the south end of Echo Lake stands one of the oldest inns in Vermont, Echo Lake Inn. This settlement was densely populated in the mid-1800s and was known as Tyson Furnace. Small by today's standards, the blast furnace and forge in Tyson were known throughout the East. Numerous types of iron-ore deposits were mined in this area, but the most important was one from which steel could be produced. The forge produced fireboxes, stoves, pots, kettles, plows, hinges, fixtures, nails, and a great variety of other products. Most people are familiar with the famous Civil War naval battle between the *Monitor* and the *Merrimack* in 1862. Both ships were ironclads, the Confederate *Merrimack* having multiple cannons and the *Monitor* a revolving gun turret. The iron plates for the *Monitor* were made in this small village of Tyson.

A portion of the first road in the state (the Crown Point Military Road, circa 1759) went through Plymouth (or Salt Ash as it was once known). The road came west over the hills from what is now Route 106, crossed the Black River on the north side of Amherst Lake, then continued around the south side of Salt Ash Mountain to Shrewsbury to what is now Route 103. British Major General Jeffery Amherst marched his troops along this road when returning to Boston after capturing Montreal in 1760; the lake is named for him. At the end of hostilities between England and France in 1763 the early settlers used this military road to reach and settle the interior wilderness of The Grants.

63.6   In the narrow valley between Salt Ash Mountain and Mount Tom lies the small village of Plymouth Union and the junction of Route 100A. *Take this route if you are planning to: 1) go to Woodstock or east on Route 4 to New Hampshire; 2) take Route 12 north to Montpelier; 3) go on Route 14 to Barre or Newport; 4) travel north or south on Route 5 from White River Junction; or 5) return to southern Vermont on Route 106.*

SIDE TRIP *Calvin Coolidge Birthplace*

It's only a mile to the village of Plymouth and the Calvin Coolidge State Historic Site. The village is easy to miss. The modern highway bypasses the several buildings that make up Plymouth, and the modest white wooden sign is the only advertisement for the historic site.

Calvin Coolidge and the Calvin Coolidge Birthplace

Calvin Coolidge, the thirtieth president of the United States, was born and grew up in this small village. A Vermont historic site marker on the old road in the center of the village reads: Calvin Coolidge 1872-1933. Born July 4, 1872, in a house back of store. Calvin Coolidge from 4 years of age lived in the homestead across the road now owned by the State of Vermont. Here on August 3, 1923, he was inaugurated president and here he spent many vacations. In the Notch Cemetery he rests beside his wife and son and 4 generations of forebears.

Coolidge was vice-president under President Harding in 1920.

While he was vacationing with his family, news of Harding's death reached this village by messenger—the nearest telephone was in Bridgewater, eight miles away. In the early hours of August 3, 1923, by kerosene lamplight in the parlor of the home he grew up in, Calvin Coolidge was sworn in without fanfare as president of the United States by his father, John Coolidge, a notary public. The story of Silent Cal is part of the American legend of how a poor boy could grow up to become president of our country.

It's an interesting historical coincidence that the two Vermonters who were vice-presidents acquired the presidency upon the death of the elected president.

The village of Plymouth consists of just over a dozen buildings, including the newly erected stone house for the Vermont Department of Historic Sites. Most of the other buildings, including the store, are museums. A rural Vermont village looked like this at the turn of the last century.

Just up the street you'll find the Plymouth Cheese Corporation founded by Calvin Coolidge's father in the late 1800s. Closed during the Depression and reopened in 1960 by Calvin Coolidge's son, John, the company makes curd cheese by hand, using the same family formula they started with. In the late 1960s and 1970s they introduced sage, caraway, pimiento, dill, and garlic flavors to their traditional mild, medium, and sharp cheeses. The small factory produces forty-five to fifty tons of cheese each year, sold exclusively in the factory's salesroom and by mail order. There are no computers in evidence here. Customer names are on index cards in filing drawers in the salesroom. These cheeses are a treat. If you are used to mass-produced commercial cheeses and have never had a homemade cheese, I suggest picking up some Vermont Crackers and a chunk of Plymouth Cheese for lunch or for an evening snack.

Picnic tables under the trees by the parking lot offer shade and an idyllic view. If you stop at the right time and miss the crowds, you'll be able to capture part of the feeling of old Vermont.

63.6   The next five miles along Route 100 north of Plymouth Union are a geological enigma. In this valley you'll see marble outcroppings in some of the road-cuts and limestone caves on the south side of Woodward Reservoir. I've collected impressive calcite crystals in the Coultry Quarry. A superior limestone was mined on Salt Ash Mountain for the production of lime; various types of iron ore, including spathic iron, were mined in this area; and the gold mines of

Bridgeport and Plymouth were the center of Vermont's gold rush. The Valley of Vermont is just over the mountains to the left (west) and is the site of the state's marble deposits. As a gemologist and mineral collector, I know that it takes tens of millions of years of seashell (calcium carbonate) deposits to form limestone (sedimentary deposits); that limestone when cooked by geological forces (metamorphism) produces marble; that gold is found in seams of quartz formed deep in the earth's crust (igneous formation); and that iron ore (of the type mined here in colonial times) comes from the erosion of metamorphic rock over 200 million years older than the marble! It's strange to find all these mineral types in such close proximity. There's more to this valley than what meets the casual viewer's eye.

68.9   Route 4W merges with Route 100N in West Bridgewater. **Bear left.**

Now the road changes, becoming wider and straighter, with more traffic. It's the main road between Woodstock and Rutland and, in the winter, the primary route to the Killington and Pico ski areas from New Hampshire and Massachusetts. Traveling north in this deep valley you'll see several access roads and ski lifts to Bear Mountain and Killington on the left.

The valley was formed during the last great glacial epoch. As the massive blanket of ice slowly moved southward it carved and shaped much of New England's present topography. This valley is U-shaped and similar to the gouges that now form New York's finger lakes and Lake Willoughby in northern Vermont. You are gaining altitude as you ride north along the valley, but it feels as if the road is following level terrain.

75.1   Routes 4 and 100 divide on the north side of Sherburne village.

The road leading to the Killington ski area is on the left, almost directly across from the intersection. You'll find numerous restaurants and lodging accommodations along the first 3.5 miles of this access road. In fact, Killington is now a village in and of itself, with a fire department, post office, gas stations, specialty shops, delis, a bakery, and much more.

There's an abundance of motels on Route 4 as you climb Mendon Mountain—even more should you continue ten miles to Rutland.

Turn right to continue on Route 100N.

For those who prefer to camp out, the Gifford Woods State Park is just .5 mile north of the intersection. One of the state's best parks, it contains one of the few virgin forests in Vermont. From the fieldstone ranger's station, which was built circa 1933–1934, one can hike the Appalachian Trail or connect with the Long Trail. The

Cave at Sherburne Pass is located at the junction of the two trails.

The highway begins a twisting, ten-mile, fast and exciting descent to Pittsfield. Because this is part of the primary east-west route across the middle of the state, you might get stuck behind a slow-moving vehicle. Should you find yourself behind a truck hauling a mobile home, don't attempt to pass because these rigs are always escorted by a state sheriff!

Pittsfield sits in a beautiful valley with the Tweed River flowing through it. These fertile valleys nestled in the midst of mountains are always a delight to discover.

From Route 4 to the village of Warren the highway follows the eastern edge of the Green Mountain National Forest. Except for the gap highways, the land to the west of Route 100 is rugged wilderness.

85.7   Route 107 junctions at Route 100 at the end of the valley and the foot of Wilcox Mountain. **Bear left.** *Route 107 continues east, following the White River through Bethel to Route 14; it intersects with Route 12 and I-89.*

86.8   This is the village of Stockbridge. All of it.
Caution: This is a dangerous four-way intersection. Motorcyclists should be careful of gravel.

The winding road follows the northern portion of the White River for the next eighteen miles. The mountains, covered with hardwoods, rise steeply on either side of this narrow valley, making this an exquisite drive during foliage season.

93.5   The junction of Route 73W is on the left in what used to be known as Talcville. *Route 73 winds through the Green Mountain National Forest, over the Brandon Gap between Goshen Mountain and Mount Horrid, before descending into the Champlain Valley.*

94.7   The village of Rochester looks like a Vermont postcard. Inner Traditions International and Schenkman Books, two internationally known publishing houses, are located here, and the famous verde antique marble (serpentine) has been mined since 1850 on the mountain that rises abruptly on the eastern edge of the village. On a hot summer day the shaded town green with its gazebo is a great place to stop and take a break from driving. Walk over to The Store or to the minimart to get snacks and a cold drink.

95.5   Just outside of Rochester, on the western side of the highway, you'll find a small park sponsored by the Lion's Club. If you didn't take advantage of the green, here's another opportunity to rest.

98.3   As you enter Hancock you'll pass the Chesapeake Hardwood finishing plant on the left.

Lumbering, sawmills, and wood manufacturing plants are one of Vermont's primary industries. Much of the early prosperity of the state was based upon lumbering. Burlington and the towns along the Connecticut River were dependent upon the business of transporting cut timber or sawn lumber. The first mills built in Vermont were for lumber, and numerous small operations still prosper throughout the state. The Ethan Allen Furniture Company, one of Vermont's largest manufacturers, is but one example of a thriving wood products industry.

98.9   The junction of Route 125W is on the north side of the village. *Route 125 goes through the national forest, over the Middlebury Gap, along the Ripton Gorge, and into the Champlain Valley in East Middlebury and meets Route 7.*

The Old Hancock Hotel is located at this junction. No longer a hotel, it houses a fine restaurant, bakery, and a great little bookstore.

103.0   When you reach Granville you can see that you're running out of valley, and the mountains begin to reach for the stream and the highway that follows it.

104.3   The White River Valley ends when you enter the Granville Gulf and the six miles of preserved wilderness called the Granville Reservation. Here you find yourself climbing on a narrow, winding road with steep mountainsides leaving just enough room for the pavement and the fast-moving stream. Moss Glenn Falls, a popular place to stop, especially on a hot summer day or during foliage season, offers two beautiful waterfalls that drop from the heights into clear pools. Parking is available, but beware of southbound traffic. You can find the last patches of the winter's snow here, sometimes as late as June.

When you reach the top of the gulf, you've crested the Granville Gap and find yourself in upland beaver meadows hemmed in by rising mountains. Watch for ducks, herons, beaver, and moose, and possibly black bear. This is my favorite section of Route 100.

Once you leave the reservation the highway descends into "The Valley," known for some of the best skiing in the East. In the summer it becomes a virtual playground offering swimming, bicycling, hiking, horseback riding, polo, sail gliding, local theater, concerts with top bands, crafts shows, art exhibits, and much more.

110.2   The entrance to the village of Warren is on the right.

The Mad River runs through the center of the village, and the gorge is a popular swimming hole; just ask someone how to get to it. This community of very creative people is widely known for throwing the best Fourth of July party in the state. The main street quickly takes you back to Route 100.

113.1 On the left, the access road to the Sugarbush Ski Resort can also be used as a shortcut to Route 17W. *To reach Route 17 take the access road up the mountain. At the Sugarbush Inn take a right onto German Flats Road. Follow this road to Route 17 and take a left to climb through the Appalachian Gap.*

Ben & Jerry's, Inc., holds its annual stockholders' meeting each June at the Sugarbush Ski Resort. Unlike those held by other major American corporations, their stockholders' meeting is a rock festival. Ben & Jerry's One World, One Heart festival is free to the general public, and performers such as Bo Diddley, Taj Mahal, Pete Seeger, The Woods Tea Company, and The Band are featured. Organized letter campaigns to lawmakers—especially on issues concerning children—are part of the festival, as are crazy events like organizing the world's largest blues harmonica jam (it made the *Guinness Book of World Records*). You'll find great food, fun workshops, and, of course, free ice cream. If you're touring Vermont in late June be sure to include this event on your itinerary.

Just past the Sugarbush Access Road, Route 100 crosses the Mad River on an old iron-truss bridge. Watch for a large hand-painted sign advertising glider rides. Airport Road, the gravel road along the river, leads to the Warren Sugarbush Airport. For a modest fee you can rent a pilot and a sailplane and find yourself riding the thermal currents high above the mountain peaks.

118.8 The junction of Route 17W is in the village of Irasville, but this whole area is usually referred to by the township in which it resides, Waitsfield. *Route 17 goes over the spine of the Green Mountains through the Appalachian Gap and across the Champlain Valley to Crown Point, New York.*

> **Caution:** *As you enter Irasville, the junction of Route 17 has limited visibility, traffic usually exceeds the speed limit, and cars may be exiting from three restaurants.*

You can get a cup of coffee at Green Mountain Coffee Roasters in the Green Mountain Shopping Center on the left. The Waitsfield Farmers Market, rated the best one in Vermont, opens here on Saturday mornings. To discover what's going on in town or to get additional travel information, visit the Tempest Bookstore in the Mad River Shopping Center.

119.8 Another good place to take a break is in the center of Waitsfield. Turn right onto Bridge Street and park before the second oldest covered bridge in Vermont. You'll find additional parking, a couple of picnic tables, and access to the river (including the swimming hole) behind the stores to the right of the bridge. Take time to have lunch and browse the shops located here.

124.2 Slow down as you approach the junction of Route 100B. Route 100B continues straight as the primary highway. **Route 100N is a ninety-degree turn left.**
　Caution: There is usually gravel on the pavement as you make this ninety-degree turn left.

The covered bridge in Waitsfield is the second oldest in Vermont.

Route 100B is an alternate route leading to the junction of Route 2 in Middlesex (7.8 miles) and then south to Montpelier (5.8 miles) or north to Waterbury (4.4 miles).

As you travel over the ridges through Duxbury, you will have glimpses of the Worcester Range ahead.

131.2 Route 100N merges with Route 2 in Waterbury. **Turn left (north) on Route 2W.**

As you drive along South Main Street in Waterbury, the large complex of brick buildings on the left houses various departments of the state government. This used to be the state mental hospital, and many of the old isolation cells still exist on the lower levels of many of these buildings. I've often wondered if they should be used to restrain overzealous bureaucrats.

Waterbury was established by a royal charter from King George III on June 7, 1763 (the end of the Seven Years' War), but wasn't settled until James Marsh built a cabin in 1783; the first organization of the town took place in 1790. Most towns in Vermont were established by royal charters, but most were not settled until after Vermont became an independent republic in 1776.

132.2 Stowe Street is at the second stoplight in the center of the village. There are two good restaurants here, a great bagel shop, and the local sports bar. Just ahead is the Stage Coach Inn. *Stowe Street leads to Route 100.*

132.4 Routes 2W and 100N divide. **Turn right.** Just ahead is Exit 10 of I-89. The Holiday Inn is on the knoll to the left after crossing I-89. This centrally located hotel is extremely popular, not only for lodging but also for local dining.

A little farther on is the Inn at Thatchers Brook. This beautiful inn has expanded since it first opened and gives its customers plenty of the personal attention that makes Vermont inns and bed and breakfasts so popular.

133.7 The entrance to Ben & Jerry's main plant, a major tourist attraction (for some a mecca), is on the left. Once known as Colbyville, this area is frequently referred to as Ben and Jerryville.

Traveling through Waterbury Center you'll notice another tourist attraction, the Cold Hollow Cider Press. This stretch of Route 100 caters to the tourist trade, with outlets offering Green Mountain Chocolates, Cabot Cheese, Miguel's Salsa, and more.

Past Waterbury Center you have a splendid view of the Presidential Range to the left and the Worcester Range to the right. If you're visiting during one of the weekends when an antique, classic, or fifties auto show is taking place, I suggest stopping somewhere and just watching the traffic. This road is always busy and some days the traffic moves with agonizing slowness.

140.1 The junction of Moscow Road is on the left. *This leads to Route 108 about midway along the Mountain Road. If you're planning on doing The Notch, consider taking this road. You'll avoid the traffic congestion of downtown Stowe and much of the commercial development along the lower section of the Mountain Road.*

142.5 The junction of Route 108 is in the center of Stowe village at the blinking red light. Here traffic from three directions stops and each vehicle alternately takes turn in proceeding.

At only 743 feet in altitude, the village of Stowe sits between Mount Mansfield (4,393 feet), Hunger Mountain (3,620 feet), and Mount Worcester (3,286 feet). Stowe is called the Ski Capital of the East, where the first modern ski trail in the United States was built by the Civilian Conservation Corps in the 1930s; the National Ski Patrol formed in 1938; and the first chair lift in the country was built in 1940. Stowe has many fine lodging and dining facilities. The commercial part of Stowe is along the Mountain Road (Route 108) and not along Route 100.

The Village of Stowe

Stowe, the Ski Capital of the East, is probably the only town that is internationally associated with Vermont. This little Switzerland was made famous in the film The Sound of Music, and The Trapp Family Lodge remains one of the town's most popular inns.

It wasn't until just prior to the Civil War that tourism developed in Stowe. Then, as now, people would come to climb to the top of Mount Mansfield for the exceptional view. In 1858 a commercial lodge was built on the mountain's summit. The tavern-hotel that opened in 1814 grew into the two-hundred-room Mount Mansfield Hotel. The Green Mountain Inn, still in business, was built in 1833. In 1918–1919 the wagon road through Smugglers Notch was rebuilt to accommodate automobiles, quickly becoming one of the favorite touring roads in the state. Vermont's highest mountain became big business for this isolated village decades before the first ski trail cut its slopes.

Downtown Stowe (Center Village) is not very large and Route 100 quickly takes you through what was North Village. As you leave Stowe, the valley begins to widen and becomes prime agricultural land.

SIDE TRIP   *Moss Glen Falls*

145.5 On the right, on a curve, Randolph Road forks from Route 100. **Bear right** and travel for .4 mile; **turn right onto Moss Glen Road** (a well-maintained gravel road). Continue for .5 mile to a parking area on the left (it appears to be in front of you as you approach it because the road curves to the right). You'll see a hand-painted sign nailed to a tree that reads Falls. Park and follow the trail for approximately five minutes to the base of the falls. Moss Glen Falls is one of the highest waterfalls in Vermont with a drop of over one hundred feet in two cascades.

After leaving the falls consider taking a **right turn** onto Randolph Road. A local road with far less traffic than Route 100, it junctions with Route 100 on the edge of the village of Morrisville.

149.1 The Morrisville-Stowe Airport is on the right. Like the Warren Sugarbush Airport, this is an active center for sailplaning (gliders). On most weekends, you can rent a glider (if you're certified) or hire a pilot for a great ride, well worth the price. I recommend taking one of these rides during foliage season—there is no better way to view the spectacular color than by sailing over it.

150.6 The village of Morrisville is located along the Lamoille River Valley at the head of both the Worcester and Stowe valleys. Elmore Mountain (2,608 feet) rises on the eastern side of the village; on the western side is the majestic Sterling Range with White Face (3,715 feet) and Morse (3,380 feet); while to the north stretch the Green Mountains with the peaks of Butternut (2,715 feet), Bowen (2,340 feet), and Belvidere (3,360 feet) predominating. The scenic panorama is spectacular from here.

Morrisville is a true Vermont community, and its geographic location makes it the commercial center for many towns. The village is built around the twisting turns of the Lamoille River, and Lake Lamoille is the reservoir for the hydroelectric dam located in its center.

151.3 At the traffic light and four-way intersection in downtown Morrisville, **turn left** to continue on Route 100. This is the northern end of Route 12. If you continue straight you'll reach Montpelier in 26.3 miles. If you're planning to take Route 15E to Danville, continue straight for two blocks and turn onto Park Street (Route 15A).

Route 100 twists and turns as it follows the local streets to the north side of town.

152.5 Route 100N merges with Route 15W at this busy intersection. **Turn left** to continue on Route 100. *Turning right will take you to Hardwick (Routes 14 and 16) and onto West Danville (Route 2).*

I usually stop at the gas station to get a cup of Green Mountain Coffee Roaster's brew and fill the gas tank before heading into the rural lands to the north. Many people recommend the Charlemont Restaurant.

155.6 Routes 15 and 100 divide in Hyde Park at the intersection with the overhead flashing light. The village is to the left; **turn right.** *Route 15W continues straight, eventually entering Burlington.*

158.7 On the mountain that's ahead on the right, you'll see a smaller hill of white or gray. This is the dump pile for the Vermont Asbestos mine on Belvidere Mountain, renowned among mineralogists worldwide for the green garnets once discovered here. I've found gold orange grossular (hessonite) garnets, green diopside crystals, green vesuvianite, white aragonite, and red almandine garnet at the dump pile. A faceted orange garnet from this site convinced the Vermont legislature to adopt this variety of garnet as the state gemstone.

160.6 The junction of Route 100C from Johnson is on the left in North Hyde Park.

164.9 The junction of Route 118 is on the left. *Route 118 goes to Montgomery.*

166.2 Route 100 becomes a wonderful, winding road with an uphill grade as you go through Eden Mills; Lake Eden is on the right as you crest the hill. As you proceed north, you are imperceptibly climbing in elevation. This is dairy country, where the growing season is not as long as it is in southern Vermont or in the lower elevations along the Champlain Valley.

174.0 Route 58 intersects Route 100 in Lowell. *Route 58E leads to Lake Willoughby and Route 5A. Route 58W turns to gravel outside of the village. This is the old Bayley-Hazen Military Road that goes through the notch between Haystack and Buchanan Mountains, built by Jacob Bayley in 1776 from Wells River to Peacham; by 1779 Moses Hazen completed it from Peacham to the notch. It's a beautiful road that leads to Montgomery Center.*

Jay Peak (3,870 feet), seen ahead on the left, is identified by the tall white tower on its peak. The beautiful vistas and the mountains unfold across this high plateau. This far north Route 100 has little traffic.

177.4 The large brick structure in the field to the right is a Benedictine monastery.

180.3 North Hill Road branches off to the left at the small green in Westfield. *This is the best road to take to reach Route 242 in Jay.*

181.8 The junction of Route 101 is on the left at the green in Troy. Route 101 goes north to Route 242 and Route 105; it will take you to North Troy or Granby, Quebec.

187.6 Route 100 meets the northern end of Route 14 to the west of Newport. **Turn left** at the large traffic island that has a barn in its center. *If you continue straight you'll be on Route 14 heading south; it's about forty-five miles to St. Johnsbury.*

188.1 Route 100 ends at Route 105. *Route 105E leads into the city of Newport; Route 105W goes to Lake Champlain.*

You may elect to make a left turn and travel west to Lake Champlain, New York, or into Canada, but my advice is to go into Newport first. The best views of Lake Memphremagog are from Route 105 as you drive into the city.

191.9 Route 105E becomes Highland Avenue and merges with Route 5 (Pleasant Street) inside the city limits. **Bear left onto Pleasant Street**, which ends at Third Street. **Turn left and drive for a block and a half to West Main Street, then turn right.**

Traveling through downtown I always feel as if I've returned to the late 1950s or early 1960s. Newport is the economic center of the Northeast Kingdom and south-central Quebec; the city and township abound with viable retail, wholesale, and service businesses.

193.1 The small park on the left before the bridge, located on the very end of the peninsula that separates South Bay and Lake Memphremagog, is the best vantage point from which to watch the lake. Just over the bridge are two other good places to take a break: the back of the Grand Union parking lot and in Gardner Park, opposite the shopping plaza on the banks of the Clyde River.

Newport

Newport is Vermont's northernmost city and has a population of over 4,400. Lake Memphremagog (5,847 acres of which is in

Vermont) is the prominent feature of the city, while South Bay (470 acres) seems virtually ignored. This long, narrow lake stretches through the remote woods and farmlands of Quebec to the city of Magog in the north. At one time a vital port for shipping lumber into Canada, in another era it was a notorious smuggling route for bringing Canadian whiskey into the states.

This town, a vibrant community prior to the Great Depression, had electric lights in the 1890s, was a major railroad depot, and a summer resort area for people from Boston and New York. Old photos, circa 1919–1920, reveal a wide, concrete-paved Main Street lined with sidewalks, iron lampposts, and beautiful buildings. The city has lost its visual cohesiveness over the intervening years, but its surprising vitality remains.

ROUTE 7:
Vermont's Western Corridor

Coming into Vermont from Montreal, Canada, you'll find Route 7 as the first exit past the U.S. Customs checkpoint. Route 7 runs along western Vermont from Canada to the Massachusetts border. Although much of Route 7 remains the primary highway west of the Green Mountains, the section from Canada to Burlington has essentially been relegated to a local road by the parallel Interstate 89.

Route 7 goes through several distinct regions along its length. From Canada to Middlebury, the highway runs through the Champlain Valley with spectacular views of New York's Adirondack Mountains, Lake Champlain, and the Green Mountains. Passing through Burlington, Vermont's largest city, it offers exquisite dining, nightlife, shopping, and a vibrancy that mirrors both Boston and Montreal. South of Middlebury, Route 7 enters the marble region of Vermont, then narrows into the Valley of Vermont between the Green Mountains and the Taconic Mountain Range. From Dorset to Bennington is one of Vermont's most historic regions and a tourist mecca for tens of thousands of people each summer.

Like most Vermonters, I treat Route 7 as if it were three distinct routes: Burlington to Canada; Burlington to Rutland; and Rutland to Bennington. For this reason I've broken Route 7 into those three sections, adding a fourth, historic Route 7A.

Route 7S: Canada to Burlington

0.0   The highway begins just beyond the United States Customs checkpoint. Route 7 follows I-89 all the way to Swanton, so there's little traffic. You'll get glimpses of Lake Champlain, especially when you cross Rock River, but this is not a scenic road. In fact, this section of I-89 offers better views than does the old highway.

Vermont's earliest settlers lived along the Missisquoi Bay in Highgate. Archaeological sites confirm the existence of permanent Indian settlements in this area eight thousand years ago. The lake was the traditional boundary between the Iroquois tribes to the west and the Algonquins to the east. In Vermont many place names, such as Missisquoi and Memphremagog, derive from the Algonquin language; in New York they derive from the Iroquois. When white settlers began exploring this region they found a large settlement of Abnakis—part of the Algonquin tribe—at the mouth of the Missisquoi River. Today, the majority of Vermont's Abnaki Indians still reside in Highgate and Swanton.

8.3   In the center of Swanton, at the north end of the long rectangular green, Route 78 intersects Route 7. *Route 78W leads to Route 2 and the Champlain Islands; it also leads to Route 36, which follows the shore of the lake and rejoins Route 7 in downtown St. Albans. Route 78E leads to Route 105W, which crosses northern Vermont to the New Hampshire border.* Most people first encounter Route 7 here at the green. Coming south from Montreal, many visitors will take Exit 20 from I-89 or come into Swanton on Route 78E from New York's I-87.

From the late 1700s to as recently as 1970, this area was known for producing the finest quicklime in the United States. Quicklime, produced by mining limestone and then roasting it in kilns until a limestone powder is created, is the primary ingredient in plaster, cement, and mortar, and is also used in producing paper, tanning leather, sugar refining, and glass manufacturing. Lime is also essential to agriculture, especially to neutralize Vermont's acidic soil.

9.4   The highway crosses the Missisquoi River south of Swanton suburbs.

10.8   The road on the left goes to Highgate Center.

From Swanton to St. Albans is a rapidly growing residential area where once-prime farmland now supports small residential lots with fine views of Lake Champlain and the Adirondacks to the west. You'll enjoy them, too.

Vermont is known for its dairy farms. The familiar images of black-and-white cows in their green pastures popularized by Ben & Jerry's has almost become a symbol of Vermont. Franklin County and the adjoining county to the east, Orleans, are two of the three primary dairy-producing counties in Vermont (Route 7 also goes through the third county, Addison, south of Burlington). In the 1890s the Franklin County Creamery in St. Albans was the largest in the world. However, it is a myth that there were ever more cows than people in Vermont. There might have been more sheep, yes; more cows, no.

14.7 The access onto I-89 (Exit 20) and the junction of Route 207 are on the left. *Route 207 goes to Highgate Center and Route 78, then through farmland to Canada.*

15.8 The junction of Route 105E is on the left as you enter the city limits of St. Albans. *Route 105E crosses the top portion of Vermont, through Newport, to the Connecticut River.*

St. Albans

St. Albans, a vigorous town since it was first settled in 1785, was originally located on the shore of Lake Champlain as a major port for the shipping of goods to Canada. The economy of the town was placed in jeopardy by the unpopular Embargo Act of 1807 and the subsequent War of 1812 against British Canada. In response to this unpopular act of Congress, St. Albans became a center for smugglers. Goods were smuggled into Vermont by boat along Lake Champlain and into Canada by land. Smugglers took the land route through Smugglers Notch in Jeffersonville or the water route through Carry Bay in North Hero. The smuggling ceased as public opinion quickly shifted after the British attacked Plattsburgh in September 11, 1814, and the citizens of St. Albans watched the battle from the eastern side of the lake.

After the first train arrived in 1850, the center of town shifted two miles east from the shores of the lake to its present location in the city. St. Albans became the headquarters of the Central Vermont Railway, and once the railway's maintenance shops were moved here, it had the largest railroad depot in New England. In 1895 St. Albans had a larger population than it does one hundred years later. In 1895 the downtown area was gutted by fire, destroying well over a hundred buildings. The homogenous feeling of the present commercial area is due to the rebuilding of the center of town during that prosperous period in the history of St. Albans. As a result of the town's growth, and probably in part due to the pride of a newly rebuilt commercial district, St. Albans incorporated as a city in 1897.

On October 19, 1864, a group of Confederate soldiers staged a rear-action raid into Vermont. The soldiers had infiltrated St. Albans during the previous days, and in a well-coordinated plan, robbed all of its banks, killed a man, and escaped to Canada. Although the men were arrested in Canada, they were tried and acquitted because the Canadian government determined that the raid was a legitimate act of war—the northernmost Confederate action during the Civil War.

Another raid that is part of United States history happened two years later in 1866. In June a special train from Boston brought thirty-five hundred Irish, known as the Fenians, to St. Albans. The Fenians were dedicated to capturing Canada from Great Britain and to setting up an Irish Free State. Martial law was declared in Canada, and United States troops were sent to stop the invasion. Although this effort was thwarted without much violence, it set the stage for a further attempt a few years later. Before returning to Boston, the Fenians enjoyed the hospitality of the citizens of St. Albans for several days. I'm sure that the locals were still upset with the Canadian authorities for releasing the Confederate raiders and that it encouraged the people of St. Albans to support this group of Irish, who promised to give the Canadians a bit of trouble.

15.8   St. Albans's downtown is centered around the green known as Taylor Park. The eastern side of the green is bordered by Church Street with the brick Congregational Church at the north end, followed by the courthouse, the United Methodist Church, the beautiful St. Albans Historical Museum, and the Episcopal church all facing Main Street. In this beautiful tree-filled park you'll find the traditional fountain, park benches, and even a couple of picnic tables. On the western side of the green is the commercial district of the city.

TJ's Bread and Pastry is across from the southern end of the green. You can stop here to get a loaf of bread and a sandwich or a pizza. On a nice day you can make use of the picnic tables on the green.

The intersection of Route 36W is on the right on the southern side of the green. *This route (Lake Street) leads to the railroad station and then to St. Albans Bay on Lake Champlain.*

17.0   The junction of Route 36E (Fairfield Street) is on the left at the southern end of Taylor Park. *Route 36E goes through Fairfield to Route 108 in Bakersfield.*

17.3   The access to I-89 (Exit 19) is on the left. *This is the St. Albans*

State Highway and leads to Route 104 and the interstate highway.

19.3   South of the city the highway gains a little elevation, and you again have beautiful views of the lake and the Adirondacks.

22.9   This small village green is the center of Georgia.

Laughing gas (N_2O—nitrous oxide) was discovered by Gardner Colton of Georgia, but it was Horace Wells of White River who first used it in 1844 as an anesthetic for pulling teeth.

24.1   Just ahead of you on the left are the first good views of Mount Mansfield and Sterling Mountain.

25.4   This, and the next left, .3 mile farther, are the accesses onto I-89 (Exit 18) in Milton.

25.9   The junction of Route 104A is on the left. *Route 104A goes along the northern shore of Arrowhead Mountain Lake, then through East Georgia to Route 104.*

26.2   On the left is Arrowhead Mountain Lake, the impoundment of the Lamoille River for the hydroelectric plant in Milton. An important nesting area for American bittern, belted kingfisher, osprey, hooded merganser, wood duck, great blue heron, green heron, common goldeneye, and other waterfowl, it also abounds with muskrat, otter, mink, and other wildlife.

29.6   The hydroelectric dam adjoins the iron bridge where you cross the Lamoille River and enter into the village of Milton.

29.8   On the left, in the center of the old village, is a turn leading over to Westford. **Continue straight.**

Milton spreads along Route 7 for the next 4.5 miles. From the dam, through the big sweeping curve that marks Checkerberry Village, to the Catamount Industrial Park, the highway is lined with commercial development.

35.3   Route 2 merges with Route 7 in Chimney Corner in Colchester. The access onto I-89 (Exit 17) is to the right. *Route 2W goes through the Sand Bar Wildlife Management Area and State Park, across the lake, and north through the Lake Champlain Islands. For those who wish to avoid the traffic of Winooski and most of Burlington, take I-89 south to I-189 (Exit 13); I-189 connects I-89 with Shelburne Road (Route 7) in South Burlington.*

38.1   The junction of Route 2A is on the left. *Route 2A is a bypass around the cities of Burlington and South Burlington. If you are planning to travel east on Route 15 or south on Route 2, take this highway. (See Route 2, page 223.)*

From here Route 7 goes south through the most densely populated area of the state. Of the roughly half a million Vermont residents, about 20 percent live in the greater Burlington area; the combined population of the village of Essex Junction and the cities of Burlington, Winooski, and South Burlington is over sixty-five thousand. During the last twenty-five years these large towns grew into small cities and then expanded into the neighboring townships. During the 1980s this was the fastest-growing county in Vermont and, by percentage of population, the fourth fastest-growing urban area in the country.

38.8   The intersection of Route 127. *Route 127W leads to Malletts Bay and then into the north end of Burlington.*

41.1   You've entered the outskirts of the cities and need to be alert for entering, exiting, and lane-changing traffic.

41.5   The Hampton Inn and the Colchester Reef Lighthouse restaurant are on the left. From here you get a beautiful view of Mount Mansfield.

41.6   The I-89 access (Exit 16) marks the boundary of the city of Winooski. Two industrial parks and numerous commercial firms are located here, due in part to the combination of lower taxes in Colchester, access to I-89, and the nearby city of Burlington. Route 7 (Main Street) is now a busy commercial thoroughfare.

42.6   At the main intersection in downtown Winooski, Route 7S briefly merges with combined Routes 15W and 2. The post office is ahead on the right. The Champlain Mill shopping complex is ahead on the left. Route 15E is to the left.

Continue straight. Position yourself in the left lane if you plan to visit the Champlain Mill or continue straight (recommended) into Burlington; position yourself in the right lane if you intend to enter Burlington on Riverside Drive.

42.9   You'll find a few fine restaurants in Winooski including a couple in The Champlain Mill retail complex.

The city is built along the river, where the Winooski River flows through a gorge and then down a series of rapids to the Winooski Falls—located under the bridge—and into Salmon Hole. Ira Allen built the first of many mills to harness the power of this river, but it was the woolen mills for which this town became known. As late as World War II, the American Woolen Company employed as many as twenty-eight hundred people, but the mills have been shut down now for more than twenty years.

As you go through the series of traffic lights and cross the concrete bridge over the Winooski River, **you need to position yourself in the left lane.** *I recommend going straight and up the hill (Colchester Avenue) to enter into Burlington, but you can also take the turn right and enter Burlington on Riverside Drive.*

43.5 At the traffic light, East Avenue enters on the left and Trinity College is on the right. *East Avenue leads to Route 2E on Williston Road in 0.8 miles.*

To continue on Route 2E to Route 100, Route 116, or Montpelier without stopping in downtown Burlington, turn left. (See Map on page 268.)

To go to downtown Burlington, to Route 7S, or to the ferry dock, continue straight. You'll pass the Medical Center Hospital of Vermont and the Fleming Museum, both on the left. This is the campus of the University of Vermont.

43.9 On the left is the Ira Allen Chapel and the grave site of educator and philosopher John Dewey, a Burlington native who graduated from UVM before gaining worldwide acclaim for changing the nature of education in this country.

On the left is the UVM green, the heart of the UVM campus. Properly called the University of Verd Mont or the University of the Green Mountains, it is commonly called the University of Vermont. UVM was founded in 1791 by Ira Allen, one of the original founders of Burlington in 1763, who played a major role in the formation of the Republic of Vermont.

43.9 At the traffic light is the intersection of Prospect Street, with the UVM green on the left. Colchester Avenue now becomes Pearl Street. *Pearl Street goes down the hill to Battery Park, which overlooks the lake.*

To go to Route 7S without going through downtown Burlington, turn left onto Prospect Street. *You can also go to downtown Burlington or to the ferry docks by turning left onto Prospect Street and then taking either of the two next right turns and riding down the hill.*

(See Map on page 268.)

Prospect Street to Route 7S

(See Map on page 268.)

43.9 Turn left onto Prospect Street with the green on the left. The Fletcher Allen Hospital is now on the right. Across the green you can see the brick building with the turret, Billings Center—the student center, a classic Richardsonian Romanesque, the last edifice designed by famous architect Henry Hobson Richardson. Next to it is the Williams Science Building (now the art building) a Gothic-style brick structure. The cornerstone of the next building was laid by General Lafayette in 1826. Rarely does one have the opportunity to compare in one venue the differences in architectural style seen on this campus. On the right is the neo-Federal style (1926) brick Waterman Building (UVM administration) and at the corner of Prospect and Main Streets is the Wheeler House, an authentic Federal-style home, although it's been modified several times.

The architecture of Burlington is diverse, from the brick and stone buildings near the docks to the mansions commanding a view of the lake from strategic locations on the hill. A walk along any of the streets between the lake and the UVM campus will delight the architect, home builder, or decorator.

44.1 At this traffic light at the intersection of Main and Prospect Streets you can turn right and go down the hill to downtown Burlington and the ferry docks.

Continue straight on South Prospect Street to go to Route 7S. The UVM properties are on the left while the Champlain College properties begin one block down the hill on the right.

44.6 The Redstone Campus of UVM is on the left, then the Burlington Country Club. From the country club South Prospect Street continues straight but you **bear right**, following the main road (Ledge Street) winding downhill through a residential neighborhood.

The main buildings on this campus incorporate the red stone that used to be quarried in Burlington. Redstone was built as the estate of one of Burlington's lumber barons.

45.5 Ledge Street ends at Shelburne Road (Route 7). **Turn right and immediately round the small traffic island in order to continue on Shelburne Road.**

Shelburne Road has numerous motels, restaurants, fast-food eateries, gas stations, shopping malls, and retail stores.

46.0 At this traffic light, Flynn Avenue is on the right.

46.7 The entrance onto I-189E is on the right. Here I begin mileage on Route 7 south to Rutland and Bennington.

Pearl Street to the ferry dock

(See Map on page 268.)

43.9 **Continue straight through the traffic light onto Pearl Street.** As you're going down the hill you'll get glimpses of the lake. The building with the roof proportionally shaped like the great pyramid once housed the Masonic lodge. You pass the end of the Church Street Marketplace on the left and the Unitarian Church (1816) on the right.

44.7 A modern church is on the left and soon after it is another, built of concrete. In the early 1970s a crazed arsonist torched several buildings here, destroying these two churches and one whole business block. The fires threatened to engulf the other buildings of the downtown district—a scenario repeated in many of Vermont's downtowns during the nineteenth century.

44.9 Pearl Street ends at Battery Park. *To get into Battery Park you have to turn right and go around the park to enter from the other (North Avenue) side.* Turn left onto Battery Street and down the hill past the Radisson Hotel on the left. The lake is on the right and you'll go through several traffic lights.

45.3 **Turn right** and down to the ferry dock. *The Lake Champlain Transportation Company will convey you across the widest part of the lake to Port Kent in New York.*

Route 7S: Burlington to Rutland

The central section of Route 7 travels through the lower Champlain Valley into the Valley of Vermont. In the summer one can easily travel from the eastern to the western side of the state by using the highways winding through the gaps—Routes 117, 125, and 73—in the Green Mountains, but in the winter most people travel to Burlington and then take Route 7 south. Route 7 also provides access to the highways leading west to New York State—Routes 17, 73, 125, and the major Route 4.

Not everyone wishes to experience Burlington. People who want to avoid the traffic of Winooski and Burlington often use I-89 from Chimney Cor-

ner (Exit 17) or Winooski (Exits 16 and 15) to Route 189; those coming from Route 2W usually use I-89 from Richmond (Exit 11) to Route 189 (Exit 13). From the ferry dock continue straight for two blocks, turn right onto Pine Street, and continue to Flynn Street. At the traffic light turn left and climb the hill to Shelburne Road. Take a right. If you have taken the time to enjoy the city, you can reach Shelburne Road by taking Pine, St. Paul, South Winooski, or South Union Streets.

0.0   The mileage for the central section of Route 7 begins at the junction of Routes 189 and 7S in South Burlington. For the next four miles Shelburne Road (Route 7) is a continuous series of restaurants, motels, hotels, car dealerships, retail stores, antiques shops, and small shopping malls. Only one small apple orchard now stands against the tide of strip development. Over the past thirty years the growth of Burlington and the high cost of business space in the downtown district has pushed businesses farther from the center of town.

The center of the village of Shelburne is at the traffic light and the Shelburne Inn is on the left. The road on the right leads to Shelburne Farms and Shelburne Point. As you continue through the village you'll see some of the buildings that are part of the Shelburne Museum on the right.

5.4   The entrance to Shelburne Museum is on the right at the crest of the hill, from which you can see magnificent views of the Adirondack Mountains. I suggest stopping at the museum and, if you can, devoting most of a day to it. The last of the great Lake Champlain steamships, the *Ticonderoga*, is a museum in itself, but the old Colchester Lighthouse; original paintings by Monet, Rembrandt, Picasso, and other masters; antique dolls; Americana; and many other great exhibits are also located on these spacious grounds.

Continuing south, you'll soon see large, exclusive, residential homes being built on the slopes to the right. When you reach the top of the rise (6.9 miles), you'll be presented with one of the most beautiful views in the eastern United States. In the town of Charlotte, the Adirondack Mountains of New York seem close enough to touch, and Lake Champlain stretches north and south in splendor. On the left are the Green Mountains with Camel's Hump and Mount Mansfield, the prominent features of the Presidential Range.

Descend down Church Hill and enjoy the view of the lake reaching south to Crown Point.

9.8   There's a traffic light at the intersection in Charlotte, but no village. *The road to the right is Route F-5 and leads to the Charlotte ferry*

crossing to Route 22 in Essex, New York. The road to the right leads over to the village of Hinesburg on Route 116.
  Continue straight.
  The small hills in this area, Church Hill, Pease Mountain, and Mount Philo, are the high points in the Champlain basin and mark a portion of the Champlain fault where older, harder rock was pushed westward over the younger sedimentary rock of the Champlain Valley. The summit of Mount Philo, Mount Philo State Park, is accessible by a paved road and affords splendid views of the lake and the New York mountains. At one point this land was under water, a vast inland sea connected by the Saint Lawrence to the Atlantic. In 1849, while building the railroad right-of-way, the bones of a whale were discovered in Charlotte in an era when the scientific theories of the great glaciations were first being postulated. This discovery was controversial news in both Europe and America. This skeleton, of a species similar to the Beluga, is on display at UVM.

13.5   This is the village of North Ferrisburgh. Great views of the Adirondacks are visible at times from Charlotte to Ferrisburgh.

17.3   The village of Ferrisburgh has the green and a brick church on the left and the town clerk's office on the right. *To the right, Little Chicago Road leads to the Lower Otter Creek Waterfowl Area, Kingsland Bay State Park on Lake Champlain, and the Little Otter Creek Wildlife Management Area.*

18.9   The junction of Route 22A, on the right, leads into Vergennes past the Kennedy Brothers factory outlet, which is now a series of crafts and gift shops. *Route 22A goes south from Vergennes through the open Champlain Valley to Fair Haven before entering New York. It is also a shortcut to Route 17 for those planning on crossing the Crown Point Bridge into New York and on to Ticonderoga or Lake George.*

19.8   The right turn at the shopping center also leads into Vergennes. You can see the eastern edge of the city on the right after passing it. (For more on Vergennes see Route 22A on page 205.)
  Vergennes is the third oldest city in the United States, incorporated on October 23, 1788, and is also the smallest, population twenty-five hundred. Located eight miles from Lake Champlain at the first major waterfall on Otter Creek, Vergennes is not a city one would associate with naval warfare. However, it was here that Benedict Arnold built the fleet with which he stopped the British advance in 1776, and here that Thomas Macdonough built the ships that defeated the British navy at the Battle of Plattsburgh in 1814.

20.2 This right turn also leads into Vergennes. Continue straight and climb the hill. After passing Vergennes, Route 7 heads southeast and the Green Mountains become visible on the left.

23.7 If you look at the Green Mountains from the ridge before descending into New Haven Junction, the gap where Bristol is located—and through which Routes 17 and 116 pass—is readily visible. The mountains to the north (left) are the Hogback Mountains, the high mountain behind the gap is Lincoln Mountain, and the one to the south (right) with the rocky sides is Robert Frost Mountain.

The ancient New Haven River flowed out of this gap and created a delta, upon which the village of Bristol is built, where it entered Lake Champlain ten thousand years ago. All the land between you and the mountains was once under water, as well as all the land for ten miles to the west. The modern New Haven River still flows through this gap and winds its way to the modern Lake Champlain via Otter Creek, but it is no longer the mighty river it once was.

24.2 In New Haven Junction, Route 17W is on the right just before the railroad tracks. *Going west on 17W will take you to the Crown Point Bridge crossing Lake Champlain. Take this road if you plan on going to Ticonderoga or Lake George.*

Continue straight. The old brick depot building is on the left.

24.3 To the left, just past the 7&17 Corner Store, is Route 17E leading over to Bristol and to Route 100 in Waitsfield.

26.1 From this vantage point you have another view of the rocky slopes of Robert Frost Mountain and a different perspective of Bristol Gap. For the next couple of miles you'll be treated to views of both the Green Mountains and the Adirondacks. The mountain ridge that stands between you and Lake Champlain is Snake Mountain and is part of the overthrust of the Champlain fault, as were the low hills in Charlotte.

31.3 Middlebury may feel like a small city, but it is an incorporated village located on the western edge of a township that wraps itself around the borders of the southeastern corner of the town of Weybridge. In Vermont, cities and villages are located within townships. To confuse matters some settlements, which may look like small villages, are governed by the township and some areas, called gores, have no local government at all!

(See map on page 269.)

Middlebury

Middlebury is known for education. Middlebury College, established in 1800, is one of the most sought-after private schools in the country. The Bread Loaf Writers' Conference and the Russian School are two internationally recognized summer programs of the college. In 1814 Emma Willard established the first women's college in the nation here.

Middlebury was once an industrial town, harnessing the power of the second falls on the Otter Creek. Marble was discovered in 1802, and some of Vermont's first marble quarries were established here. Isaac Markham developed the process for sawing marble, using a wire charged with grit in conjunction with water, still used today to saw marble and granite. The sawmills on Otter Creek lead to Jeremiah Hall's invention of the circular saw. Middlebury was also known for its early ironworks, and the method of welding cast steel was invented and patented here. It's not surprising that Rutland boy John Deere came to Middlebury to learn his trade as a blacksmith before joining the mass emigration west, where his iron plow tamed the western prairies. The falls also supplied power to the woolen mills and to other enterprises that made Middlebury one of the wealthier towns in the state.

Today this shire town (county seat) has a population of over eight thousand, and education is the primary industry with tourism a strong second. The marble mills of yesterday are restored and house local stores and business. The stone mills and warehouses on Mill Street below the falls are restored and occupied by stores and the Vermont Craft Center at Frog Hollow. The ever popular Bakery Lane Cookbook came from the restaurants on Bakery Lane along the creek. The Congregational Church, the Community House, the Sheldon Museum, and other historic buildings attract thousands of visitors each year.

32.0   The green in the center of the village of Middlebury is often a confused tangle of moderate to heavy traffic, and people who are not familiar with this junction often make wrong turns. It's best to decide whether you're continuing on Route 7S, stopping in town, or changing to Route 125 or Route 30 before reaching the green.

As you approach the green the Middlebury Inn is on the left. *The right turn takes you into downtown along Main Street, to Middlebury College, to Route 125S, and to Route 30S.*

To continue on Route 7S, continue straight between the two greens and turn left.

Caution: Cars entering from the lower green and from the street directly ahead should go around the green in a counterclockwise direction,

Accidents frequently happen here! This second narrow green acts as a rotary with one-way traffic. **At the end of the green, turn right** onto Routes 7S and 125E.

32.9   You'll find three motels on the south side of town.

35.9   The junction of Route 125E is on the left. *Route 125E leads over through Middlebury Gap to Hancock on Route 100.*

36.3   The junction of Route 116N is on the left; it intersects Route 125E in approximately .5 mile. *Route 116 goes along the western edge of the Green Mountains north to Burlington.*

39.1   The junction of Route 53 is on the left. *This highway goes to Lake Dunmore and around its eastern side to Forest Dale and Route 73. This delightful road is squeezed between the lake shore, the steep slopes of Mount Moosalamoo, and Oak Hill. Branbury State Park offers camping and a network of rugged nature trails, including those leading to Silver Lake. This road is not a shortcut; it will take you longer than continuing to Brandon before taking Route 73E.*

As you approach the northern end of the Valley of Vermont in which Brandon sits, you get the first glimpse of the northern end of the Taconic Range.

48.1   Entering into the village of Brandon, you might notice an old marble quarry on the left (east) side of the road, which marks the beginning of Vermont's marble belt.

When most people think of Vermont, what comes to mind are either majestic mountains or small farms on rolling hills, but not the swamps of the Champlain Valley. South of Middlebury and west of Route 7 the swamps stretch south to Brandon along the headwaters of Otter Creek. Critical habitat for countless waterfowl, many wildlife management areas have been established here. Route 73W goes through one of the largest, Brandon Wildlife Management Area in Long Swamp, otherwise almost impenetrable. For the patient wildlife photographer, many roadside opportunities exist, especially during the fall migrations of geese.

48.2   The merging of Route 73 is on the right at Brandon's northern green. *Route 73W leads to Route 30 and Route 22A.* **Continue through downtown Brandon.**

Brandon was the home of Thomas Davenport, builder of the first electric motor (in 1834), the electric printing press, the electric piano, and the electric railway, and editor of the first electrical journal.

Unfortunately, his vision was ahead of his time, and this man, whose inventions changed the world, died a pauper. Stephen Douglas, the great American orator from Illinois, was born and grew up in Brandon. The "little giant" didn't endear himself to his fellow Vermonters when he made the comment, "Vermont is the most glorious spot on the face of this globe for a man to be born in, provided he emigrated when he is very young." When running for the Republican nomination for president, Douglas was firmly defeated in Vermont by Abraham Lincoln.

48.6   Route 73E divides to the left at the end of Brandon's southern green. *Route 73E leads through the Brandon Gap over the Green Mountains to Route 100 in Rochester.*

It was just outside the village, along the Neshobe River on Route 73, that John Conant built one of this country's first stove factories. The famous Conant stove, first of the modern cast-iron stoves, was built using the ore for which this region was known. Vermont was a leader in the development of heating stoves—necessity being the mother of invention—and Bethel, about twenty miles due east, is still the world's leading manufacturer of cast-iron stoves.

Brandon hosts over a dozen motels, inns, and bed and breakfasts, including the Brandon Inn, the centerpiece of its downtown. If you turn left onto Route 73E, Park Street, you'll ride past beautiful homes, two of which are bed-and-breakfast inns. Houses along this street are often photographed for magazines and calendars, especially during foliage season.

Continue straight on Route 7S.

49.2   As you're leaving the village another old marble quarry, now filled with water, is on the left. White marble with black streaks can also be seen in the road-cuts along the highway as you crest the slight hill. This is the northern end of the Valley of Vermont and the beginning of the marble belt that stretches along the eastern length of the Taconic Mountains.

51.3   Across the field to the right you can see a cliff of solid marble. Not all marble was used for building; much was quarried to produce lime, which is still used to neutralize the acidic soil of the state. Lime was also used in tanning leather, making glass, producing paper, and as the primary ingredient in mortar. The earliest use of polished marble was in the production of tombstones; it replaced slate for headstones until granite supplanted it. You can quickly date the age of a remote cemetery—useful if you're doing genealogy research—by the proportion of the types of stone used for grave markers.

52.8   Here is a magnificent view looking south down the Valley of Vermont, with the Taconic Mountains on the right and the Green Mountains on the left. The Taconic Mountains were originally the top of the Green Mountains, which were sheared off and pushed westward in a cataclysmic event over 300 million years ago. The process produced so much heat that the sedimentary limestones of this valley, and those under the Taconic Mountains, metamorphosed into marble.

56.0   In the center of Pittsford the green is on the left and a broad but tight curve is at its end. The signs say 15 MPH, and I recommend that you heed it.

The Vermont historical site marker here states that in 1790 the first U.S. patent was issued by George Washington to Samuel Hopkins of Pittsford for the process of making potash out of wood ashes.

56.6   The Pittsford Historical Museum is on the right. Pittsford is part of the West Rutland marble district, and the museum documents the role Pittsford played when this was the marble capital of the world.

57.2   At the bottom of the hill in Pittsford Mills the junction of Route 3S to Proctor and West Rutland is on the right. **Continue up the hill on Route 7S** unless you plan to take Route 4 west or wish to visit the Vermont Marble Exhibit. If you plan to go over to the western side of the state or to New York, consider going down Route 3.

SIDE TRIP OR SHORTCUT TO ROUTE 4W:
Proctor and the Vermont Marble Exhibit

0.0   Route 3 winds and twists southward into the throat of a narrow valley that can be seen ahead. This is an area of new residential growth and in places looks like Vermont's version of the suburbs. Its view certainly makes it an attractive place to live.

7.5   The village of Proctor is across the river. **Turn right**, cross both the beautiful marble bridge (1915) spanning Otter Creek and the wrought-iron bridge over the railroad tracks, proceeding down to the village square (.3 mile). The marble buildings on the left are a fitting prelude to the Vermont Marble Exhibit on the right. Stop and visit the exhibit or turn around and cross back over the bridges.

Much of the history of Vermont and even of the United States resulted from the wealth and political influence of Vermont's marble barons. The Vermont Marble Company was formed in 1880 from the merger of two former marble companies and became the largest in the world under the management of Redfield Proctor. The vast wealth generated by the Vermont marble industry enabled the Proctor dynasty to have a huge impact on the history of Vermont. Redfield Proctor served as secretary of war under Benjamin Harrison, while another Vermonter, Levi Morton, was vice-president. It was Redfield Proctor's influence as a U.S. senator that prompted America to enter the Spanish-American War. Redfield Proctor's son, Redfield, Jr., and grandson Fletcher were both governors of Vermont. Presidency of the Vermont Marble Company continued to be passed from father to son until the mid-1960s. Proctor is not named after this Vermonter, but after his grandfather, a Revolutionary War hero.

Continue down the narrow valley with the Otter Creek and the Vermont Railway on the right, a beautiful country ride for the next four miles.

11.8   (or 12.4 if you went into the village of Proctor) The junction of Route 3 at Route 4 in Rutland.

There are two ways to return to Route 7. To avoid the congested traffic of commercial Rutland, turn right and follow Route 4A west for 1.5 miles; access Route 4 going east; another 3.8 miles and Route 4 junctions with Route 7 on the south side of the city. To go through Rutland turn left and follow Route 4A east. In a mile, at the traffic light, turn right and cross the railroad tracks. Follow this commercial road into downtown Rutland. Ride up the hill; Route 4A meets Route 7 only 2.1 miles from the junction of Route 3.

The village of Pittsford Mills is behind you, but you are still in the town of Pittsford when you pass a car dealership on the left.

62.8   This is the city limit of Rutland. You'll find numerous motels and restaurants along Route 7 in the city. Several of them, including the Seward's Family Restaurant, are located prior to the intersection of Route 4. Adjoining the Seward's Family Restaurant is the Seward's Dairy, where tours of the milk processing plant and ice-cream manufacturing are given four mornings a week.

64.1   Route 4 merges on the left.

This concludes the central section of Route 7. Many travelers, both tourists and locals, cross Vermont on Route 4 or Routes 100 and 107 to reach Route 7 in Rutland before continuing south on the western side of the Green Mountains. The southern section of Route 7 begins where this one ends.

Route 7S: Rutland to Bennington

This is the main western corridor for southern Vermont. Route 7 follows the Valley of Vermont from Rutland to Bennington. Sections of this road are modern highway and portions are the old winding Route 7. This is the quickest way to get from Rutland to southern New England, especially if you stay on Route 7 instead of historic Route 7A.

0.0   Route 4E is on the left in the city of Rutland. At the next traffic light, Route 4A (going west) is on the right. The Rutland green is just after this light.

Continue straight through a series of traffic lights with the green to the right. Almost any of the streets on the right will take you into downtown Rutland.

0.7   The Midway Diner is set back on the left at the bottom of the hill, and its large parking lot is a good place to regroup if there are numerous vehicles touring together.

As you crest the next small rise and cross the railroad tracks, the Rutland Fair Ground is on the right. The Rutland Fair, held during Labor Day week, is a county fair with livestock, poultry, and commercial vendors. Of course, most people come for the midway rides or for the evening events that range from stock car racing to country-western music stars.

You'll find plenty of places to eat and stay along this 1.5-mile stretch of Route 7. Dunkin Donuts, KFC, Comfort Inn, McDonald's, Sirloin Saloon, Bagel Cafe, Sunset Motel, Lum's, Day's Inn, car dealerships, and gas stations line this four-lane highway. As you approach the junction of the modern Route 4W you'll see Denny's, the Howard Johnson Inn and restaurant, Holiday Inn, Ponderosa, and the Green Mountain Plaza. You won't find many restaurants or much lodging on Route 7 until you reach the Bennington area.

2.2   If you're going to New York or want to go to Manchester the roundabout way on Route 30S, turn right onto Route 4 west. *You can create an alternate route or a leisurely day trip by taking Route 4W to West Rutland; Route 133S to Pawlet; and then either Route 30E to Manchester Center or Route 30W to Route 4 in Fair Haven.*

Continue straight on Route 7; from here the signs say it's twenty-nine miles to Manchester and fifty-four miles to Bennington.

3.5   Route 7B on the right is the old Route 7 and leads to Route 103 before winding back to this one.

5.0   The junction of Route 103 is on the left. *Route 103 will take you southeast to Route 100 in Ludlow and Route 5 in Rockingham (Bellows Falls).*

6.4   Straight ahead you get a beautiful view of Dorset Mountain to the south. The Taconics will be on the right (west) and the Green Mountains on the left (east) as you continue to travel south along the Valley of Vermont.

9.0   As you enter into Wallingford the modern four-lane highway ends and you're on the old Route 7. Wallingford is the birthplace of Paul Harris, the founder of Rotary International and of True Temper Corporation (True Temper Hardware), which was formed from a few local businesses in 1902 and grew to be one of America's largest companies.

10.2   At the traffic light in the center of the village of Wallingford is the intersection of Route 140. *Route 140W cuts through the Taconics, intersects with Route 133, and ends in Poultney at Route 30. Route 140E twists through the Green Mountains to East Wallingford and Route 103.*

Farther down the street on the left is The Old Stone Shop with a Vermont historic site marker that reads: "The Old Stone Shop, built in 1848 by Batcheller and Sons, makers of pitchforks. For many years after 1848 farm implements were manufactured here. Lyman Batcheller and his sons brought the forge in 1835 and their forks became famous throughout the U.S. and Europe. In 1902 they merged with the firm making True Temper products which rebuilt the inn."

12.6   On the right is a road-cut showing the sedimentary layers which, through pressure and tectonic activity, have been altered into metamorphic rock. These are banded dolomitic marbles and red-brown quartzite of the Cambrian Monkton Formation found as far north as Winooski.

14.6   This is South Wallingford.

This narrow valley is filled with sandy hills (moraines) that formed as the last glacier retreated northward ten thousand years ago. You may also notice quarries alongside the road from which rock may have been quarried for building material or to produce lime. Directly ahead you can see the valley narrowing at the base of Dorset Mountain as you approach Danby. Vermont's premier marble comes from under this mountain. The Imperial mine is completely underground and is now over twenty acres in extent! Trucked to Proctor for finishing in blocks that may weigh up to forty tons, the marble mined here has been used in many structures, including the U.S. Supreme Court and the U.S. Senate Office buildings.

12.9   A classic example of French–Second Empire architecture can be seen on the small hill to the right.

18.9   Here you get a sense of how the Taconics were sheared off the top of the Green Mountains and moved westward to form the mountains on the right. Of course they have both been scoured by glacial ice four times in the 300 million years since this transpired, so the contours don't exactly match.

19.6   The turn to Danby is on the right. *By turning into the village and then following Danby Road, you can travel through the Taconic Mountains to Route 133 in Pawlet.*

Looking at this side of Dorset Mountain in the spring or late fall, you can see the small abandoned mines, or at least their dump piles. South of Danby is the narrowest part of the Valley of Vermont. Under certain conditions, the wind in this valley can become violent. When wind is channeled from either the north or the south, a tunneling effect, a shirkshire, develops, for which this portion of the Valley of Vermont is famous.

The entrance to Emerald Lake State Park is on the right in North Dorset. From this park numerous hiking trails range across the eastern slopes of Dorset Mountain through old-stand forest.

24.9   The gray dolomite marble showing in the road-cut on the left is one example of the marble quarried in this area for building.

27.4   There's a ledge on the right in East Dorset that is formed of still another variety of marble.

27.9   In East Dorset, the junction of Route 7A is on the right; **Route 7 continues straight**. Route 7A, called Historic Route 7A, is the old road, while Route 7 is the modern highway. Route 7A travels through the villages of the valley, while Route 7 bypasses them. Route 7A follows the western side of the valley along the base of the Taconic Mountains, and Route 7 is built on the lower slopes of the Green Mountains. Route 7A has many points of interest, places to stop, and numerous restaurants, hotels, and motels. Route 7 is a much faster highway than Route 7A, suitable for making good time getting from point A to point B, but it has no services.

Continue straight. Bennington is only twenty-nine miles, and you'll find exits to Manchester and Arlington along the way. The Valley of Vermont widens from this point south, and from Route 7 you get great views of Mount Equinox to the right.

32.2 Exit 4 is for Manchester, Manchester Center, Route 30, Route 11E, and Route 7A. To the right you have views of Mount Equinox, the highest peak in the Taconic Range at 3,835 feet, which is owned by the Carthusian monks who have a monastery on the southwestern side. To the right you also catch glimpses of the villages of Manchester and Manchester Center and the Mettowee Valley (Route 30) cutting through the Taconics.

42.8 Exit 3 goes to Route 313W to Arlington, the former home of author Dorothy Canfield Fisher and artist Norman Rockwell who lived in East Arlington from 1939 to 1953. Many of his famous Main Street America series were painted here. Over two hundred local residents were used in his portraits, some of whom are the guides through the exhibition housed in the Arlington Gallery.

Most of the lodging in this area is located on Route 7A between Exit 3 and Exit 2.

47.5 You are now at the highest elevation along Route 7—1,504 feet above sea level— here in Shaftsbury.

52.5 Route 7 begins its descent from the slopes of the Green Mountains into the village of Bennington. With a population of 16,451, Bennington is larger than all but two of Vermont's cities, but remains a village with a town manager and selectmen instead of a city government.

53.1 Exit 2 on the right goes to Route 7A just south of Shaftsbury.

54.3 Exit 1 on the right goes to Northside Drive, Bennington College, North Bennington, and Route 67A. **Continue straight** toward Bennington.

54.9 The Bennington Monument, visible to the right in Old Bennington village, stands 306 feet tall. I suggest taking the side trip to Old Bennington while you're here. (See Old Bennington, Route 7A, page 95.)

55.7 The traffic light marks the end of the modern Route 7 highway. On the right is the old Route 7 (7A) on Northside Drive; to the left is Kocher Drive. **Continue straight** on North Street (Route 7S).

56.4   Just past the traffic light, on the right, you'll see the Blue Benn Diner, a vintage diner car located here since the 1940s. Most of the numerous restaurants in Bennington are within walking distance of the intersection of Route 9.

56.9   The intersection of Routes 9 and 7 is in downtown Bennington. There's a vintage street clock on the corner of Main and South Streets directly across from the old Hotel Putnam (now retail shops). *Turn left to go on Route 9E to Route 100 or to Brattleboro; turn right on Route 9W to visit Old Bennington or to go to Albany, New York; continue straight on Route 7S to go to Pownal and Massachusetts.*

You'll find lodging on both Route 9W (West Main Street) and on Route 9E (East Main Street).

Route 7S: Bennington to Massachusetts

0.0   From the intersection of Routes 7 and 9 in downtown Bennington, continue straight on South Street. As you drive down South Street, notice the beautiful marble Federal building on the left and the police department, made of local dolomite, just ahead on the right.

0.5   Unlike the sprawl on the north side of Bennington, this side quickly becomes residential, and then you're out of the village entirely. Only five motels are located on the south side of the village.

6.0   Pownal Center is a collection of houses at the end of the Valley of Vermont. As the highway begins to descend down the shoulder of Mann Hill, you are presented with a beautiful view of the northern end of the Hoosic Valley. From here the Green Mountains begin to blend into the Hoosic Mountains.

Both James Garfield (twentieth president) and Chester Arthur (Garfield's vice-president) taught school in North Pownal. Chester Arthur became the twenty-first president after Garfield was assassinated. Since there was only a difference of three years in their ages, I wonder whether they knew each other while teaching in the town, whether the experience was something they shared.

9.0   Route 346 on the right follows the Hoosic River northwest into New York. *This is a nice highway to take if you wish to travel through New York's Catskill region.*

10.4 On the left is a great moraine or kame terrace and several commercial sand and gravel pits quarrying this deposit. You can almost visualize the last remains of the great glacier melting in this narrow valley, the great rivers of ice melt running along the edges, the sand, gravel, and boulders that the ice collected for fifteen thousand years being deposited upon the bare rock of the mountain's slope.

10.9 This is the southern border of Vermont. Route 7 continues into Williamstown, Massachusetts. The northwestern part of the Bay State is a beautiful area, but that's another book.

ROUTE 5:
Brattleboro to Newport

Until the building of the interstate highway in the 1950s, this route was one of the two primary north/south highways in Vermont. The Connecticut River was the transportation route used by Indians, explorers, and the first settlers and, until the 1870s, was the primary method of shipping goods in and out of Vermont. The first blazed paths followed the river; the first post roads, turnpikes, and stage routes were built upon their predecessors. In the mid-1800s the railroads came to Vermont, and as their railways followed the river valleys, these river towns grew even more prosperous and played an even greater role in the building of the United States. Route 5 follows these original roads, connecting the cities, towns, and villages that grew along the river.

Brattleboro
Readers of mystery novels may already be familiar with Brattleboro, where fictitious police detective Joe Gunther lives and works. Archer Mayor's series of novels is set against an accurate background of this southern Vermont village, but the vitality and diversity of the community can best be experienced by walking around the downtown area. You'll find great food from Elliot Street to the north end of Putney Road and lodging from the Art Deco Latchis Hotel on lower Main Street to the convenience lodging around Exit 3 of I-91.

Archer Mayor is not the first author to be associated with Brattleboro. Royall Tyler, writer of the first American comedy and a novelist, was a local resident, and both Harriet Beecher Stowe and Henry Wadsworth Longfellow frequented the village when they came for the famous hydropathic cures. Rudyard Kipling finished both Jungle Books *and* Captains Courageous *while living here. Perhaps you're more familiar with the works of the famous American painter, William Morris Hunt, or with the work of his younger brother, Richard Morris Hunt, who designed the base of the Statue of Liberty, the Biltmore in Asheville, North Carolina, and the Breakers in Newport, Rhode Island. Larkin Mead, a famous American sculptor, and Jubilee Jim Fisk, partner with Jay Gould, who almost cornered the gold market but caused the Panic of 1869 instead, lived here.*

Although Route 5 comes north from Massachusetts through Gilford and then struggles through the congestion of downtown Brattleboro, let's begin Route 5 on the north side of Brattleboro at the major intersection of Routes 9E, 5, and I-91. Most visitors coming into Vermont from the south will be traveling on the interstate highway and have only to take Exit 3 to arrive at this intersection. Those coming across Vermont on Route 9E have only to access I-91N at Exit 2 and drive for 3.3 miles before taking Exit 3. Travelers coming from Route 30E pick up Route 5 in downtown Brattleboro and have to ride north for 2.1 congested miles. Many will reach Route 5 coming west from Keene, New Hampshire.

0.0   The route begins at the major intersection of Routes 9E, 5, and I-91.

This is an extremely busy location, with traffic exiting the interstate and traffic entering Vermont from New Hampshire on Route 9. Within 0.5 miles north or south are numerous motels and restaurants, many catering to truckers and business travelers. As you head north on Route 5 for the first 0.75 miles, you'll encounter trucks entering and exiting the major industries, including Vermont's largest company, C&S Wholesale grocers, and After the Fall, producers of juice and juice drinks.

0.8   Route 5 quickly leaves Brattleboro behind. While continuing north to Putney you'll enjoy farmland and views of New Hampshire's mountains to the east. Since I-91 runs parallel to Route 5, you are spared the heavy traffic that used to travel on this highway. About 2.5 miles north from the intersection of Routes 9 and 5 is the Hidden Acres Campground on the right. There is a nice public picnic area in the pines on the right about 0.2 miles beyond this campground.

3.4   The Brattleboro North KOA campground is on the right (east). The vistas to the right of the river and the hills of New Hampshire are part of the ancestral African continent that is divided from the proto-North American continent by a deep fault line over which the Connecticut River flows. Vermont feels and looks different from New Hampshire and Massachusetts because the geology is different. The Connecticut River flows over the ancient fault line that used to be the edge of the North American plate; the land on which you are traveling was the basal rock and sedimentary deposits of a shallow sea; and the land across the river is composed of rock from a volcanic archipelago and a portion of the ancient African continent. The geological formation of Massachusetts is a combination of the collision and the withdrawal of the ancient African tectonic plate. There are other differences between Vermont and her neighbors, but this one "hits bedrock," so to speak.

6.1   Exit 4 of I-91S is on the right just after the gas station. Route 5 follows this interstate highway all the way to Newport. You can always use I-91 to bypass any of the towns and cities along this route.

6.4   The access road to I-91N is on the right.
To the left is the Community Deli, and to the right is a gas station; just down this road, next to I-91, is the Putney Inn.

Putney used to be the home of Windham College, one of the creative enclaves of the hippie culture in the late 1960s. The town remains a very creative arts community, but it is much quieter—with fewer people—since the closing of the college. The counterculture of the 1960s was not the first of Putney's avant-garde movements. In 1838 Humphry Noye's community, espousing free love and shared wives, flourished briefly here. Fleeing local persecution in 1847, the community fled to the wilds of western New York where they established Oneida.

Putney was the home of Senator George D. Aiken, one of the most beloved of Vermont's statesmen, who served as both governor and U.S. senator.

6.8   In the center of the village is the traffic island in front of the Putney General Store. Ahead and to the right is Basketville, a popular tourist stop since I was a boy; on the left is the mill where baskets are made. This company is the major manufacturer of American splint baskets, but the baskets and wicker in the store come from around the world. **Continue past Basketville** and climb the hill as you leave the village.

The Connecticut Valley from Putney to Bellows Falls contains some of the best farmland in Vermont. The rich soil plus the slightly longer growing season and localized weather conditions make this land suitable for orchards and berry and vegetable farms. You'll ride by fields of strawberries, blueberries, and numerous apple orchards. Harlow's Sugar House is the place to stop to pick strawberries (June), blueberries (July–August), raspberries (July–August), or apples (fall). North of Westminster you'll find fields of sweet corn, green and wax beans, squash and pumpkins, and various other summer vegetables. Stop by any one of several produce stands along the highway to get the freshest berries, fruits, or vegetables you'll find anywhere.

In the southern Connecticut Valley the weather is slightly warmer and the growing season slightly longer than in any other part of Vermont except the Champlain Valley. The extra twenty, sometimes thirty, frost-free days allow some plants to grow here that are not found in other parts of the state. Sycamore and dogwood trees can be found here, and I have not seen pear trees growing anywhere else in the state. The steep slopes of the eastern-facing hills in combination with the Connecticut River produces a localized climatic condition in the fall, heavy fog. The slope, the fog, and the eastern orientation all contribute to preventing the formation of frost on the vulnerable orchards. Usually the fog lifts by around 10:00 a.m., but if you find yourself driving through mile after mile of this, detour on inland roads or those that rise into the hills.

15.5   When you reach the southern end of the village of Westminster, notice the unusually wide and straight main street. In 1737, the village was laid out this way so the militia would have a place to muster and practice. The brick house on the left (1814) is a wonderful example of a Federal-style home. The First Congregational Church (1767) and the Westminster Institute (the brick building) are on the right in the center of the village. Next to the post office is a splendid example of a colonial homestead, lovingly restored inside and out.

Both New York and New Hampshire originally claimed the region now known as Vermont. The old Cumberland Courthouse, the seat of New York's colonial administration in The Grants, was located at the north end of the village. Here, in March 1775, the Westminster Massacre took place, when Yorkers shot the locals who had taken possession of the courthouse protesting New York's right to issue land grants in this area. This incident was the beginning of the independence movement in The Grants. In Westminster on January 16, 1777, The Grants declared their independence and the formation of New Connecticut.

Westminster was also the site of the first printing office and the first newspaper in Vermont. The press used was the Stephen Daye press, the first printing press in America, that now resides in the Vermont Historical Society's Museum in Montpelier.

16.4   On the flats of Lower Westminster you'll find the MG Museum ironically located behind a local garage specializing in Volkswagens.

16.8   The junction of Route 123E is on the right at what is locally known as Westminster Depot. **Continue straight.**

The road winds up and around the hill, affording a great view looking north up the river. On the far side, the access road leading to Route I-91 (Exit 5) is on the left. From here to Bellows Falls are the truck farms (small commercial vegetable farms) for which the area is well known.

18.8   The restaurant on the left after the Ford dealership is a popular local dining spot. Route 5 winds up the hill after passing the restaurant. At the crest of the hill, notice the large bank of clay on the left riddled with holes indicating where a colony of bank swallows has dug tunnels in which to build their nests.

Ahead you can see Fall Mountain and the village of Bellows Falls, where the clock tower of the town hall and the gray stone Immanuel Episcopal Church are clearly visible. Crossing the bridge over the Saxtons River, you can see the ruins of the old paper mills on the right.

Bellows Falls

Bellows Falls, referred to locally as BF, is named after its first settler, Col. Benjamin Bellows, but the village was originally known as Great Falls. Here was a gorge so narrow and a drop so great that shad coming up the river from the Atlantic Ocean could go no farther; only the Atlantic salmon could make it up past the falls, but only when the river wasn't running high. The first bridge over the Connecticut River (1785) and the first lock canal in America (1791) were built here, creating a crossroads of river and overland traffic. Indians continued to come to Bellows Falls as late as the early 1800s to fish for salmon.

Bellows Falls was also known for its log drives in which trees felled during the winter in the northern forests of Vermont and New Hampshire were floated down the river in late spring and summer. The logs would jam trying to make the ninety-degree turn into the gorge and, as this section of the river was always a trouble spot, extra hands were always needed. The last log drive took place in

*1915, when a scant sixty-five million board feet of spruce logs went
over the dam and through the gorge.*

*This village was one of New England's largest industrial centers
from the 1870s to 1927, producing paper, silk, wool, and farm implements. The first paper mill was built here in 1802 and the
world's first pulp paper mill in 1869. (When I was a boy, the village
still had six paper mills.) Bellows Falls was home to other industries: the Derby & Ball scythe snath factory was the oldest and
largest snath factory in the world; the Vermont Farm Machine Company was the largest manufacturer of dairy machinery in the world;
and the Casein Company of America produced, as a milk byprod-
uct, the red paint used on barns throughout the United States.*

*Bellows Falls, like many Vermont towns, was at the center of
things in the late 1800s and not considered a rural town. The devastating flood of 1927, coupled with the depression and the flood
in 1932, destroyed most of the commercial base of the village. This
was a time of change in American industry that affected the fortunes and future of the town.*

*Bellows Falls is where I grew up, where my family grew up. In
school, we learned not only U.S. history but also Vermont's and our
own rich local history.*

20.1   In Bellows Falls at the bottom of Old Terrace Street (Red Light
Hill) is the junction of Route 121. *Route 121 goes between Bellows Falls
and Grafton.* Going straight on Atkinson Street is the quickest and
easiest way through town, although the mileage is the same as going
through the square; this street is residential and joins up with Route
5 on the north side of the village. Turning right leads down Westminster Street to "The Square" and then up Rockingham Street to
where Atkinson Street joins it.

**Continue straight on Atkinson Street or detour and take the
alternate route to the square.**

ALTERNATE ROUTE:
The Square

0.0   On Route 5, at the bottom of Red Light Hill (Old Terrace
Street, Route 121) **bear right** and drive down Westminster Street. On
the right you overlook the river and the hydroelectric plant built in
1927-1928.

On the left are three interesting buildings. The brick armory
(1915), now retirement apartments, is a uniquely styled structure

that, with its narrow slit windows, resembles a medieval castle; the Rockingham Public Library (1908), donated by Andrew Carnegie, is a neoclassical-style building made of imported beige brick; the Masonic temple is a renovation (1909) done in the French–SecondEmpire style with Italianate-style trimming. Bellows Falls has a variety of architecturally important buildings, including the Gothic-Revival Immanuel Episcopal Church built by Richard Upjohn, who popularized this style, complete with bells made by Paul Revere. Half the surviving bells made by Revere and Sons reside in Vermont.

Just as you're about to go down into the square you'll see the First Vermont Bank on the left, the site of Hetty Green's house. Known as the "witch of Wall Street," Hetty Green was the richest woman in America at the turn of the twentieth century but lived like a pauper. The story of Hetty Green, and of Bellows Falls during its heyday, is written about in the book, *The Day They Shook the Plum Tree*.

0.3   Downtown Bellows Falls is built upon an L-shaped square, unlike most Vermont villages that formed around a green.

To the right the base of the L leads to the canal, the island, and the river. The canal, begun in 1791 and finished in 1802, was originally built for transportation with eight locks and an elevation of fifty-two feet, allowing boats to navigate around the tremendous falls on the river. The canal also supplied the water power for the mills on the island and on the south side of the village. The first hydroelectric facility was built in 1898, but the present power station was built in the late 1920s. The canal was enlarged for the power plant and delivers 4,200,000 gallons per minute to it. The fish ladder, completed in 1982, is open to the public; here you can watch the salmon and shad during their migration up the river.

Island Street, on the left after crossing the canal, leads to the train station, where you can take a round-trip tour from Bellows Falls to Chester on the Green Mountain Flyer. Just beyond Island Street is the Vilas Bridge over the Connecticut River. Park in the large lot on the left just before the bridge. Just over the bank on the right side (south) of the concrete bridge is a series of Indian carvings (petroglyphs) that can be seen from the bridge. No one knows whether these carvings were made three thousand or three hundred years ago, but they have been cut deeper by the local D.A.R. chapter. The traditional fishing place of the Abnaki Indians, the great falls was also the site of the first bridge built over the Connecticut River (1785). The gorge was widened when they built the hydroelectric dam in the late 1920s, again in the late 1930s or early 1940s, and still again during the 1970s. As a boy, I was able to jump across the lower gorge when the water was low, which shows how narrow the channel used to be. The spring runoff provides an awesome spectacle of raw power, vibrating the bridge and the earth around it.

You can cross the bridge into New Hampshire and continue north along the river on Routes 12 and 12A to Windsor or go south to Keene, New Hampshire. **Turn around and go back into the square.**

Devastating fires in 1860 and 1912 destroyed most of the wooden buildings in the square. These fires occurred during the era of the village's prosperity, so the commercial buildings built to replace them are of brick and of high-quality construction. More than modernization or urban renewal, fires and floods have transformed the downtowns of Vermont. The Bellows Falls square has been altered by several major fires in the past twenty-five years.

The central building in the square, the town hall, was built in 1926 and is an amalgam of several different architectural styles. Its clock tower can easily be seen as one approaches the village on Route 5 from either the north or the south. The movie theater in the town hall is now owned by the village. Where else can you see a feature film for $2.50—and on a full-sized screen at that?

At the end of the square, on the right, is the head of Canal Street that leads down and along the canal. You can cross onto the island to the train depot. Canal Street will lead up to join with Rockingham Street.

You leave the square along Rockingham Street with the old railroad hotel (Hotel Rockingham, circa 1883) on the right and, just beyond it on the left, the Miss Bellows Falls Diner, the only surviving barrel-roof diner in Vermont. Built in the late 1920s by the Worcester Lunch Car Company, it was moved here in 1942 and has since become a classic site for diner enthusiasts.

0.6   Canal Street and the hydroelectric dam are on the right. The bridge leads over to North Walpole, New Hampshire, and Route 12. Rockingham Street continues along the elevation above the river.

0.8   Atkinson Street, on the left, ends here.

20.1   **Continue straight on Atkinson Street.** This residential street has some interesting houses. Foremost among them is the gray-shingled Queen-Anne-style home at 47 Atkinson. This house is the finest example of this architectural style in the state.

20.9   Atkinson Street ends at Rockingham Street. The Connecticut River, now backed up behind the power dam, is on the right.

21.5   There's a motel here, on the edge of the village.

21.7 A bed-and-breakfast inn is located on the terrace to the left, and there is a restaurant on the right. From the vantage point of the inn or the dining room of the restaurant, you can enjoy a fantastic vista of the river and the setback, which is separated from the water by the railroad bed. Perch, pickerel, pike, and record-sized small-mouth and largemouth bass abound.

22.9 At the top of the hill you'll find tourist cabins on one side of the highway and a motel on the other. The town's industries are now located in this area.

23.7 Route 5N takes a ninety-degree turn right. This is the junction of Route 103; the access onto I-91 (Exit 6) is a hundred yards ahead. *If you continue straight you'll be on Route 103 going to Chester, Ludlow, and Rutland.*

Caution: The turn to continue on Route 5 is actually an S-turn and is often sandy.

Going down the hill you'll pass over the Williams River. The entire area to the right, lush wetlands where mud, snapping, and painted turtles abound, is also a popular fishing area for bass, pickerel, pike, perch, and brown trout.

Route 5 follows the river north to Springfield, twisting and turning, going through shaded woods and open fields along the river. This section of Route 5 is known as the Missing Link Road because it took almost a decade after the flood of 1927 to rebuild the road between the junction of Route 103 and the Black River in Springfield. This is a very beautiful section of highway, with views of the river and New Hampshire on the right. Route 5 crosses the Black River within view of the junction ahead.

30.8 Route 5N briefly joins with Route 11E on the north side of the river. There's a gas station/minimart on both sides and a restaurant and lodging directly ahead. *To go into Springfield or to go west to Route 100 or Route 7A, turn left.*

Turn right. In 0.3 miles you'll access I-91 (Exit 7) and pass under the interstate highway.

31.6 Route 5N takes a ninety-degree turn left. Route 11 continues east, crossing the toll bridge over the Connecticut River into Charlestown, New Hampshire. On the right is the Holt Landing and Fishing Access.

Just across the river in Charlestown is the site of Old Fort Number 4, now recreated and open to the public. This was the northernmost British fort during the early colonial period and the French and Indian Wars. Built in 1759 by order of General Jeffrey Amherst and under the command of Captain John Stark, the Crown Point Military Road transversed the Vermont frontier from Fort No. 4 to Crown Point. This road was essential to the successful capture of Montreal by General Amherst in 1760; it was also used by the early settlers to reach the interior of The Grants when settlement became feasible at the conclusion of the Seven Years' War in 1763.

37.0   The junction of Route 143 is on the left. *Route 143 leads over the ridge to downtown Springfield.* This is wonderful touring along the river and through farmland. In the summer the fields of the upper Connecticut Valley are filled with corn. This is my favorite stretch of Route 5.

38.7   The Bow Baptist Church on the left and the William Jarvis House ahead on the right are located in Weatherfield Bow.

It was William Jarvis, U.S. Consul to Portugal, who in 1811 brought four hundred of the world-famous Merino sheep to Vermont—the beginning of the commercial wool industry here.

41.6   The Wilgus State Park on the right is a great place to have a picnic lunch and take a break under the pine trees overlooking the river. The state park has camping as well.

42.7   Suddenly you emerge from the woods and you're in the village of Ascutney with its traffic light at the junction of Routes 12E and 131W with access to I-91 (Exit 8). *Route 131W goes to Route 106 and Route 103 in Proctorsville. Route 12E goes to Claremont, New Hampshire.* **Continue straight on combined Routes 5N and 12N.** The 1799 House is on the right and the Ascutney General Store is on the left. There's a motel 0.5 miles ahead on the left.

Mount Ascutney, on the left, is the prominent peak you see as you drive up Route 5 from Springfield. This solitary mountain, just over three thousand feet, was formed beneath the surface of the earth. Known as a monadnock and composed of hard igneous rock, it has resisted the erosion of glaciers, wind, and water better than the softer metamorphic rocks that once covered and surrounded it. Of course, this process has taken millions of years, wearing the metamorphic rock down to the level we travel on and leaving the granite towering above the landscape. The study of Mount Ascutney and Mount Monadnock in New Hampshire lead to the understanding of the principals and cycles of erosion.

43.9   The junction of Route 44A on the left leads to the Ascutney

State Park in approximately a mile. There's a paved toll road leading up the mountain to about the 2,800-foot level, and hiking paths from the parking lot lead to the summit. The trails on Mount Ascutney inspired the creation of the Long Trail and the Appalachian Trail. Camping, picnicking, hiking, and hang-gliding are offered in this state park.

47.6   As you enter into Windsor, the American Precision Museum is on the left. At the first traffic light is the junction of Route 44W on the left. *Route 44W leads to Route 106.* On the right is Route 12A that takes you across the Connecticut River on a magnificent covered bridge to Cornish, New Hampshire. The row of apartments on the left (on Route 44W), one of the largest tenement blocks in northern New England, was built in 1922 for the employees of the National Acme Machine Company (NAMCO)

Windsor

Windsor is considered the birthplace of Vermont and of the American machine-tool industry. Vermont was one the leaders of the Industrial Revolution in the United States, and Windsor was where precision machining began.

The American Precision Museum, just south of the junction of Route 44, was the actual site of the birth of this industry. Sometime prior to the Civil War a gun shop was located here. The machines invented at this gun shop, the shaper (crank planer), an early turret lathe, a profiler, and the disk grinder, were then manufactured and sold to other companies. The gun shop grew to become the Robins & Lawrence Company where the development of interchangeable parts created a revolution in manufacturing. The breech-loading rifle was invented by machinist Christian Sharp, and the five-shot pistol was invented by another employee, Baird Wesson. Robins & Lawrence produced the Sharp Rifle and muskets for the U.S. government, but prior to the Civil War the company went bankrupt and was purchased by E. G. Lamson. In 1863, a lever-action, breech-loading, repeating rifle was patented by Alfred Ball, produced by E.G. Lamson & Company, and used by Union troops at the end of the Civil War. E.G. Lamson & Company went on to become the Jones & Lamson Company of Springfield.

But guns and machinery to produce armaments were not the only inventions to come out of Windsor. Here Lemuel Hedge invented numerous machines including one for ruling paper in 1815—previously it was done by hand—another for dividing scales in 1827, and the band saw in 1849. Asahel Hubbard invented the revolving hydraulic pump in 1828. Glazier's points, still used to se-

cure glass in wooden window frames, were invented in Windsor.

It was here, in Elijah West's tavern on July 8, 1777, that the constitution of the Republic of Vermont was ratified by the delegates from the towns in "The Grants." This process had begun a year earlier in Kent's Tavern on the other side of the Green Mountains in Dorset, with the drafting of the Articles of Association. Who knows how long it would have taken the delegates to agree on the constitution if the news that General Burgoyne's redcoats had captured Fort Ticonderoga and were matching south to Bennington had not arrived just as a violent summer thunderstorm delayed their hasty departure for their home towns?

47.9   The Windsor Diner is on the right.

Continue straight along Windsor's main street, where you'll see many fine examples of Federalist architecture, including the beautiful

The Old South Congregational Church in Windsor was designed and built by Asher Benjamin in 1799.

Old South Congregational Church built in 1799 by Asher Benjamin. The Windsor House, housing the Vermont State Craft Center, and the Old Constitution House (formerly Elijah West's tavern) are also on the left.

51.7   Here is another access onto I-91 (Exit 9).

52.8   The division of Routes 12N and 5N occurs in the village of Hartland. On the left Route 12N leads to Route 4W and Woodstock while **Route 5N bears to the right.** The Hartland General Store is here at the junction.

Daniel Willard, president of the Baltimore and Ohio (B&O) Railroad and often referred to as the dean of American railroad men, was born in Hartland. (An incredible number of Vermonters were instrumental in the building and managing of America's railroads during the period of western expansion; only a few are mentioned in this book.)

Route 5 follows along I-91, first on the right and then on the left, as you continue north to White River Junction.

57.2   This is the green in the small village of North Hartland. Route 5 crosses under I-91 once again. Just north of the village you come to the beautiful yellow-painted buildings of the Lemax Farm on both sides of the road.

The North Hartland Dam on the Ottauquechee River can be seen to the left.

60.8   Ahead you can see the Veterans Hospital. Once you pass under I-91, you're in White River Junction. (See Map on page 273 in the appendix.)

White River Junction

White River Junction, usually referred to as White River by Vermonters, is a village in the town of Hartford. Before the coming of the railroads in 1847 only one farm existed in White River, but by the mid-1860s there were five railroads here, and this became one of Vermont's famous railroad towns.

While growing up I played with trains. Real trains. My favorite engine had eight drive wheels, each taller than I was, and weighed over a hundred tons. It was one of the largest steam locomotives ever built, and it was used to pull entire trains—engines and all— over the passes of the Continental Divide. The trains I played with weren't mine, of course, they were part of a millionaire's private collection that was stored in the rail yard at the base of Fall Mountain, before Steamtown U.S.A. became a reality.

I wasn't the first Vermonter to be fascinated by the iron horse. The first steam train pulled into Bellows Falls in January 1849. Twelve months later you could ride from Boston to Burlington, and more important, ship products south to the population centers of coastal New England. Vermonters learned much in building these railways and went beyond the borders of the state to build the railways of the West. Famous railroads such as the Canadian Pacific, the Union Pacific, the Northern Pacific, the Erie, and the Chicago and Northwestern were built by Vermonters. The Baltimore and Ohio, the Illinois Central, the Fort Worth and Rio Grande, the Fort Wayne and Chicago, and the Grand Trunk Railway were among the famous lines run by Vermonters. The Atchison, Topeka, and Santa Fe Railroad was run by no fewer than six different Vermonters. John Converse was the president of the Baldwin Locomotive Works; Elisha Harris designed the hospital railcar; William Chandler invented the refrigeration car; and Benjamin Field was partners with George Pullman. One Vermonter designed the layout for Grand Central Station in New York City, while another built the New York Elevated. Thomas Davenport ,of Brandon, invented the electric train, but it was Charles B. Holmes, of Springfield, who became the "Street Railway King of America."

61.4   There are several motels and restaurants within the next half mile. The access onto I-91 and to I-89 is on the left as you go under the interstate highway once again. *You can avoid the traffic in the next couple of miles by taking I-91 north to Exit 12.*

61.9   At the traffic light you can see the Vermont Transit bus terminal ahead to the right (behind the gas station), and past the gas stations Route 5 goes down the hill.

62.2   At the blinking light, Route 4W is on the left directly across from the landmark tourist haunt 25,000 Gifts. *Route 4, the major east-west highway in the middle of the state, leads to Woodstock, Rutland, and finally to New York state.*

62.6   At this light, **turn left and cross the bridge** over the railroad tracks and the White River. *Continuing straight takes you into downtown White River Junction.*

62.8   The intersection of Routes 14, 4, and 5 is on the other side of the bridge. *Route 14N on the left leads to Barre and eventually to Newport. Route 4E on the right leads to West Lebanon and Concord, New Hampshire.*

Continue straight through the traffic lights and up the hill. After 0.5 miles you begin to leave this residential section and White River Junction.

63.6 On the left is an access onto I-91 (Exit 12).

64.5 This is the village of Wilder.

67.2 The intersection of Routes 10, 10A, and 5 is at another I-91 (Exit 13) access. This is the primary road leading to Dartmouth college in Hanover.
Turn left to continue on Route 5N.

67.6 At the green, you have the center of the village of Norwich on your left. At one corner is the junction of Route 132E, which continues straight, while **Route 5 takes a ninety-degree turn right.** *Bear right. Route 132 goes to Strafford and Sharon.*

The was the site of the first grammar school in the United States, and Norwich University was founded here in 1819 by Captain Alden Partridge. After the building that housed the university was destroyed by fire in 1866, the campus moved to its present site in Northfield. Norwich is very much a part of Dartmouth College, just across the river.

Norwich is now the corporate headquarters for King Arthur Flour.

68.6 There is a reverse Y on the right leading to Hanover, and Route 5 returns to the edge of the Connecticut River. This stretch of river is the reservoir behind the power dam in Hanover and provides a popular recreation area for boating, water-skiing, canoeing, sculling, and fishing. You might even see one of Darmouth's teams out practicing. At the mouth of the Ompompanoosuc River, you may see ducks, geese, heron, and other waterfowl in the setbacks, especially during the fall migrations.

77.4 On the right is a road leading over to Lyme, New Hampshire, followed by the junction of Route 113 on the left here in East Thetford. *Route 113 leads to Chelsea on Route 110.*

When you go through the village of North Thetford you probably won't even realize it. Less than a mile later Route 5 runs next to I-91, as both roads find themselves squeezed between the Vermont Piedmont and the Connecticut River. The next several miles will offer beautiful views of New Hampshire on the right.

Vermont is geologically different from New Hampshire. The land you're seeing to the right in New Hampshire is known as the Benson

Hill Formation. At one time, about 440 million years ago, there was an archipelago of volcanic islands off the coast of the ancestral North American continent. Around this time the earth's continents began to move toward each other, and as that happened, over millions of years, the volcanic islands were pushed by the continent of Africa. This arc of volcanic islands acted like a giant bulldozer blade plowing up ocean sediment, volcanic debris, and even continental bedrock that was miles in depth, pushing it up onto the North American tectonic plate. When the ancestral continents finally met 375 million years ago, the chain of volcanic islands was squeezed in between them. The Connecticut River follows the fault line—the precise dividing line—between the western edge of the volcanic islands and the stuff it plowed up. What you see to the right is the geological remains of land formed as an archipelago between two ancestral continents. Vermont is made up of what was plowed up from the shallow seas where life first began.

84.7   On the left is access to I-91 (Exit 15), to Lake Morey, and to the splendid Lake Morey Inn.

Rumor has it that the remains of the first steamship built in the United States rest on the bottom of Lake Morey. Samuel Morey, of Fairlee, built the first steamboat in America in 1793 and plied it up and down the Connecticut River fourteen years before Robert Fulton built the *Clermont.* Eleven years prior to Fulton's success, Morey was operating a dual-paddlewheel steamship on the Delaware River, carrying passengers between Bordentown, New Jersey, and Philadelphia. There is even documentation that Fulton's partner, Chancellor Robert Livingston, came to Fairlee to see Morey before building Fulton's famous steamship. But Morey's fame didn't begin or end with the steamship. In 1826 he patented the first internal combustion engine, using spirits of turpentine for fuel and a carburetor to mix the fuel and air. Another of his twenty recorded patents was in 1818 for the creation of hydrocarbon gas, which became the standard component of city gas plants. Besides being an inventor, he was a civil engineer in charge of all the navigational canal locks on the Connecticut River, and was recognized as one of the leading authorities in the field of ichthyology on freshwater fishes.

85.2   In the village of Fairlee the long, thin green is on the left. The junction of Route 25A to Orford, New Hampshire, is on the right. The cliffs, known as the Palisades, on Morey Hill rise up behind the village hiding Lake Morey from view.

88.0   On the left the rocks and cliffs fall from the heights to the shoulder of the road. Here I-91, Route 5, and the Boston and Maine Railway are squeezed between Sawyer Mountain and the Connecticut River.

90.6 The busy junction of Route 25, a restaurant, and a minimart are on the left. *Route 25 leads to Route 302 in Orange.* The Bradford Motel is about the only place to stay in this area.

The old beautiful village of Bradford, a classic Vermont image, is just over a mile north of the modern village, which has grown around the junction of Route 25. In this village the first globes in the United States were made.

North of Bradford the river valley widens as the Connecticut River makes graceful loops and oxbows, while Route 5 follows the base of the piedmonts on the edge of the valley.

98.7 The center of Newberry is another great Vermont village with beautiful homes, white picket fences, and large lawns.

Newberry, one of the state's early settlements, was founded by Jacob Bayley who named it after his hometown in Massachusetts. It was this Revolutionary War general who cut a road from Charlestown, New Hampshire, to Peacham in 1777. The Bayley-Hazen Military Road served to encourage settlement in the interior of the new republic at the end of the Revolutionary War.

As the road follows the valley, you can see Mount Washington and the White Mountains of New Hampshire to the right. These mountains of granite were formed after those in Vermont, when the single land mass, Panagea, began to separate into individual continents 200 million years ago at the end of the age of the great dinosaurs. As this separation was taking place, molten magma from deep inside the earth welled up to form the White Mountains of New Hampshire and the Northeastern Highlands of Vermont. The area to the right between the river and the mountains is still the Bronson Hill Complex.

102.8 One of Vermont's few remaining round barns is on the right. The explanation often given for the barn's shape was that the devil couldn't corner you in it. The truth is that these barns were part of the experimentation with modern agricultural techniques that was popular at the turn of the twentieth century. Although it may have been easier or faster to milk and feed the cows using a circular layout, these barns were more expensive to build and wasted more space than the conventional rectangular structures—hence their brief popularity and rapid decline.

104.4 As you enter into Wells River, Route 302E, that goes to neighboring Woodsville, New Hampshire, is on the right. *It leads to the Kancamangus Highway that weaves through the White Mountains and is one of the best touring roads in the Northeast.*

Prior to the building of the railroads, most freight moved by riverboat. Wells River was the northernmost port on the Connecticut River, and thus became a transportation crossroads along with its sister town, Woodsville, New Hampshire.

104.5 The junction of Route 302W is on the left; *this leads to Barre and Montpelier and, after about 3.0 miles, the access to I-91 (Exit 17) and the P&H Truck Stop.*

108.3 The small village of East Rygate sits along the river on the right. If you didn't know this village was there, you'd pass by without realizing it.

109.0 On the right is a facility for chipping wood used as fuel in some home furnaces and in larger electric generating plants such as the McNeil Generating Plant in Burlington. Wood chips are also used for cattle bedding and mulching.

112.4 In the village of McIndoe Falls, you can turn right if you wish to cross into Monroe, New Hampshire.

114.9 There's an access road to I-91 (Exit 18) on the left just before the village of Barnet. *The on-ramps to I-91 are another 0.7 miles ahead,* and Karme Choling, the Buddhist Center founded by Chogyam Trungpa Rinpoche, is 1.5 miles on the right.

115.2 Even before you know you're entering the village of Barnet, you'll see the falls of the Stevens River on the left. Immediately after the falls there is a turn left, leading up the short hill to the Barnet Village Store.

Barnet is known for its two Buddhist centers. Karme Choling (originally Tail of the Tiger) was the first Buddhist center founded in the Western Hemisphere. From this core have sprung Buddhist centers in Colorado, Newfoundland, and Vancouver, as well as the Naropa Institute, a liberal arts college in Boulder, Colorado.

117.7 The Passumpsic River joins the Connecticut River here in East Barnet. Ahead, off to the right, you can catch a glimpse of the Comerford Dam. When this dam was completed in 1930, most of the farms and seventy-five towns in Vermont didn't have electricity. The reservoir behind this dam also covers the fifteen-mile falls, a stretch

A round barn, Route 5, Barnet. These structures were part of the experimental agriculture movement of the 1880s. Designed to be more efficient for milking, they turned out to be more expensive to build and maintain. Round barns soon fell out of favor, and few remain today.

of intense rapids that created the northernmost boundary of shipping on the river in the 1800s. This is the last glimpse of the Connecticut River as you follow Route 5 north.

118.8 On the right is a second round barn. Few of these structures still exist, and in another twenty years perhaps only three or four will remain. This is the lower Passumpsic River valley, and the road rolls along its edge. This is a pleasant but short stretch of road.

123.0 St. Johnsbury, St. J as the locals call it, is a major crossroads for touring traffic, and many who have been riding north on Route 5 will undoubtedly plan to leave it upon reaching this town. *From St. J you can head west on Route 2 to Montpelier and even to Burlington. Route 2 also leads to Route 15, which also goes to Burlington, but by a more northerly path. Route 15 borders the Northeast Kingdom and intersects Routes 16, 14, and 100—all of which take you north, like Route 5, to the city of Newport. I-93, Routes 18 and 2E all lead to the White Mountains of New Hampshire, but Route 2E continues through northern Maine. I would suggest taking Route 2W if you plan to travel to central Vermont, western Vermont, or to loop back to any part of southern Vermont. Routes 2W and 15W are best if you're heading to Burlington, northern New York, or Montreal. If you wish to ride through the White Mountains, then leaving Route*

5 in Wells River on Route 302E is the most enjoyable route, but the faster, busier Route 2E has some beautiful scenery as it passes the northern base of Mount Washington. Route 2E is the fastest highway to Maine.

123.1 On this four-lane highway on the south side of St. Johnsbury are the ramps onto Route I-91 (Exit 20). *You can drive through the city or use the interstate highways to bypass downtown traffic. You have the following options:*

1) Take I-91 south and then almost immediately take I-93 east (Exit

North Congregational Church in St. Johnsbury was built in 1828 by Lambert Packard using limestone quarried in Isle La Motte, on Lake Champlain. The original design by H.H. Richardson was intended for Trinity Church in New York.

19). Exit I-93 to Route 2E (turn left off the exit ramp) or Route 18E (turn right of the exit ramp). Route 18E and Route I-93 go to Littleton, New Hampshire. Route 2E goes to Route 102N and Lancaster, New Hampshire. Both routes will take you through the White Mountains.

2) Take I-91 north and the next exit (21) onto Route 2W or the second exit (22) onto Route 5N. Route 2W takes you to Montpelier and Burlington. Route 5N is a continuation of this route. If you don't plan on touring St. J , then I would suggest getting on I-91 north and rejoining Route 5 off Exit 22.

123.4 The left turn is South Main Street. Exactly one mile from here South Main Street joins Route 2W at the St. Johnsbury Academy where Main Street begins. I recommend this as the route through the town if you are continuing north on Route 5. (See Map on page 272 in the appendix.) See Route 2W, page 210, for a side trip on Main Street.

123.4 **Continue straight** on Railroad Street, Route 5, into downtown St. Johnsbury. Consider tanking up with gas and perhaps getting a snack or a quick lunch before heading into the Northeast Kingdom. It will be about fifty additional miles before you reach the abundant services of Newport.

123.9 Route 5N merges with Route 2E for 0.1 miles in downtown St. J. *Route 2W turns left on Eastern Avenue and goes up the hill to Main Street.* **Continue straight on Route 5N.**

125.0 On the left at the traffic light is Hastings Hill.

125.9 An intersection with the access to I-91 (Exit 22) is on the left.

126.7 This is St. Johnsbury Center. It's been developed commercially from downtown St. J to the Green Mountain Mall. If you want to avoid the shopping area, use the I-91 bypass. The road is more enjoyable and less congested after the shopping area.

128.0 A motel with cabins is on the right. Within the next four miles you'll find three additional motels, ranging from family operations to one of the national chains.

131.2 This is Exit 23 on I-91 (Exit 23) on the outskirts of Lyndonville, a small college town.

132.7 You now enter the village of Lyndonville, home of Lyndon State College.

Here, in a speech in 1949, Senator Aiken coined "the Northeast Kingdom" in reference to the northeastern portion of the state.

Notice the large green rectangular tin box attached to one of the buildings just prior to turning onto the main street. Produced here, Bag Balm is an ointment originally developed to prevent chapping on cows' udders, and it became popular during the late 1960s as a natural product used on chapped hands and lips.

The dowsing conventions are now held here during early August, and in mid-August you can catch the Caledonia County Fair. (See Danville, Route 2, page 214.)

132.9 Many of the houses facing the green were built by Lambert Packard of St. J. The road leading to Lyndon State College is on the far side of the green.

134.5 The junction of Route 114 is to the right, while Route 122 and **Route 5N bear left**. The Lynn-Burke Motel is on the left. *Route 114 leads past Burke Mountain through Island Pond to the Canadian border.*

From here the highway becomes pleasantly rural. To the right (east) the predominate peak is Burke Mountain, 3,267 feet.

138.1 You'll find a couple of picnic tables located under the pines in the turnoff to the right. A couple of paths on the far side of the pines lead down the steep bank to a shallow, secluded swimming area. If you need to take a dip—not a swim—on a hot summer day and forgot to pack bathing suits, you can take advantage of this spot.

140.9 Ahead to the right you can see the cliffs of Mount Pisgah. Route 5A skirts around the base of those cliffs, around Lake Willoughby.

141.8 The junction of Route 5A is on the right in the village of West Burke. (See Alternate Route 5A, page 82.)

Route 5, from West Burke to Crystal Lake, follows the Canadian Pacific Railway along a shallow, glacier-gouged valley. This is not a road frequented by tourists. This valley is typical of the northern boreal forest found in Vermont's northeastern counties. Bogs and swamps line the road, and evergreen trees predominate. You won't see the majestic landscapes found on Route 5A.

152.2 The public boat launch on your right is located at the southeastern end of Crystal Lake. This finger lake, like Lake Willoughby a few miles to the east, was created by the gouging effects of ice during the Wisconsin glaciation; you can see the evidence of this glacial gouging in the rock on the eastern side. This lake is also famous for its rainbow trout.

153.9 You now enter Barton, one of two major villages located in the township of Barton. The northwestern end of Crystal Lake is here, and on a hot summer day enjoy yourself on the public beach.

154.7 The Barton General Store is on the left, and to the right Route 16 crosses the railroad tracks and leads up the hill. *Route 16 goes to the north end of Lake Willoughby and junctions at Route 5A.* **Route 5 continues straight** into downtown Barton.

155.0 In the center of Barton Route 5 continues straight , while Route 16S is on the left.

You quickly leave the village and follow the Barton River northward. There's a beautiful stone railroad bridge on the right, but you must be looking at the river to notice it.

As you approach the village of Orleans, the second major village in Barton, you can see the lumberyard and the Ethan Allen Furniture plant on the right. Ethan Allen has five manufacturing plants in Vermont and produces exceptionally fine furniture that is sold throughout the United States.

159.8 Route 5 briefly joins Route 58 on the western edge of the village of Orleans. Turn right to go into the village. **Turn left to continue on Route 5.** You immediately pass under the I-91 bridges at Exit 26. *The quickest way to get to Newport is to take the interstate north to Exit 27.*

160.2 *Route 58 turns to the left and continues west to Route 14 and Route 100.* **Continue straight.**

164.9 Route 5 joins Route 14 just south of the village of Coventry.

165.4 Route 14 turns to the left in Coventry. There's a nice rest area with picnic tables on the left, but it's hidden from the highway by a hedge of cedar. **Route 5 continues straight.** This is a beautiful stretch of road as it winds its way along the Black River, with plenty of turnoffs for the next five miles.

169.9 Here the road forks. **Continue straight going up a slight hill on Pleasant Street.** There are no signs to indicate this is Route 5N. If you continue on Coventry Road, the road to the right, you will still end up in downtown Newport.

170.3 The Motel Bayview, on the right, is one of the few located in the city.

170.5 Route 5N merges with Route 105E. **Turn right and continue on Pleasant Street** and Routes 5N and 105E.

170.9 Pleasant Street ends. **Turn left onto Third Street. Go .1 mile and turn right onto West Main Street.** This is downtown Newport.

171.2 The gas station next to the park and the bridge over the lake is where I have begun or ended all of my mileage measurements on tours and routes that pass through Newport.

(For more on Newport see Route 100, page 36.)

ALTERNATE ROUTE 5A:
West Burke to Newport

140.8 The junction of Route 5A is on the right, and the West Burke General Store is on the left. *Route 5 continues straight going to Barton, Orleans, and Newport. Route 5 is a shorter, quicker route to Newport than Route 5A. However, I still prefer and strongly recommend taking Route 5A.*

Turn left onto Route 5A. This road slowly increases in altitude and meanders through some beautiful country. Long before you can see Lake Willoughby, you'll see Mount Pisgah and its sheer cliff face. Approaching the lake, you get a spectacular view of the effects of glaciation where the ice tore its way between the two mountains, gouging out this deep northern lake. To the west (left) of the highway is the Willoughby State Forest, while to the east (right) and north is wilderness with few roads.

147.1 This is the south shore of Lake Willoughby. White Cap Campsite, located here on the right, is where the best hiking trails to the top of the mountain begin. This spring-fed lake is known for its clear water and spectacular fishing. Many record-sized lake trout, landlocked salmon, and smelt have been caught here.

Local dive clubs, scuba shops, and individuals use this lake for training in altitude diving. The lake's altitude above sea level causes depth gauges to read incorrectly and adjustments to navy dive tables are necessary to prevent decompression sickness. The lake's clear water and dramatic underwater landscape—the rocks and cliffs continue plunging into the depths—make it one of Vermont's most popular dive sites.

Route 5A was cut out of the mountain at the edge of the lake making a spectacular five-mile route to ride along. There's an inn and restaurant on the right toward the north end of the lake. This small collection of cottages is the village of Westmore.

152.2 The intersection of Routes 16 and 5A is at the northern end of the lake. *Route 16 goes to Barton where you can rejoin Route 5N to Newport.*

The most rural approach to Newport, Route 5A is a beautiful touring road, traveling north and northeast past numerous small lakes. About a half mile past the intersection of Route 16, at the top of the hill, is Will-o-wood Campground on the left, one I recommend.

Lake Willoughby is not the only lake in the Northeast Kingdom famous for fine fishing. Crystal Lake on Route 16 in Barton is known for rainbow trout; Seymour Lake to the east has lake trout, bass, salmon, and pike; Echo is fished for lake and rainbow trout, salmon, and bass; Lake Salem is populated with bass, salmon, and pike; and even little Pensioner Pond has fine bass fishing. You'll find exceptional trout fishing in all the streams and rivers in this area.

153.6 The junction of Route 58 is on the left. *This leads east to Route 5 and I-91 in Orleans, Route 14 in Irasburg, and Route 100 in Lowell.*

159.5 On the right is Pensioner Pond.

160.4 Route 5A ends at the junction with Route 105. **Turn left onto Route 105W.** This junction is located at the Great Falls of Clyde River. To check out the gorge, turn right onto Route 105E and immediately turn onto the small road to the left.

161.0 Lubber Lake, on the right, is really a large pond. At the northern end of the lake, the local road leads over to Morgan and Seymore Lakes on Route 111.

164.5 Lake Salem is on the right. The Clyde River connects Pensioner Pond, Lubber Lake, Lake Salem, Clyde Pond, and Lake Memphremagog.

166.5 You're entering Derby Center.

166.8 The junction of Route 111E is on the right.

167.3 This is the merging of Route 105 with Route 5. *Continuing straight on Route 5N will bring you to Derby Line and the Canadian border.* There's a gas station on the left, a restaurant on the right, and the Border Motel is just ahead on Route 5N.

Turn left at this reverse Y to continue to Newport on Routes 5S and 105W.

168.3 This access onto I-91 (Exit 28) is a busy one because it's the last full-service exit before the Canadian border. You can continue on this busy commercial road into Newport or take the interstate bypass to get to downtown.

There are numerous motels, gas stations, and eating places along this section of highway from the interstate to Newport, including the Miss Newport Diner. The commercial traffic can be slow along this road, especially as you approach Newport.

The Waterfront Plaza is located on the right at the southern end of Lake Memphremagog. The Grand Union has a great deli, and the back of the parking lot is right on the water's edge. Across the street is the Vermont North Country Chamber of Commerce where you can pick up additional information on places to visit or stay here in the Northeast Kingdom.

171.5 After crossing the bridge you're in downtown Newport on Main Street.

ALTERNATE ROUTE
To Downtown Newport

168.3 Travel south on I-91 to the next exit (27), Route 191.

170.9 Clyde Pond is visible on the right from this access road.

172.6 Route 191 intersects Western Avenue. **Continue straight through the traffic lights.**

173.0 Route 191 junctions with Routes 5 and 105. **Turn left** and ride by the shopping plaza on the right. I've found that two of the best places in Newport to stop, park, and take a short break are in the back of the Grand Union parking lot and in Gordon Park opposite the plaza on Glen Road.

On the right is the southern end of Lake Memphremagog and South Bay is on the left.

173.3 After crossing the bridge, you're in downtown Newport. There is a small municipal park on the right along the railroad track.

Massachusetts to Route 4

ROUTES 8, 100, AND 112:
The Southern Green Mountains

Route 8N

This road actually begins in the old mill town of North Adams, Massachusetts, where Route 8 follows the North Branch Hoosic River through Clarksville to the Vermont border. Route 100 begins at the headwaters of the Deerfield River, but it can only be reached by traveling on Route 8. These two highways cut through the southern end of the Green Mountain National Forest. Filled with twisting turns, radical climbs and descents, and bucolic villages nestled in deep valleys, they offer premium auto and motorcycle touring, but I don't recommend them for RVs.

0.0   At the Vermont-Massachusetts border you enter into the small village of Stamford that looks as if it were taken from the pages of a glossy magazine. The large attractive homes sit in a beautiful valley with the rounded mountain ridges protecting it from storms.

This valley was shaped from the gouging ice of the Wisconsin glaciation, and the numerous boulders found here were carried south by a mile-and-a-half-thick blanket of ice.

The valley ends and Route 8 climbs into the mountains within the Green Mountain National Forest. Both sides of the highway are wilderness for many miles. A great touring road, Route 8 twists and climbs to the collection of dwellings known as Heartwellville.

7.8   On the right is the junction of the southern end of Route 100, the highway that runs the length of Vermont in the Green Mountains. The beautiful building on the right just past Route 100 is the old stagecoach inn built in 1783, a time when Vermont was still an independent country.

Route 8 continues to be a great drive, continuously climbing in elevation with lots of tight corners and few trucks. The woods are the prevalent feature of this stretch of highway as it continues through the national forest.

12.4   In this area you'll see beautiful views of the Green Mountains to the right (east). After reaching the highest elevation on Route 8, the road dips down to Searsburg.

24.9   Route 8 ends as it junctions with Route 9 in Searsburg.
Route 9W leads to Bennington and Route 7. Route 9E leads to Wilmington and Route 100.

Route 100N to Wilmington

7.8   From Heartwellville and the junction of Route 8, Route 100N follows the west branch of the Deerfield River. At first the road is nice, straight, and open, but then it gets more twisted as it follows the river's descent.

11.01   On the left is a great turnoff along the river. Once part of the main road, it's now a popular place to stop and sit next to the iron-stained waters of this fast-flowing river.

The next 1.5 miles are a fast downhill drive along the rock cliffs and the gorge cut by the fast-flowing water.

12.6   After making the S-turn by the lumberyard, you find yourself in the village of Readsboro, which is in the town of Readsboro. The village of Readsboro sits in the deep valley carved by the Deerfield River; the southern Green Mountains rise steeply on all sides of this village. *The right turn across from Jerry's Hardware heads south along the river and the Sherman Reservoir to Rowe and Monroe Bridge, Massachusetts.* **Continue straight, crossing the bridge over the gorge and high above the river.**

The next five miles of Route 100N are filled with tight turns, shady woods, and a dramatic rise in elevation.

17.1   Lake Whitingham can be seen on the left. This man-made lake is over two thousand acres in size and contains more shoreline than any other lake within the boundary of the state.

17.7   In the village of Whitingham, Brown's General Store is on the right and the historic site marker for Brigham Young on the left. The birthplace of Brigham Young is just a couple of hundred feet off Route 100 on the shore of Sadawga Pond. Brigham Young lead the Mormons from Illinois, after the death of their prophet, Joseph Smith (see Route 14, Sharon), to the shores of the Great Salt Lake in Utah.

Route 100 winds up through the village, past Sadawga Pond on the right, and continues to climb in elevation.

19.5   You crest the ridge and now descend all the way to Jacksonville, the last section twisting on an 11 percent downgrade—a descent of over a foot for every ten feet traveled!

21.3   Routes 121 and 8A junction with route 100N as a reverse Y at the bottom of the hill in the village of Jacksonville. Greenfield, Massachusetts, is only twenty-six miles away.

Turn left at the Jacksonville General Store—don't be confused by the old Community Store sign hanging from the front porch—and begin the climb back up the mountain.

21.9   As you begin to climb the mountain, you'll see a concrete basin with a black plastic hose on the left. This is good drinking water so fill up the canteen or water bottle.

26.8   The merging of Routes 100N and 9W are on the east side of Wilmington village. *Route 9E leads to Brattleboro.*

Route 112

Another entry into southern Vermont and Route 100 is Route 112. From the Mohawk Trail (Route 2) in Shelburne Falls to the Vermont border is a mere 10.8 miles as the rural highway follows the east branch of the Deerfield River through the rounded hills of central Massachusetts.

0.0   When you enter Vermont you're in the town of Halifax.

This is a narrow rural road without a shoulder that twists and turns as it follows the rocky East Branch North River. There are few homes along the highway in this wooded section of the state, and the hills become steeper as you continue riding northwest.

5.8   The junction of Route 8A is on the left. *Route 8A goes south to Charlemont, Massachusetts.*

6.7   You begin to enter into the village of Jacksonville.

7.1   The North River Winery is located on the right just across the stream.

7.3   Route 112 junctions with Route 100. A restaurant is located on Route 100 just across from the junction.

ROUTE 9W:
Brattleboro to Bennington

Route 9, known as the Molly Stark Trail, was the path taken by General John Stark on his victorious return home from the Battle of Bennington. This route was named after his wife, Molly, who had mustered and had sent the two hundred plus men from their New Hampshire farms to join the colonials under her husband's command in time for this decisive battle.

This is the primary east-west highway across southern Vermont, and the long mountainous climb with its steep, tight corners is usually backed up with traffic. This, like Route 2 in central Vermont, is being improved section by section to remove the narrow corners.

(For more information on Brattleboro, see Route 5, page 59.)

0.0   Route 9 actually begins on the north side of Brattleboro, where it comes into Vermont from New Hampshire, but for convenience we start it at Exit 2 of I-91 on Western Avenue. *From New Hampshire and Route 9 the easiest way to reach Western Avenue is to continue straight through the intersection of Route 5 and get onto I-91 (Exit 3) going south to Exit 2 (3.3 miles).*

Continue west on Route 9W (Western Avenue) riding through West Brattleboro.

Driving through the outskirts of Brattleboro and the village of West Brattleboro is a pleasant experience; the traffic moves along well most of the time, and the road is flat and open. After passing through West Brattleboro, however, the road abruptly changes.

2.6   Here Route 9W becomes narrow as you begin to climb into the Vermont Piedmont following Whetstone Brook. Route 9 is southern Vermont's main east-west road connecting New York and western Vermont with New Hampshire and the eastern side of the state. It's also the primary access road to the major ski areas. The twisting, turning highway with its steep grades is a nightmare for truckers.

13.6   The top of Hogback Mountain has a commercial scenic pull-off on the left.

Caution: Be extra careful as you approach the top of the mountain where the commercial lookout is located. Cars are parked on both sides of the highway on a curve with limited visibility.

Underneath the gift shop is the Luman Nelson Wildlife Museum. Luman Nelson was a noted taxidermist in the early 1900s, and this museum houses one of the largest collections of stuffed birds in New England. The restaurant on the right offers magnificent views of three states from its dining room.

From here the view is magnificent, with the Holyoke Range to the south and Mount Monadnock to the east. It's interesting to note that when you pass the Hogback Mountain Ski Area you are on Mount Olga, not Hogback Mountain.

15.0   The Molly Stark State Park is located on the left (south) at the bottom of Mount Olga.

17.3   **The merging of Routes 9W and 100 is on the eastern side of Wilmington. Continue straight on combined Routes 9W and 100N.**

Route 100S will take you down around Lake Whitingham, through Readsboro; it then intersects with Route 8. Route 8S goes to Massachusetts; Route 8N brings you back to Route 9 in Searsburg.

Caution: I've seen drivers who were proceeding north on Route 100 go through this stop sign at full speed! The outdoor flea market that takes place at this intersection during summer weekends only compounds the danger.

18.4   **The dividing of Routes 9 and 100 is at the intersection and traffic light in downtown Wilmington.**

Wilmington is 1,580 feet above sea level, over 1,200 feet higher than Brattleboro.

Most of the buildings in the downtown area have been placed on the National Register of Historic Places, and you'll find the mix of architectural styles—Greek Revival, Italianate, Queen Anne, and

Colonial—a delight. Traffic can get congested downtown at the intersection with its narrow streets and single traffic light.

This resort town has numerous fine restaurants, antiques shops, and specialty shops. Consider Dot's restaurant, open at 5:30 A.M., next to the bridge if you're coming through town early. The best parking will be found by taking a left (south) at the traffic light.

19.2   On the left is Lake Whitingham, a man-made reservoir on the Deerfield River that contains more shoreline than any other lake within Vermont's boundaries. The turnoff on the left is at Ox-Bow, a great place to take a swim or soak your feet on a hot day. In about another mile, where the river enters the reservoir, there's a left turn that crosses the river into what is known as Medburyville. If you feel the need to take a break, follow the dirt road to the water and the picnic tables.

From Wilmington the narrow highway has an abundance of tight curves and climbs even higher into the Green Mountains.

21.7   There's a unique brick hydroelectric power station on the far side of the Deerfield river. A wooden conduit, running for several miles from Searsburg Reservoir, comes down the mountain to a water tower from which the water drops directly downhill to power the turbines in the brick building. The advantage of this system is that a tremendous amount of force is generated by the vertical drop of the water, and the generating plant doesn't have to rely on the flow of water in the river.

22.3   Begin the ascent up the mountain with the road snaking all the way to the crest of the hill. There is a truck lane on the steepest section.

25.6   The junction of Route 8S is on the left at the crest of the mountain in Searsburg, which has always been sparsely populated. Currently the town has 85 residents, that's 149 acres per person! The village is at an elevation of 1,734 feet, only 154 feet higher than Wilmington, but after climbing that hill it feels as if you've reached the highest point on Route 9. After only .1 mile the road begins to descend again.

28.1   The Red Mill Campground is on the right.

Approximately a mile after the Red Mill Campground you begin to enter Woodford, a concentration of houses built along Route 9. Although it feels as if you've been descending the mountain for the last 2.5 miles, this village is listed as being the highest in Vermont at

2,215 feet above sea level—481 feet higher than Searsburg. From Wilmington to Searsburg feels like a great climb, not 154 feet; from Searsburg to Woodford feels like a descent, not a climb of 137 feet per mile! From Woodford to Bennington is only 10 miles, but the drop in elevation is 1,465 feet, and you get the sensation of descending on this stretch of road.

31.8   You now have three miles of steep downgrade with signs recommending that trucks descend at 5 MPH. You may get stuck behind some slow-moving traffic in this section, but be patient—this is not a good hill to pass on.

32.1   You'll find a restaurant, lodging, and camping on the left.

33.0   On the left is a dirt turnoff with potable water coming from the old spring. This is an ideal place to stop and get water, especially if you're stuck behind traffic.

34.7   You've crossed the Long Trail, the hiking trail that runs along the crest of the Green Mountains for the entire length of Vermont. You're also leaving the Green Mountain National Forest.

35.9   The descent down the western side of the mountains finally ends here in the village of Woodford Hollow.

37.0   You are now on East Main Street as you enter the village of Bennington. You'll find numerous motels and restaurants along Main Street, both east and west. More fine restaurants can be found on those streets leading north from Route 9 to Routes 7 and 7A.

39.8   The intersection of Routes 7 and 9 occurs in downtown Bennington. *Continue straight on Route 9W to Old Bennington or turn right onto Route 7N to travel to Manchester or on Route 7S to go to Williamstown, Massachusetts.*

On Route 9W to Old Bennington

40.0   At the next traffic light Depot Street is on the right with Paul's, a burger and fries drive-in, on the corner. Depot Street leads to Route 7N. The next street on the right, just past the stone church, is Benmont Avenue, which leads to Northside Drive and Route 7A. Just past Benmont Avenue on the right is the Hemmings Sunoco. Headquartered in the adjacent building, *Hemmings Motor News* is the largest and best publication for finding vintage cars and trucks. If you're not familiar with Hemmings, make sure you stop in at the gas station to check out their books and magazines.

40.2   There are several good motels on this part of West Main Street.

40.6   On the left, on the hill leading into Old Bennington, is the Bennington Museum, which houses the largest public collection of paintings by Grandma Moses, the oldest United States flag (carried in the Battle of Bennington),and the only surviving example of the luxury touring car known as the Wasp, designed and built by Karl Martin in Bennington. The museum has an outstanding collection of American glass, Bennington pottery, American furniture, and other Americana. There is an extensive genealogy library open by appointment only.

40.8   **Turn right at the top of the hill** and ride up the street to the Bennington Battle Monument. Magnificent homes line both sides, including the old academy building, made of brick with a bell tower, on the right.

The 306-foot-tall monument was built to commemorate the Battle of Bennington, which took place on August 16, 1777, and is considered to be the turning point in the Revolutionary War, when the troops under Major General John Stark stopped the British advance intended to cut the American colonies in half. Interestingly, the fighting actually took place in Walloomsac, New York, but the British troops were after the stockpile of food and supplies in a storehouse on the hill where the monument now stands. The cornerstone for the monument was laid in August 1887, and the capstone was placed in November 1889.

Circle around the monument and head back into Old Bennington.

41.8   This is the center of Old Bennington, with the green and the Old First Church, 1805, on the left. Behind the church is the Old Burying Ground, which stretches down the hill to the museum. Robert Frost and many other notable Vermonters are buried here.

The Walloomsac Inn, 1766, listed as the oldest inn in Vermont, is on the right just before turning right and continuing on Route 9W to New York. Thomas Jefferson and James Madison are among the notables who have slept here.

Bennington

Bennington is Vermont's southwestern gateway, just as Brattleboro is the southeastern. Bennington, like Brattleboro, was one of

the state's first towns, settled in 1761. Here the similarity ends, because until the advent of the automobile and reliable highways, the
towns and villages on the eastern side of the Green Mountains were
effectively divided from those on the western side.

Vermont's independence arose from the conflicts over land
grants between New Hampshire and New York at the end of the
Seven Years' War (French and Indian Wars). Land speculators, most

The First Congregational Church in Old Bennington was designed
and built by Lavius Fillmore in 1805.

notably Ethan and Ira Allen, and others who would be dispossessed of their land by grants made by New York's governor, became the core of a radical military movement—The Green Mountain Boys— to protect their interests. The center of armed resistance was in Bennington, but the organization of the separatist movement was joined by the communities in the Connecticut Valley. The Declaration of Independence by the thirteen colonies turned everyone's attention toward the British, and the Green Mountain Boys went north to capture the strategic British forts on Lake Champlain. The settlers of the disputed territory called The Grants had had enough. Even as the British under General Burgoyne were moving south and the Green Mountain Boys were heading north to intercept them, these settlers were signing the Vermont Constitution, making it independent of both Great Britain and of the United States.

These days this village of sixteen thousand people is not a hotbed of political activism. Tourism seems to be the primary industry, replacing woolen mills and other manufacturing from the nineteenth and early twentieth centuries. Bennington Potters carries on a manufacturing tradition that began in the early 1800s—making stoneware out of the local red clay. The most extensive collection of Bennington Pottery in the United States can be viewed in the Bennington Museum. You'll find interesting shops, some good restaurants, and excellent places to spend the night.

ROUTE 7A:
The Valley of Vermont

Whether you're entering Vermont from New York on Route 9E or from Massachusetts on Route 7N, you'll enter into the Valley of Vermont in Bennington. From Bennington Route 7A (old Route 7) and Route 7N (the modern highway) follow the valley north to East Dorset, where they merge, and continue on to Rutland. Route 7S from Swanton to Bennington is detailed in "Route 7: Vermont's Western Corridor" on page 37. Route 7A is a slow-moving tourist road with motels, restaurants, places to visit, and things to see. If you've come to see Vermont, travel up the valley on this road.

Access to Route 7A from Downtown Bennington

0.0　From the intersection of Routes 9 and 7 at the traffic light in downtown Bennington, turn onto North Street. If you are on Route 9W turn right; if you are on Route 9E turn left; if you are on Route 7N (South Street) continue straight.

This is downtown, so you'll find plenty of shops, restaurants, and traffic.

0.5　The Blue Benn Diner, a vintage diner car that has been located here since the 1940s, is on the left just past the traffic light.

1.2　At this traffic light **turn left** onto Northside Drive, the beginning of historic Route 7A.

Another option is to continue straight, up the access ramp onto the interstate-like Route 7N, and then take Exit 2 onto Route 7A.

Old Bennington

The center of Old Bennington is at the green and the Old First Church, 1805. Behind the church is the Old Burying Ground, which stretches down the hill to the museum. Robert Frost and many other notable Vermonters are buried here.

The Walloomsac Inn, 1766, opposite the Old First Church, is listed as the oldest inn in Vermont but is now a private residence.

At the end of the green is Monument Avenue. Magnificent homes line both sides of this street, including the old academy building, made of brick with a bell tower, on the right. The street ends at the 306-foot-tall Bennington Battle Monument, built to commemorate the Battle of Bennington. Fought on August 16, 1777, the battle is considered to be the turning point in the Revolutionary War. Here, troops under Major General John Stark stopped the British advance that intended to cut the American colonies in half. Interestingly, the fighting actually took place in Walloomsac, New York, but the British troops were after the stockpile of food and supplies in a storehouse on the hill where the monument now stands. The cornerstone was laid in August 1887, and the capstone was placed in November 1889.

There's more history to be discovered in this early Vermont town. Just down the street, on the other side of the Old Burying Ground, is the Bennington Museum. If the weather is nice, take a walk, and don't forget your camera.

Access to Route 7 and Route 7A from Old Bennington

If you're coming into Vermont on Route 9E or have come from Route 9W or Route 7N to see Old Bennington, there's no need to fight traffic in downtown Bennington to reach Route 7A; there are a couple of shortcuts to Routes 7 or 7A from Old Bennington you can use.

0.0   The Old First Church is on the right and the turn on the left goes up to the Bennington Monument.

1) Go up the street to the Bennington Battle Monument. When you reach the monument turn left onto Walloomsac Road and then take the next right onto Fairview Street. Turn right onto Silk Road and cross the covered bridge. The road ends at Northside Drive in front of Bennington College. Turn right, and at the second traffic light, turn left onto historic Route 7A. In another 1.5 miles you see an access onto Route 7 on the right.

2) Go up the street toward the monument but turn right onto Bank Street before reaching it. Bank Street becomes Hunt Street, which joins at the junction of Benmont Avenue and Northside Drive. If you turn left, you'll be on Route 7A. To access Route 7N, turn right and then immediately get into the left-hand lane to make a left turn at the traffic light.

1.0   Paul's, a burger and fries drive-in, is located on the corner of West Main and Depot Streets. **Turn left** onto Depot Street. Just .1 mile farther is the Historic Bennington Station Restaurant and Lounge on the left.

1.3   There's a four-way stop at the intersection of Depot and County Streets. On the left you can see the Holden-Leonard Mill. *To go to the Bennington Potters Yard, turn right onto County Street, crossing North Street at the traffic light, and it's on the left.*

1.4   Depot Street ends at North Street (Route 7). The Blue Benn Diner is just around the corner to the right.
Turn left onto Route 7.

2.0   At the traffic light turn left onto Route 7A (Northside Drive). *To go north on Route 7 continue straight through the traffic light.*

(For more information on Bennington, see Route 9W, page 91.)

Historic Route 7A

0.0   At the traffic light at the intersection of Route 7, Northside Drive, North Street, and Kocher Drive, **turn left onto Northside Drive (Route 7A).**

0.5   In Bennington and on Route 7A you'll have your choice of a multitude of places to stay. This is one of Vermont's traditional tourist highways, and you'll find everything from rustic cabins and vintage strip motels to bed-and-breakfast inns and world-class accommodations from here to Manchester. During foliage season there will NOT be any rooms available, so please make reservations during the summer if you plan to tour when the leaves turn.

0.8   **Bear right** after the Best Western because Route 7A turns and goes north while Northside Drive continues straight. *Northside Drive leads to Bennington College and to North Bennington.*

1.2   You finally leave the village when passing under the Route 7 bridges.

2.5   The access onto Route 7 (exit 2) is on the right.

3.8   This is the village of South Shaftsbury.

4.3   The junction of Route 67W is on the left

5.9   Jonas Galusha, one of the first settlers of the town, served nine terms as governor of Vermont. These days, it's a major political victory if the governor is elected for more than two terms.

6.7   In Shaftsbury village you get the first beautiful views of the valley to the north.

7.6   Serenity Cabins, from another era, are on the left. This area has the last concentration of 1950s strip motels in the state. I enjoy staying in this type of place and will choose one over the giant franchises whenever possible. Even the names of these smaller motels are more interesting: The Iron Kettle, Governor Rock, The Cut Leaf Maples, and The Valhalla.

9.9   Lake Shaftsbury State Park on the right is a great campground, but call ahead because it has only a few sites and it's very popular.

12.8   On the right, just as you're entering Arlington, is Route 313E, the access road to Exit 3 off Route 7 that follows the eastern side of the valley.

Route 313E also leads to the village of East Arlington.

13.8   This is the edge of downtown Arlington.

Arlington was a hotbed of politics in The Grants, with Green Mountain Boys Ethan Allen, Seth Warner, Thomas Chittenden, and Remember Baker living here. The Green Mountain Boys were formed to keep the Yorkers out of The Grants in the early 1770s, but became the nucleus for Vermont's role in the Revolutionary War. It was Ethan Allen and the Green Mountain Boys who captured Fort Ticonderoga in May 1775. Seth Warner and his men fought the Battle of Hubberton in July 1776 and reinforced Colonel John Stark at Bennington in August. Thomas Chittenden became the governor of the independent republic of Vermont (1777–1791) and was the first governor of the fourteenth state in the Union.

14.1   On the right in the village is the Arlington Gallery featuring the work of Norman Rockwell who lived in East Arlington from 1939 to 1953, and many of his famous *Main Street America* series were done here. Over two hundred local residents were used in his portraits, and some of these former models are your guides through the exhibition housed in the gallery.

Next to the gallery is the Chittenden House, home of one of Vermont's founding fathers and first governor, and the road to East Arlington. East Arlington is a beautiful village. You'll find the modest beginnings of numerous up-scale retail stores located on this road.

14.3   The junction of Route 313W is on the left just after the gray stone Gothic–Revival–style St. James Episcopal Church, 1832. *Route 313W leads to West Arlington and to Route 22 in Cambridge, New York.*

Author Dorothy Canfield Fisher was another celebrated resident of Arlington who was known beyond the boundaries of this small state.

15.3   The scenic views of historic Route 7A are seen almost exclusively as you travel north. Traveling south is quite different.

17.4   On the left along this stretch are moraines, vast sand banks left as the last glaciers melted. These sand banks follow the pattern of the miles-thick glacier melting, with the accumulated sand, gravel, and stones eventually settling on the hills and in the valleys of the land. Rocks, being the heaviest, stayed on the hillsides and didn't wash down the icy rivers into the valleys as the ice melted over hundreds of years.

17.8   The Ira Allen House bed and breakfast on the left has a historic site marker out front next to the highway. This is where Ethan and his youngest brother, Ira, had their homes, where Ethan Allen wrote his *Oracles of Reason,* and where Ira, as secretary of the Council of Safety, drafted many of Vermont's early documents. These two brothers were political opportunists, land speculators, soldiers, statesmen, and the core of the famous Green Mountain Boys. These two were involved in the pioneering of The Grants, the capture of Ticonderoga, the American Revolution, the creation of the independent Republic of Vermont, the maneuvering to having Vermont accepted as the fourteenth state in the Union. At one time the State of New York had a bounty of $20,000 in silver on Ethan Allen's head, yet he lived and moved openly in the towns of The Grants, immune from the wrath of New York's colonial governor.

18.3   The toll road up Mount Equinox is on the left.
Caution: You shouldn't take this side trip if you are driving an RV, towing a trailer, or uncomfortable with extremely tight corners.

SIDE TRIP *Equinox Sky Line Drive*

There are several mountains in Vermont that feature a touring road to their upper peaks, but the most popular are The Toll Road to the top of Mount Mansfield and this one to the summit of Mount Equinox.

The Equinox Sky Line Drive begins at the tollhouse on Route 7 where you purchase your ticket. You will be cautioned about the corners on the road. The narrow road begins to climb the shoulder of Little Equinox, and despite a couple of tight corners, this portion is easy. Just before you reach the second parking area, the road begins a series of nasty switchbacks, and the pavement in the right lane is banked at what seems to be a thirty-degree angle. The road straightens out as it climbs to the summit of Little Equinox (3,320 feet).

On the summit of Little Equinox are several three-bladed wind turbines. These 100-kilowatt generators are the second largest collection of wind turbines in southern Vermont. You can get an idea of just how strong the winds can be on this mountain by looking at the bent and stunted trees growing on this ridge.

Just beyond the first summit is the saddle between Little Equinox and the summit of Mount Equinox (3,385 feet). There's parking on both sides of the road. The view to the west (left) looks deep into the Taconic Mountains. Below you in this wilderness is a massive granite monastery built by the Carthusian Order and the man-made Lake Madeleine and Barbo's Lake. The view to the east (right) overlooks the Valley of Vermont and into the Green Mountains. From this vantage point you'll notice how flat the top of the Green Mountains are in southwestern Vermont. About 350 million years ago the top of this section of the Green Mountains was sheared off and forced westward. The Taconic Mountains are the remains of these majestic peaks. The heat generated by this cataclysmic event cooked the limestone bedrock turning it into marble and dolomite. The marble for which Vermont is famous is found in this valley or under the Taconic Mountains.

After you cross the saddle you'll encounter another series of nasty switchbacks with radically banked pavement. These blind corners require first gear. Look out for gravel wash on the pavement and the cars coming downhill. Expect strong wind gusts. It's now a short straight stretch into the parking lot and to the comfort of the Equinox Mountain Inn.

From the vantage of Lookout Point you can gaze down upon Manchester, or from the upper porches of the inn, look at the rolling peaks to the west. The land to the west, or at least seven thousand acres of it, are owned by the Carthusian Order. The granite monastery—the only Carthusian monastery in the Western Hemisphere—was built in majestic isolation on the acres donated to the order.

When you're ready, negotiate the 5.2 miles down the mountain to your starting point. Again, be careful of the gravel and of cars on the blind corners.

18.8 The next 2.5 miles have several motels. As you approach Manchester, the quality, and generally the cost, of lodging increases.

21.8 Hildene is on the right as you enter the village of Manchester. This Georgian-Revival mansion was built as the summer home for Robert Todd Lincoln who lived here until his death in 1924. Hildene stayed in the Lincoln family until 1975 when it was purchased by a local foundation. Still furnished with the Lincoln family's possessions, Hildene should not be missed by anyone interested in U.S. history.

I have always called this stretch of Route 7A from Hildene to the Equinox House "Mansion Row," and there's no other place like it in Vermont.

22.5 The Equinox House is on the left with the majestic Mount Equinox behind it. Built on the site of William Marsh's tavern, this grand resort hotel was built from several existing inns by Franklin Orvis in the 1850s. Catering to the rich and famous, the Equinox House flourished during the Civil War, the Great Depression, and two world wars, but it declined in the 1950s and 1960s and finally closed down in 1974. Fortunately it was purchased, restored, and re-opened in 1985.

On the left, two buildings beyond the Equinox House is the American Museum of Fly-Fishing. The early wealth of this resort town, coupled with the famous fishing gear of the Orvis company and one of this country's best trout streams, the Batten Kill, made this a destination for celebrities who were serious about fishing. The museum shows the evolution of sport fishing in this country and displays gear from some of the celebrities who frequented Manchester.

22.8 The Rose Room at the Village Country Inn, The Reluctant Panther, and The Equinox House are some of Vermont's most expensive lodgings. These and other specialty inns and bed and breakfasts in Manchester offer an experience, world-class dining, or both. The Equinox has one of the better golf courses in New England. The Reluctant Panther has rooms with individual fireplaces, private Jacuzzis, and is rumored to have one of the best wine cellars in the state. If you desire a gourmet dinner followed by a walk in formal gardens or a room furnished in antiques, then the Village Country Inn would be your choice.

23.1 The famous Orvis outfitters is located on the right.

Manchester Center is filled with factory outlet stores, specialty stores, gourmet foods, restaurants, and up-scale shopping plazas. If you're looking for a wristwatch, stop in the Movado company store, or get outfitted at factory stores by Ralph Lauren, Calvin Klein, Anne Klein, Saville, or Orvis. To be fair, the Orvis store is the original and is not a factory outlet and was founded in Manchester by Charles Orvis in the 1850s.

23.8 The junction of Route 11E and the intersection of Route 30E are on the right in what is known locally as "Malfunction Junction" because of the traffic jams. Route 30W goes left (west) and Route 7A continues straight.

There are no traffic lights, all pedestrians have the right of way, and if there are Yield signs, they are not visible among the other signage. If you want to stop in this village, I suggest taking the first parking space available to you.

Route 7A junctions with Route 7 three miles north of the village. I strongly recommend having lunch or an early dinner in Manchester no matter what route you're planning to take. For those traveling to Lake George, take Route 30W through the beautiful Mettawee Valley to North Pawlet and the junction of Route 149. The most scenic way to Rutland is not on Route 7. Route 30W goes to Pawlet where Route 133N junctions; drive through the Taconics on this highway to West Rutland. Route 7 is the fastest way to reach Rutland. Route 30E takes you over the Green Mountains to Bondville and the access to Stratton Mountain or Route 100S. Route 11E goes over the shoulder of Bromley Mountain, intersects Route 100 in Londonderry, and continues to the Connecticut River in Springfield. By taking the combination of Routes 11E, 100N, and 155N, you will travel more miles, but will return to Route 7 on the southern edge of Rutland.

24.0 The Chamber of Commerce is on the right at the small green. Stop by and pick up a selection of guides on where to eat, stay, and play in the area.

24.4 On the northern outskirts of Manchester you'll find the last of the readily available lodging until Rutland.

28.8 Historic 7A junctions with Route 7. **Turn left and continue north on Route 7.**

ROUTE 30W:
The West River Valley

Brattleboro to Route 100 and Alternate Roads

This is a short portion of Route 30 that takes you north and west from Brattleboro to join Route 100 in East Jamaica. If you plan to travel on Route 100 through Vermont, Route 30W is an important option if time or traffic is a consideration. Taking this highway to Route 100N, instead of Route 9W to Wilmington and then north, can save more than the twenty-seven-mile difference; it can save a tremendous amount of time on a weekend, especially during foliage when traffic can move with agonizing slowness through Wilmington and the Mount Snow area. If it's a hot day and you've been traveling for two or three hours already, you might consider this option just to take advantage of the swimming holes on the West River.

By taking Route 35 in Townshend and traveling to the village of Grafton or Chester, you are presented with a number of alternate ways in which to reach Route 100. You can also create a series of afternoon tours on the roads of southern Vermont by using Route 30W and these alternate highways. However, these are for those who wish to experience southeastern Vermont, not those who want to save time.

Route 30W goes from Brattleboro to Middlebury but, like so many highways in Vermont, it's rarely traveled from one end to another. This is a major access to the ski areas of southern Vermont and is used in conjunction with Routes 100, 7, and 11 to reach them. Route 30W goes from Brattleboro to Route 100; in this book, Route 30S, goes in the opposite direction—from Middlebury to Route 100. If I had to travel from southern Vermont to Middlebury, Crown Point, or another portion of the Champlain Valley, I'd go Route 30W to Route 100 and then north to one of the roads leading over the Green Mountain gaps (Routes 73W, 125W, or 17W) to reach my destination. If, for some reason, you wish to take Route 30 to Fair Haven, just follow the section on Route 30S in reverse.

Access to the beginning of Route 30W is made by riding into downtown Brattleboro. If you're coming north on I-91 take Exit 2, turn left, and ride down Western Avenue (it turns into High Street at the Y) to Main Street, then turn left and travel to the north end of Main Street. From New Hampshire and Route 9 the easiest way is to continue straight through the intersection of Route 5 and get onto I-91 (Exit 3) going south to Exit 2 (3.3 miles). You can also turn left at the intersection of Route 5 and ride south on Putney Road through 2.1 miles of strip development until you get to the green (on the right). You can either turn right at the southern end of the green or go another block into downtown before turning so that your trip odometer matches the mileages listed in this tour.

0.0   **In Brattleboro, at the end of Main Street or at the green, bear right onto Route 30W.**

Route 30 begins by the Gothic-style building that houses the municipal offices and the police station where Joe Gunther, the fictitious police detective in the series created by author Archer Mayor, has his office.

Leaving Brattleboro, you drive through the Brattleboro Retreat, originally built in 1834 as the Vermont Asylum for the Insane and later used as a military hospital during the Civil War. Going west on Route 30 follows the West River headed toward Newfane. You will probably see many people canoeing, rubber tubing, and fishing in the river's clear water. There are many popular swimming holes along the highway. Most of them are easily recognizable, as the turnouts sometimes have a couple of dozen cars parked in them. One popular swimming hole, especially for those with children, is located under the West Dummerston covered bridge (6.7 miles) where it crosses the West River.

8.6   Another swimming area is located under the steel bridge at the mouth of the Rock River (8.6 miles) and has ample parking on the right. A beautiful, deep ravine, this is one of the best swimming holes on the river. This area used to be called Williamsville Station.

On the left is a road leading west through South Newfane and East Dover to Route 100 in West Dover.

11.6   The Newfane green is famous for its colonial architecture, including the Windham County courthouse with its four majestic columns, circa 1825, and the Congregational Church, 1839. The Newfane Inn, in operation since 1793, is the second oldest inn in Vermont. The county jail used to abut the inn, and the inmates were fed the same meals as the paying guests. There's an old story about Theodore Roosevelt's once remarking that someday, when he had time on his hands, he would come to Newfane and commit some petty infraction.

12.6   On the right is the location of the famous Newfane Flea Market, one of the largest flea markets in Vermont, open on Sundays during the summer.

16.4   The junction of Routes 30W and 35N is at the Townshend green *where the alternate routes begin.*

Townshend once looked much like Newfane, but fires in 1894 and 1918 ravaged the town. Many of Vermont's towns suffered devastating fires, especially in the era when wooden buildings were heated by wood stoves and illumination was by lamp oil. Many of the downtown areas in various villages have a predominate period style because of rebuilding after these fires.

Continue on Route 30W through Townshend and up the West River valley.

On the left, the Scott covered bridge spans the West River. This 276-foot wooden bridge, built in 1870, is a fine example of the numerous covered bridges in Vermont. This one is now restricted to foot traffic.

18.4 The entrance to the Townshend Recreation Area is on the left after the covered bridge. This flood-control dam on the West River provides a man-made lake with picnic and swimming areas.

22.4 Route 30W merges here with Route 100N in East Jamaica.
Continue on combined Routes 30W and 100N, or turn left onto Route 100S and circle back to Brattleboro.

THE ALTERNATE ROUTES
Townshend to Grafton

16.4 **Turn right at the junction of Routes 35N and 30W at the Townshend green and head north to Grafton.**
This road was part of the major stage route to Montreal in the middle of the 1800s. It hasn't changed since I was a boy—not a single new house or garage has been built along its path in the last forty years.

19.9 Three and a half miles outside of Townshend village the road forks, with Route 35 going to the right and Townshend Road going to the left. **Take the left fork.**
Route 35 is a beautiful ride to Cambridgeport and then on to Grafton, with a short stretch of dirt road in Athens. Both roads are extremely beautiful country rides, but I recommend the left fork.
The road continues climbing the hill and runs through the woods, with trees arching overhead. At various points you emerge from the quiet woods into beautiful open meadows. On the right you'll pass the Grafton Cheese Factory and, as you enter into the village, the Grafton Inn is on the left.

26.3 **Turn right at the T in the village next to** the Grafton Inn. On the other side of the small concrete bridge you reconnect with Route 35N.
Turn left and continue on Route 35N to Chester or go straight on Route 121 to Bellows Falls. In Chester you have several options: 1) you can take Route 11W to Londonderry (Route 100); 2) Route 11W coupled with the Andover Road will take you to Weston (Route 100); 3) you can travel on Route 103W to Route 100 in Ludlow; and 4) you can connect with Route 5 by traveling on Route 11E to Springfield or on Route 103E to Bellows Falls.

Grafton

Grafton, population 602, is the stereotypical image of Vermont, with its immaculate colonial homes. Supported by The Windham Foundation, which owns most of the property in the village, Grafton is the archetype of a small Vermont town at the turn of the last century. The famous Grafton Inn was built in 1801 and then expanded to its present appearance in 1865 by Harlan Phelps with the money he made in the California gold fields. As it was situated along the stagecoach road from Boston to Montreal, the inn prospered. Ralph Waldo Emerson, Henry David Thoreau, Rudyard Kipling, Theodore Roosevelt, and Woodrow Wilson often stayed here. Most of the fine brick buildings in town date from the 1830s to 1850s, when Grafton was the crossroads in this neck of the woods, and the wool industry was still prosperous.

In 1850 there were over 10,000 sheep in Grafton and 568,553 sheep in all of Windham County. The mills of Grafton produced over 75,000 yards of wool cloth annually, but the lifting of U.S. tariffs on foreign wool coupled with the floods of 1869—which destroyed the mills—and the opening of the western prairies after the end of the Civil War, brought an end to the woolen industry in most of Vermont. By 1895 the town had shrunk to a population of eighty people.

Grafton to Chester

26.3 **Turn right on Route 35N** to begin some of the most beautiful country touring imaginable. Traveling up the mountain from Grafton village, headed toward Chester, you ride through woods with a network of branches from the trees on both sides of the road providing cool shade. Rocky ledges and steep hillsides are covered with lush ferns for several miles along this section of highway. When you crest the ridge you'll find yourself quickly dropping down into the village of Chester. As the old stagecoach road into Grafton, this was the northern route into town from the establishment of the town in 1754 until the road was built from Saxtons River in 1814.

26.5 **The junction of Route 35 with Routes 11E-W and 103N-S is in the center of Chester. On the left, Route 11W leads to Route 100 and to Manchester Center and Route 7.** *Across from the junction is Depot Street, which merges with Route 103N. On the right, after about 175 yards, South Main Street becomes Route 103S to Bellows Falls or Route 11E to Springfield. The Country Girl Diner is located on South Main Street, just before Route 11E divides from Route 103.*

Chester is famous for its "flagstone" houses, and although the majority of these buildings are on Route 103N in what is known as the Old Stone Village, you will see a couple of them on Route 11W. Among the seventy-five structures built by the Clark Brothers of Chester Depot between 1835 and 1845, these are made of gneiss (silent g) mined from nearby Mount Flamstead (Chester was originally called Flamstead). These beautiful homes are found almost exclusively in the townships of Weathersfield, Springfield, and Chester, with the greatest concentration in Chester Depot (Route 103N).

You'll find a number of fine bed-and-breakfast inns in the village, especially centered around the green, .3 mile ahead on the left.

ROUTE 121:
From Dirt Track to Modern Highway

This is a pleasant route leading you on a side trip to Grafton. From Grafton you can loop back to Brattleboro, or go over the hill to Chester. From Chester you can go to Rutland on Route 103W; to Springfield and Routes 106 or 5 on Route 11W; and to Bellows Falls on Route 103E.

Route 121 is a prime example of how Vermont's roads have evolved from pioneer times to the present era. Most of the state's highways developed in a similar manner.

Bellows Falls

Bellows Falls was an early crossroads of traffic. The earliest settlers coming up the Connecticut River had to stop at the south end of town at the mouth of the Saxtons River to portage around the great falls. In 1785 the first bridge over the Connecticut River was built here, and in 1791 construction on the first lock canal in the United States was begun. The first train arrived in town in 1849, and the first car, a Stanley Steamer, arrived around 1901–1902.

The first blazed trails became paths; the paths grew to accommodate sled and oxen; and these tracks became dirt roads with bridges carrying wagons and carriages back and forth between the thriving nineteenth-century villages. In 1892 Vermont began its road improvement program, and by 1914, two hundred miles of improved gravel roads had been built.

Bellows Falls was a very modern village at the beginning of the twentieth century, and new ideas, inventions, and progress were accepted here more readily than in most parts of Vermont. In 1906 there were five or six cars in town; by 1910 fifty people had cars, and only five years later about two hundred automobiles traveled the streets. During these early years people rarely traveled more than a few miles a day in their cars, and a couple of days of heavy rain would make the roads impassable. In October the cars went into storage and out came the old reliable horse-drawn sleigh until after mud season. However, it wasn't until after World War I, in 1919, that Westminster Street became one of the first streets in the state to be tarred, as a direct result of the demands of automobile owners in town, and in 1925 Rockingham began to plow the roads in the winter instead of rolling them. In October 1929, the first concrete highway in the state, a fourteen-mile stretch from the Putney town line to the foot of Old Terrace Street, was completed. It was not until 1931 that the Vermont legislature established the present highway system with 1,014 miles of main highway.

As you ride along Route 121 and other Vermont highways, visualize that many of the houses, barns, and covered bridges you see were built decades before a highway ran between them. Many of the older houses alongside the highway were built in the days when only a dirt track suitable for travel by foot or a winter path for oxen and sled ran past their doors. This is part of the beauty of touring the roads of this state.

0.0   In the village of Bellows Falls, the junction of Route 121W and Route 5 is at the traffic island on the south side of the village, at the bottom of Old Terrace Street. This is also the south end of Atkinson Street and Westminster Street (Route 5).

Turn left at the traffic light and go up the hill. The hospital is on the left just before you crest the hill. There is only a short stretch of road between the end of the village of Bellows Falls and the next grouping of houses, North Westminster, locally known as Gageville.

As a boy I used to see the old trolley tracks exposed in a portion of the pavement on Old Terrace Street. The history of the trolley was memorable but short-lived. In June 1900 the Bellows Falls and Saxtons River Street Railway began service from downtown Bellows Falls to downtown Saxtons River, transporting people and goods along the dirt road that is now Route 121. By the end of 1924, the local trolley company, like most others in New England, was out of business.

1.4   The center of the village of North Westminster is in the town of Westminster.

The road to the left leads down to the Saxtons River, where there are some great swimming holes—one known as "twin falls" or "the puddles." Here the river flows swiftly and the first waterfall drops into a large round pothole, while the second drops into a gorge hiding two other circular depressions. This is a beautiful spot, but beware—the swimming can be treacherous for those not familiar with swimming in gorges. It was along the river that the Gage Basket Company was located. North Westminster became known as Gageville because the village grew around the prosperity of this one company. In the 1940s the company moved to Putney and changed the name to Basketville.

When you leave Gageville you'll follow the river along the valley to Saxtons River, another village in the town of Rockingham. Route 121W follows the road built in the late 1700s between Bellows Falls and Saxtons River.

If you're thirsty, you'll find a roadside spring located a few yards up Back Westminster Road on the left after going under the interstate bridges. If you're attentive you'll notice these roadside springs all across Vermont, which are still being used as an alternative to fluorinated/chlorinated town water.

Saxtons River

Saxtons River is a village in the town of Rockingham. Bellows Falls is an incorporated village in the town of Rockingham, having its own village government. Saxtons River, Cambridgeport, Bartonsville, and Rockingham are unincorporated villages in the township and are governed by the town of Rockingham. Sometimes people get confused by this system, but it was extremely valid in the previous century, when distances where measured by how far a horse and wagon could travel in a day. Often the location of the village(s) was determined in the original layout of the grant (the township), but usually certain villages, especially those with abundant water power or some other economic factor, became the primary village (like Bellows Falls) as the town's population grew.

4.4   At the traffic island the road on the left leads across the river, through Westminster West, to Putney.

Continue straight, and as you leave the village the Pleasant Valley Road, on the right, *leads over to Rockingham (4.6 miles) on Route 103. It's a winding, twisting road and rough in spots.* When you pass the Pleasant Valley Road, Route 121W winds along the edge of a field on the left. **Caution:** *The corner at the end of the field is extremely tight and is banked incorrectly.*

This section of Route 121 from Saxtons River to Grafton was built in 1814, many years after the section from Bellows Falls to Saxtons River, and has changed little since then.

7.2   I advise you to slow down as you enter the final village in the town of Rockingham. Usually there is sand on the corner and on the old concrete bridge.

Cambridgeport, one of those old Vermont villages that was so vital in the days of water power, was named after J. T. Cambridge, who opened a clothier's business here in 1825. As you enter Cambridgeport you'll see the ruins of the old stone mill, one of the many woolen mills in the area, built in 1836. Like the town, it was gutted by fire one too many times and was not considered economically viable enough to rebuild.

The center of the village of Cambridgeport was destroyed in a disastrous fire in 1930 and was damaged in the floods of 1927, 1936, and 1937, and by the hurricane of 1938. Coupled with the Great Depression, these natural disasters encouraged emigration from many small villages in Vermont.

7.5   **Route 121 merges with Route 35 in Cambridgeport at the T. You've just crossed the Saxtons River and must turn right to continue on combined Routes 121 and 35 toward Grafton.** *If you turn left, you will go through Athens to Townshend and intersect with Route 30; part of Route 35 is a gravel road.*

Just before the bridge, on the right, is a house that was a soapstone mill. Located here at the sixth dam, where the bridge now stands, this mill finished the stone quarried on Kidder Hill, on the left after crossing the bridge—the second largest soapstone quarry in the United States. Serpentine stone was quarried on the hill and hauled down to the Saxtons River on sleds pulled by oxen. Here at the mill, inkwells, sinks, griddles, and heating stones were fashioned for commercial sale throughout the United States. I once lived in this house and was always finding milled pieces of soapstone in the garden and in the river, by the bridge.

Continue along the river to Grafton. As you drive along the Saxtons River, imagine it in the 1850s when the hills were deforested and the pastures filled with sheep. The river had six dams between Cambridgeport and Grafton powering woolen mills, a gristmill, and the soapstone mill. The flood of 1869 destroyed the dams and the mills. Imagine this narrow valley with the water flowing eighteen to twenty feet higher than normal.

11.3   **The division of Route 121 and Route 35 is by the small concrete bridge in Grafton.**

I don't recommend continuing on Route 121, as part of this road is gravel between Grafton and its junction at Route 11. Route 35 leads to Chester where you can connect with Routes 11 and 103 and from these to Routes 5, 106N, and 100 (see Alternate Route on page 106 suggesting Route 30W for the road from Grafton to Chester and Weston or from Grafton to Townshend).

ROUTE 11E:
Manchester Center to Springfield

I am so used to the spectacular roads twisting along narrow valleys, climbing over mountain gaps, and passing through beautiful villages that I find myself taking a road such as Route 11 for granted. In most parts of the United States, however, this route would be considered a top-quality touring road.

0.0   The junction of Route 11E and the intersection of Routes 30 and 7A in Manchester Center is locally known as Malfunction Junction, where two primary highways meet in the middle of a downtown tourist center with no traffic lights and many pedestrians. If you can find a parking spot, this is the best place to stop and eat for many miles. For lunch or dinner you can find almost any kind of food here from pizza or McDonald's to gourmet deli and European cuisine. I suggest picking up information at the local Chamber of Commerce, on Route 7A, .2 mile north of the junction of Route 11E, about places to eat, stay, and visit.

You're now riding east on combined Routes 30S and 11E.

0.7   By now you've passed the heaviest concentration of commercial shopping, although there are still factory outlet stores for another .5 mile. If you or anyone traveling with you is a compulsive shopper, it can take hours to travel this short stretch of road.

1.4   This is the access onto Route 7—the modern highway built to replace old Route 7, now named Route 7A. *Route 7 will quickly take you north to Arlington and Rutland or south to Bennington.*

2.3   You'll find numerous motels and restaurants in this area because of the access to the ski areas from Route 7. As you leave Manchester you enter the town of Winhall. The township of Winhall is primarily forest and mountains, with the one village of Bondville located on Route 30 in the southeastern corner. This is the middle of the largest portion of the Green Mountain National Forest.

2.5   The ranger station on the right, the main public station for the southern section of the national forest, is the place to stop and ask questions about any portion of the Green Mountain National Forest or camping in it. From here the road begins to ascend the foot of Bromley Mountain.

4.5   The road makes a turn and then begins to climb the steep grade of the south shoulder of Bromley Mountain. Halfway up the hill you'll probably notice the marker for the Appalachian/Long Trail, which crosses Route 11 at this point. You can park in the pull-off area and hike north or south along this trail through some of Vermont's most extensive wilderness area.

6.3   The division of Routes 11E and 30S is at the crest of the hill with The Lodge At Trout Pond on the left. *On the right Route 30S goes to Bondville and joins Route 100S in Rawsonville. I recommend taking Route 30S if you plan to travel south on Route 100.*
    Continue straight on Route 11E.

7.3   The Bromley ski area is ahead on the left.
    The broad shoulders on this section of highway make it easy to stop and admire the incredible view. As you look into the eastern Green Mountains, the predominate peaks are Glebe Mountain, 2,940 feet, ahead to the right, and Markham Mountain, 2,509 feet, overlooking the village of Weston, ahead on the left. Both of these mountains are on the other side of Route 100. Route 11E will pass along the northern foot of Glebe Mountain and the southeastern foot of Markham Mountain in Simonsville. On the right, looking south, you can see Stratton Mountain, 3,936 feet.
    Routes 11 and 30 between Manchester Center and Route 100 are principally used to access the ski areas of southern Vermont. Here at Bromley you can see the Stratton Mountain ski area to the south and just beyond, but hidden by Stratton Mountain, are the Mount Snow and Haystack ski areas; to the east Magic Mountain ski area is on Glebe Mountain; and to the north, hidden by Bromley, is Okemo ski area in Ludlow. All of these ski areas can be reached from Routes 100, 11, and 30.

From here you begin to descend the mountain to the valley through which Route 100 travels.

13.0   You left the town of Winhall and entered the town of Peru just before the Bromley ski area. Now, as you're descending the eastern side of this ridge of mountains, you're passing through the small town of Landgrove. Southern Vermont is densely settled compared to the Northeast Kingdom, but some towns have few roads and no villages. Winhall has a population of 482; Peru, 324; and Landgrove has only 134 residents. Combining these three townships you have a population density of 10 people per square mile, or 62 acres for each man, woman, and child. This is why Vermont is ranked as the most rural of the lower forty-eight states.

14.5   Route 11E briefly merges with Route 100N here in the village of Londonderry. *Turn right if you wish to continue south on Route 100.* Londonderry survives on the ski industry. Many of the small shops catering to skiers are not even open during the summer months.

14.9   Here Routes 100N and 11E divide. *To go north on Route 100, turn left.* **Continue straight on Route 11E** across the narrow iron bridge and over the West River.

This is a popular stretch of the river for canoeists and kayakers. If people are running the rapids beneath the bridge, or if a race is in progress, park along the main highway or the dirt road on the left just before the bridge. You can sit on the bridge and have a grandstand view of the event.

16.5   The ski area directly ahead of you is Magic Mountain, located on Glebe Mountain. Access to the ski area is .75 mile ahead on the right.

After passing the access to the ski area, the highway climbs the mountain for about 1.5 miles.

19.1   On the right is the junction of Route 121, a beautiful road over to Grafton, but part of it is dirt. The mountain to the left is Markham Mountain that you viewed from Bromley.

22.3   The Rowell's Inn in Simonsville is an example of one of Vermont's old stagecoach inns. Route 11 follows the Middle Branch of the Williams River from Simonsville to Chester.

25.4   The Hetty Green Motel II is on the left at the junction of Andover Road. *The Andover Road on the left leads over Markham Mountain and into Weston.* You are now in the outskirts of Chester.

27.5 Chester is famous for its "flagstone" houses, and although the majority of these buildings are located on Route 103N in the Old Stone Village, you will see a couple of them on Route 11. Among the seventy-five built by the Clark Brothers of Chester Depot between 1835 and 1845, these stone houses are made of gneiss (silent g) mined from nearby Mount Flamstead (Chester was originally called Flamstead). These beautiful homes are found almost exclusively in the townships of Weathersfield, Springfield, and Chester, with the greatest concentration being in Chester Depot (Route 103N).

28.9 You'll find a number of fine bed-and-breakfast inns in the village, especially centered around the green. Across from the green on the left, the Chester Area Chamber of Commerce has an information booth. Stop by to pick up local information and then visit the Chester Historical Society in the building directly behind it.

29.2 On the right is the junction of Route 35, the old stagecoach road that goes over the mountain to the village of Grafton. *If you plan to travel to Brattleboro or to Keene, New Hampshire, consider taking this route south. If you plan to continue north to Woodstock on Route 106, consider the alternate Route 10. Route 103N coupled with Route 10 brings you to Route 106 in North Springfield in only ten miles—just .8 mile less than Route 11 to Route 106. Also, the alternate route avoids the traffic congestion of Springfield, and the countryside is more pleasing.*

29.3 Routes 11E and 103S briefly merge just beyond the junction of Route 35. *Route 103N on the left goes through Chester Depot, merges with Route 100 in Ludlow, and junctions with Route 7 in Rutland.* If you're staying in Chester, or would like to try another form of touring, turn left and go down to the depot. Here you can take the Green Mountain Flyer, a sightseeing train running between Chester and Bellows Falls. This railway tour goes through areas you can't get to by car or by motorcycle, and the round-trip takes less than two hours.

29.6 Just beyond the Country Girl Diner, the routes divide, with Route 103S continuing straight. *Route 103S goes to Route 5 and Bellows Falls (ten miles).*
Turn left onto Route 11E.
Route 11E from Chester to Springfield is a wide, straight road. Green Mountain Classics, a garage that sells only vintage cars, is on the left just before you enter Springfield.

35.8 As you begin to enter Springfield you'll pass the hospital on the right, and at the bottom of the hill, the Springfield Plaza is on the right and a McDonald's on the left. The Friendly's restaurant in the plaza is probably the best place for many miles to stop for an ice cream or for lunch.

36.7 Here, at this maze of traffic lights, Route 106 merges with Route 11. **Stay in the right-hand lane to continue on Route 11 through Springfield to Route 5.** *On the left, Route 106N goes to Woodstock.*

37.0 On the right along the Black River you can see the old Fellows Gear Shaper Plant, now used as rental space for a variety of businesses.

Edwin Fellows left the machine shop of Jones and Lamson and founded this company in 1896. As a leader in the development and production of precision gear manufacturing, Fellows Gear Shaper played a key role in the early development of the auto industry. These plants were so critical to America during World War II that Springfield was listed as the third most essential manufacturing site in the country.

My grandfather told me stories of antiaircraft guns that were mounted on the roofs of the machine shops during the war, and he spoke of the many security precautions everyone had to take.

37.3 Here in downtown Springfield Route 143 junctions at the traffic lights. *Route 143 is a shortcut to Route 5N and is a great, but short, touring road.*

Springfield was the birthplace of many inventions: sandpaper, gravel roofing, the jointed doll, the kitchen mop, and the mop ringer. A. H. Ellis invented a steam shovel in 1848. H. Grinnell developed the process still used in polishing marble. David M. Smith invented a combination lock and the first adding machine in America. Doll carriages, breech loading rifles, guitar cases, and much more were invented, designed, and manufactured here in Precision Valley.

38.3 On the left is the Jones and Lamson Company and Bryant Chucking Grinder is on the right. The Jones and Lamson Company moved to Springfield from Windsor after the Civil War. James Hartness, as manager of Jones and Lamson, was as responsible as any one individual for the growth of Springfield as one of America's leading industrial centers. James Harness invented the turret lathe in 1841 and patented 120 different machines. He was governor of Vermont in 1921, was an amateur astronomer, and an avid aviator. He encouraged inventiveness in an environment where inventors were highly respected.

W. J. Bryant left Jones and Lamson in 1909 to form Bryant Chucking Grinder Company, which is now one of the few survivors of Springfield's decline in the machine-tool industry. My mother, my uncle, and my grandfather all worked for Bryant's, as did the members of many other families from the towns surrounding Springfield. I grew up watching giant green machines build even larger machines. These days most of the machining is done by CAD operators, and a machinist now needs computer skills rather than manual dexterity and a precisioned eye.

Farther along on the outskirts of the village you'll see the Eureka Schoolhouse, owned by the Vermont Department of Historic Preservation. It is an authentic reconstruction of the schoolhouse that was moved to this location from North Springfield.

40.8   Route 5S on the right leads to Route 103 and Bellows Falls. Route 5N merges with Route 11E and continues straight. There is a motel and restaurant on the left.

41.1   The I-91 access (Exit 7).

41.6   Routes 11E and 5N divide here; Route 11 continues straight crossing the Connecticut River over the Charlestown Toll Bridge into New Hampshire.

Route 5N makes a ninety-degree turn left and follows the river north. The Holt Landing and fishing access is on the right and would be a good place to take a break on a hot summer day.

Just across the river is a reconstruction of Fort No. 4, the northernmost British fort from which General Amherst and Roger's Rangers built the first frontier road across the wilderness to Crown Point, New York, in 1759. After completion of this road, General Amherst lead his troops from Fort No. 4 to Lake Champlain and then on to capture Montreal. As a direct result of the building of this road, General Amherst and General Wolfe were able to capture the French in a pincer movement, and Canada became part of the British Empire.

Route 106N:
Springfield to Woodstock

This popular local road to Woodstock is often toured by vintage auto clubs. Route 106 can be reached by traveling east on Route 11 from Chester, east on Route 10 from Gassetts, and by driving 4.3 miles through the village of Springfield on Route 11W from Route 5.

0.0 The junction of Route 106N is at the traffic lights. Get in the right-hand lane and continue straight. *To continue on Route 11W to Chester and eventually Manchester Center be in the left-hand lane.* Use the left-hand lane to gain access to the Springfield Plaza on the left, which contains a Friendly's restaurant, or to gain access to McDonald's, opposite the plaza.

You'll continue to drive through commercial development between Springfield and North Springfield following the Black River on the left.

3.3 **Turn right to continue on Route 106N.** The junction of Route 10, *which leads west to Gassetts on Route 103*, is directly ahead.

4.1 The road to the Hartness State Airport, founded by James Hartness in 1919, is on the right. Besides all of his other accomplishments, James Hartness was Vermont's first licensed pilot. Ahead and to the right you can see Mount Ascutney.

6.1 Here you cross the Black River and continue up the valley with the river on the left. The valley slowly increases in elevation as you ride deeper into the Vermont Piedmont.

8.1 On the right, at the intersection of Route 131, is the Country Creemee Restaurant, a very popular local spot in the summer, offering milkshakes, fries, burgers, fried clams, and similar fare. A gas station is on the left. *Route 131E on the right leads to the village of Ascutney, Route 5, I-91, and Route 12 to Claremont, New Hampshire, Route 131W on the left leads to Proctorsville on Route 103.*
Continue straight on Route 106N.

8.9 Here Mount Ascutney can be seen on the far right and Little Ascutney on the immediate right. The rock slides are on the sides of Little Ascutney.

Mount Ascutney is just over three thousand feet high, yet it was formed beneath the surface of the earth. Being composed of harder igneous rock (granite), it has resisted the erosion of glaciers, wind, and water better than the softer metamorphic rocks (gneiss, slate, and schist) that once covered and surrounded it. Of course it's taken millions of years to wear the metamorphic rock down to the level you're now riding on, leaving the granite towering above the landscape. Mount Ascutney is known as a monadnock, and the study of this mountain and Mount Monadnock in New Hampshire lead to the understanding of the principals and cycles of erosion.

10.4   The stone house on the left is but one of about seventy examples of this type of construction found in this part of Vermont.

12.3   This is the village of Felchville, named after William Felch, with the Reading post office and Reading General Store on the right. The village of Felchville is the southeastern corner of the township of Reading, but the post office and the name of the store often creates confusion for visitors.

Tyson Road, on the left by the general store, *leads through South Reading on over the mountain to the village of Tyson and Route 100 on the southern end of Echo Lake.*

You'll see three stone houses in this village made of the local gneiss (silent g) that were built by the Clark Brothers of Chester Depot between 1835 and 1845. These beautiful homes are found almost exclusively in the townships of Weathersfield, Springfield, and Chester with the greatest concentration being in Chester Depot (Route 103). There are three other fine examples, including the South Reading Church, on Tyson Road.

13.1   You now begin a more obvious ascent in elevation, which is typical of valleys in the Vermont Piedmont.

13.6   On the right is the junction of *Route 44E, which goes to Windsor and Route 5 following Mill Brook around the northern base of Mount Ascutney.*

Approximately 1.5 miles farther on you'll ride through the small village of Hammonville. From here Route 106 begins to quickly climb out of the valley, twisting and turning as it follows Reading Hill Brook for the next five miles.

18.7   When you crest the ridge you'll start the descent into a narrow valley containing numerous horse farms and an equestrian center. In the summer scores of people arrive with their horses for training and competitions. On the right you'll see the training fields and stables. On most summer weekends there is some type of equestrian competition. The Green Mountain Horse Association and the Highbrook Horse & Harness tack shop are on the right.

There seems to be a rapid increase in horse breeding in southeastern Vermont. Farms that once stocked dairy cattle now have horses grazing in their fields. It seems that horse farms are now replacing the family dairy farm in this region. Thirty years ago, I rarely saw more than an isolated horse or two, usually owned by farmers.

On one of these hills overlooking the equestrian center is one of Vermont's major calendar sites, thought by many to be evidence of Celtic and Phoenician exploration and settlement in the new world before Columbus. The standing stones and other megalithic markers line up with a surveyor's' precision to mark specific days of the year and are similar to those found throughout western Europe. They took quite a bit of effort to build. Why didn't the early settlers destroy them when clearing their fields? Why weren't these stone structures listed in any of the early land deeds? Are the engravings found on these stones really a Celtic vowel-less alphabet (Ogham)? Could the local Indian tribes have built them? Were our Yankee ancestors into ancient customs that the church didn't approve of? The more you investigate these sites, the more questions you raise.

21.2   The highway makes a hard turn left and is posted for 25 MPH. I recommend caution on this blind curve since a hidden access road junctions on the right, and all turning traffic is hidden as you approach the curve from the south.

You now enter South Woodstock, a beautiful village with the South Woodstock Country Store and the Kendrid Inn (1828) on the left. The brick buildings date to the days of the Perkins Academy (1848), when this village was an educational center.

The road has a broad sweeping S-turn beginning at the store and ending as you leave the village. You now find yourself on a beautiful, shaded, twisting road following the brook. Resist the temptation to challenge the road as this area is patrolled, and the 50 MPH speed limit is strictly enforced by the Woodstock police.

As you approach Woodstock, the Woodstock Inn Sports Center and then the Woodstock Inn Country Club will be on the right. You are now on Park Street in the village of Woodstock.

26.7   Route 106 ends as it junctions with Route 4 here at the green in Woodstock village. The Woodstock Inn is on the right. You must turn right.

If you continue straight, you'll be in downtown Woodstock. Routes 4E

and *12S lead to Quechee or Route 12N to Morrisville in northern Vermont.*
To continue on Route 4W leading to Route 100 or to New York, stay to
the left and round the green.

(For more on Woodstock see Route 4W, page 132.)

ROUTE 103:
From the Connecticut River to the Valley of Vermont

Route 103, part of the Calvin Coolidge Memorial Highway, runs northwest from Route 5 to Route 7 in Rutland. In Ludlow Route 103 meets Route 100, allowing you the option of going back to southern Vermont or going up the center of the state as far as Newport.

0.0   The junction of Route 103 is at Route 5 just north of Bellows Falls and the access ramp onto I-91 (Exit 6) in the town of Rockingham.

1.4   The left turn leads to the Old Village, the site of the first village in the town of Rockingham. As Rockingham prospered, other villages were founded: Bellows Falls, Saxtons River, and Bartonsville. As with so many Vermont villages, this one was ravaged by fire in 1909, burning the entire village center to the ground. It never recovered.

In the Old Village stands the Rockingham Meeting House, erected in 1787. This Federal-style meetinghouse is one of Vermont's earliest public buildings in near original condition. In the graveyard are slate markers with interesting epitaphs. I've watched visitors making rubbings of these words and designs using special paper and crayons.

2.7   The Vermont Country Store is located on the left. The Orton family of Weston built this retail outlet as an extension of their famous store in the village of Weston. I have fond memories of working in this old country-store atmosphere with its soda crackers, oak barrel of dill pickles, yard goods, old advertising, and penny candies. Such memories would normally belong to a child of my parents' generation. Consider stopping and experiencing the recreation offered by an old-time Vermont general store.

3.3 The Pleasant Valley Road junctions with Route 103 on the left and *leads to Route 121 in Saxtons River.*

3.5 The Brockways Mills Road on the right leads to Brockways Mills and the gorge.

This area was built upon water power, its main mill powering a flour mill on one side and a lumber mill on the other. The lumber mill, like most of the period, produced more than just cut boards; the spindles for the pews at the Rockingham Meeting House, chair stock, legs, rungs, and other furniture parts were also made on the premises. Here L. D. Parker made violins that were sold all across the United States.

6.0 The flood of 1869, like the floods of the following century, altered the course of history for many Vermont villages. Here along the Williams River, the mills were washed away. The village of Bartonsville once had two paper mills, a gristmill, a blacksmith shop, a store, a post office, a railroad station, and a Spiritualist hall, but the flood changed the course of the river, and the mills moved to the more prosperous village of Bellows Falls. The flood of 1869, coupled with the end of the Civil War, encouraged many Vermonters to emigrate to the opening lands in the West instead of to the nearest prosperous village.

8.7 As you enter the village of Chester, the Kalico Kitchen diner is on the left.

9.2 The junction of Route 11E is on the right. *Route 11E goes to Springfield and to Routes 106 and 5.*

9.5 Route 103 makes a ninety-degree turn right in Chester village. The junction of Route 35 from Grafton is approximately .2 mile straight ahead.

Although the most interesting sights in Chester are to be seen by following Route 103, you can continue straight on Route 11 and then take the first right after the green, Church Street, which will quickly take you back to Route 103 at mile 11.0.

10.0 The Depot is the place to catch the Green Mountain Flyer train that makes two round-trips between Chester and Bellows Falls each day during the summer. It's a good break from driving, and you'll get to see places not accessible by highway.

10.3 Turn left, making a ninety-degree turn on the other side of the river, to follow Route 103 into the Old Stone Village.

The Stone Village Inn, one of the first buildings you'll see as you enter this unique community, is one of the seventy-five stone buildings built by the Clark Brothers of Chester Depot between 1835 and 1845. The house next to the old school boasts 1838 on a sign above its door. These stone houses are made of gneiss (silent g) mined from nearby Mount Flamstead and are found almost exclusively in the townships of Weathersfield, Springfield, and Chester, the greatest concentration being here in Chester Depot. Notice the difference in construction between these structures and the more modern stone church.

Several of the stone houses are reputed to have hidden rooms and were part of the Underground Railway, the established routes for the runaway slaves. Vermont was a staunch abolitionist state, and many people were actively involved in helping runaway slaves escape to Canada prior to the Civil War.

Chester was first settled in 1764 as Flamstead. Religious conflicts in 1785 lead to the division of this settlement into two parishes: the Congregationalists settled here where the stone village now stands; the Baptists settled in the village on what is now Route 11 where the Chester green is located. When the railroad was built, the depot was deliberately located between the two parishes.

11.0   On the right, just north of the village, is a classic example of a colonial home. Notice the square shape, the massive chimneys, the arched windows over the doors, and the small- paned windows.

Route 103 has been following the Williams River up through this beautiful valley. On the right along the highway you can see some of the stone walls for which southern Vermont is famous.

14.2   In the village of Gassetts is the junction of Route 10 on the right. *Route 10 leads to Route 106 in North Springfield.*

Just north of the village is the old talc mill on the left and the cliffs of schist to the right. Before the road was widened, this cliff was known for its almandine garnets. Garnets and other minerals—kyanite, staurolite, diopside, titanite—can still be found in some of the rocks along the river and in the cliffs on the opposite side. Talc, the official Vermont mineral, is still commercially mined a few miles to the east of here in Springfield.

16.3   You are entering the town of Cavendish, which received national attention when Russian author Aleksandr Solzhenitsyn moved here during his exile from the Soviet Union.

Looking ahead you can see where the valley ends. Route 103 climbs through the Proctorsville Gulf, a narrow passage winding between the two mountains for about 1.5 miles. You are now in the Green Mountains.

18.5 From the village of Proctorsville you'll get the first glimpse of Okemo Mountain.

19.2 The Castle Inn is just up the hill on the right. A motel is located just beyond on the right. There are more motels as you enter Ludlow, a town whose economic prosperity depends primarily upon the ski industry.

On the outskirts of the village, the Fletcher Farm Arts and Crafts School occupies a series of white buildings on the right. This respected summer arts center offers workshops in a variety of media.

21.2 The Timber Inn is on the left and Okemo Mountain looms ahead. You're actually entering into the village here. Route 103 gives you a sense of what Routes 5 and 14 were like prior to the building of the interstate highways that run parallel to them.

21.7 This beautiful village green shows where the center of the community used to be located.

Ludlow has many beautiful and interesting buildings, but my favorite is the Baptist Church located at the end of the green. This church, designed by George Guernsey, is considered to be a High Victorian Gothic Revival style, but it has always had a Russian-design flavor for me. The Black River Academy, attended by Calvin Coolidge, is the brick Richardsonian Romanesque-styled building just up the street beyond the church.

22.3 Route 100 merges with Route 103 in downtown Ludlow directly across from the shopping center. *Route 100S, on the left, leads over the mountain to Route 155 and the village of Weston.*

You'll find a one-hour photo lab, a bagel shop, and a Mexican restaurant set back from the street on the left, but I recommend traveling less than another .5 mile before stopping to eat.

22.7 The entrance road to Okemo ski area is on the left. The small collection of shops to the left contains the Sweet Surrender Bakery, a favorite stop. Numerous fine restaurants can be found here at the base of the mountain.

24.1 Route 100N divides from Route 103 on the right. *If you turn right and follow Route 100N, you'll travel through Tyson, Bridgewater, and Sherburne. Route 100N meets Route 4E in West Bridgewater and divides*

*from Route 4W at the base of Mendon Mountain. Route 100 is the con-
nector for almost all of the ski areas in Vermont, and in the winter there
can be considerable traffic between Okemo and Killington/Pico.*

From here you climb the heights of the Green Mountains and can
feel the change of temperature as you drive to higher elevations.
Route 103 is fairly straight and has a truck lane for the next couple
of miles as you climb through the gulf between Okemo Mountain
and Sawyers Rock.

27.2   On the left is the Crowley Cheese Shop. The variety of Colby
produced here is known by cheese lovers throughout the world. Vermont produces more than 100 million pounds of cheese a year, some
in small operations such as this, some by large producers such as
Cabot Creamery.

In December 1849 the Rutland Railroad completed the railway
line through Mount Holly, thereby connecting Boston to Burlington by rail. The Rutland Railroad was in a serious, but gentlemanly,
competition with the Central Vermont Railway to be the first to establish this important rail link. The Rutland crew drove the last
spike thirteen days before the Central Vermont crew, winning the
barrel of rum that was put up as a wager. Think of what it must have
been like to build a railway along this route without modern machinery.

33.2   The junction of Route 140 is on the left and .4 mile farther is
the junction of Route 155S next to the P.J. General Store. It's only .2
mile along Route 140 to the center of the village of East Wallingford
and the intersection of Route 155. *Route 140W leads to Route 7, Middletown Springs, and Route 30. Route 155S goes to Route 100 north of the
village of Weston.*

36.0   As you enter the small village of Cuttingsville, you'll see a
beautiful Victorian home on the left, now an antiques center and
supposedly haunted.

39.4   Directly ahead is the Valley of Vermont. The Long Trail and
the Appalachian Trail cross Route 103 at this point.

This portion of Route 103 was once part of the Crown Point Military Road, the first road in Vermont, 1759, which connected the
Connecticut River at Old Fort Number 4 in Charlestown with Lake
Champlain at Chimney Point, its narrowest spot. It was built in the
days of the French and Indian Wars and allowed General Amherst to
successfully campaign against French Canada. In 1759 when General
Amherst captured Montreal and General Wolfe captured Quebec

City, Canada became a possession of Great Britain. When England and France ended their war in 1763, this road played a crucial role in the settlement of the interior of Vermont. Ahead is the Taconic Mountain Range. You can see the notch in the mountains where Route 4W, the continuation of the Crown Point Military Road, passes. West Rutland lies at the entrance to this notch, and between here and the mountains is the city of Rutland.

41.5 This is the intersection of Route 7B that is the old highway. Route 7B to the right connects with modern Route 7.

41.7 The junction of Route 103 is at the modern four-lane Route 7 on the south side of the city of Rutland in North Clarendon. *Turn right to go to Rutland, Routes 4W or 4E, or to follow Route 7 north.*

ROUTE 140W:
The Horace Greeley Highway

R oute 140 is not one of the popular tourist highways. The first six miles of this highway are a delight for the motorcyclist and a nightmare for the trucker, as the road winds through the Green Mountains, passing between Bear Mountain and Green Hill before dipping down into the Valley of Vermont. The terrain of the last nineteen miles, in the Taconic Mountains, is very different than the first six and is what one hopes to find when touring Vermont.

0.0 The eastern end of Route 140 intersects Route 103 between Ludlow and Rutland. There is another junction just .4 mile north on Route 103.

0.2 The junction of Route 155 is on the left in the village of East Wallingford. *Route 155S goes from East Wallingford to Route 100 just north of the village of Weston.*
Route 140W goes through the village, across the railroad tracks, and climbs the hill on the other side.

3.0 Here the highway crosses the Long Trail. This is a rural road with a few scattered homes and an occasional open field. This section of Route 140, between Routes 103 and 7, is an exceptional section of highway for those motorcycle sport riders who enjoy tight corners.

6.4   The intersection of Routes 140 and 7 is in Wallingford at the traffic light. **Continue straight through the traffic light.**

Route 140 winds through the village, crosses the railroad tracks, and runs over the iron bridge spanning Otter Creek. The highway then goes around Elfin Lake, barely visible on the left, then climbs the mountain.

9.2   After climbing for almost three miles, the road crests the mountain. Despite being a state highway, Route 140 feels like a town road, not heavily traveled and used almost exclusively by the local residents.

The road makes a long, straight descent into a beautiful valley filled with farms that is known as the Tinmouth Channel. Sweeping into the valley you **make a sharp right turn**, cross the valley, and climb the ridge on the other side. *The road that goes straight at this curve leads to Danby Four Corners.*

11.5   Entering the village of Tinmouth you'll notice a green, a church, a few buildings, and even a snack bar on the right. The highway turns north and follows the ridge above the valley.

14.7   **At the stop sign turn left** on merged Routes 140W and 133S. To the right Route 133N leads to West Rutland.

17.9   Rest Awhile With Us is a great sign posted on the green in Middletown Springs giving directions and distances to towns south, east, and west. **Continue straight.** Route 133S divides to the left.

The village of Middletown Springs was once a famous resort where people came for the curative waters. The Mineral Springs Park has restored one of the spring boxes, and this is a good place to take a break or have a picnic lunch. Take either the road to the left (south) at the eastern end of the green (across from the inn) or enter it .1 mile south on Route 133.

From Middletown Springs, Route 140 twists and turns as it follows the Poultney River westward through the Taconic Mountains. It's a rural road, very much like a town-maintained highway, with blind corners and vegetation growing right to the pavement. Many of the signs indicating sharp corners are half hidden in the sumac and growing elms.

23.6   This green is in the historic village of East Poultney. Numerous buildings of historic importance are on and surround the green. Centered on the green is the beautiful Baptist Church, 1805, showing many of the classic features of the Federal style including Palladian, arched, and segmented windows. To the left is the pillared Eagle Tavern, built in 1790 and now a private residence. To the left of the church, down the street from the tavern, is the old print shop that is open to the public during July and August. On the other side of the church is the original Union Academy that has been restored to its original condition by the Poultney Historical Society, located next door to the academy in the restored blacksmith shop. True museums, these provide us with links to our colonial past.

At one time, the prominent newspaper Northern Spectator was printed here, and to this newspaper came a young apprentice named Horace Greeley. From 1826 to 1830 Horace Greeley lived at the tavern and learned his trade at this print shop. In 1841 he founded the *New York Tribune* and became one of this nation's leading editors during the Civil War era. It was Horace Greeley in one of his pre–Civil War editorials who wrote the famous words, "Go west, young man. . . . "

Another young man born and raised here, George Jones, worked at the *Northern Spectator* at the same time as Horace Greeley. He cofounded the *New York Times* with University of Vermont graduate Henry Raymond. Francis Ruggles, also of Poultney, was instrumental in helping them establish this famous newspaper.

25.1 Route 140 ends in Poultney at the traffic light at Routes 30 and 31. The town of Poultney is on the Vermont–New York border. *To reach Routes 22A or 18 in New York, continue straight down Main Street and then around Green Mountain College.*

Poultney was one of the western towns in The Grants that played a part in the formation of the Republic of Vermont. The village of East Poultney was the center of the township in colonial times, but the commercial center shifted westward with the discovery of the slate deposits. This town became the center of Welsh immigration in the mid-1800s, when these miners came to own, operate, and work in the slate quarries of western Vermont.

From Poultney one can travel north on Route 30 to Route 4 or south to Manchester.

ROUTE 133S:
Through the Taconics

The Taconic Mountains are a part of Vermont that few visitors are familiar with. Of course, tens of thousands of tourists climb the toll road on Mount Equinox each year, and even more skirt the edges of these mountains along Routes 7 and 30. Route 133 and the local town roads offer beautiful touring for those willing to take the time to explore this unique region.

0.0   Route 133S begins at Route 4A in West Rutland.

2.1   On the far left, against Boardman Hill, is a marble quarry, which, like most, produces crushed rock, not cutting marble, used as a surface on driveways, parking lots, cellars, and landscaping.

The road curves to the right at the Riverside Shops.

4.9   This grouping of homes is the village of Ira, named after Ira Allen, one of the state's founders. The villages of Irasburg and Irasville, both located far from here, are also named for the same Green Mountain Boy.

8.8   Route 133S merges with Route 140W. *Route 140E leads to Route 7 in Wallingford.* The road is wide and smooth, the corners are gentle, and numerous people live along this stretch of highway.

12.0   In Middletown Springs at the green, **Route 133S turns left** and Route 140 continues straight. *Route 140W goes to Route 30 in Poultney.*

Middletown Springs was once a famous resort where people came for the curative waters. The entrance to Mineral Spring Park is .1 mile beyond the green. The Indians first showed these springs to the early settlers in 1772; they believed these waters had curative properties. In 1811 the four springs were buried when a torrential rain caused local flooding, but another flood in 1868 uncovered them. During 1868 A.W. Gray & Son began bottling the water from the recently uncovered springs. Water from each of the four springs was said to differ in chemical composition and was bottled and sold under separate labels. By the late 1800s, when water cures were the rage, Middletown Springs became a major resort. The waning popularity of mineral waters and the 1927 flood, which again covered the springs, ended the village's resort business. Since 1970, the local historical society has uncovered the springs and built this beautiful park along the brook. Under a rectangular gazebo are two park benches and two antique marble "boxes" that are just wide enough for two people to sit side by side and be bathed by the flow of the curative water.

16.9 On the right is the road leading (west) to the village of Wells. The highway runs through mostly open agricultural land where the fields are lined by steep, round-topped, tree-covered mountains.

Most of the these mountains are under two thousand feet in elevation, but their slopes are extremely steep. Famous among geologists, this is the Taconic klippe, the top of the ancient Green Mountains, where older rock has been thrust over younger rocks. About 300 million years ago, when all the continents were connected in one vast land mass called Panagea, the ancestral continent of Africa was pushing against North America. The force from the African plate caused the modern Appalachian Mountains and the Adirondacks to form. During this period of Acadian mountain building, the tops of the southern Green Mountains were somehow sheared off and pushed miles westward. The process generated so much heat that the local sedimentary limestones and shales were cooked, or metamorphosed, into the marbles and dolomites of this region. In the vast period of geological time since then, the effects of eroding water and four continental glaciations have removed thousands of feet of rock, always removing the softer marbles faster than the harder rock of the peaks. As a result, the Taconic Mountains have steep, rounded sides that end abruptly at the valley floors.

22.0 Route 133 makes a sharp turn right in this broad valley. *The left turn is a local road that leads through Danby Four Corners to Danby and Route 7.*

The road remains fairly straight as you follow Flower Brook to Pawlet.

23.3 The southern end of Route 133 junctions at Route 30 in the village of Pawlet across from Mach's General Store. The village is built around the gorge where the water power from Flower Brook was used since 1768 when Remember Baker had a gristmill at this site. The cast-iron cookstove was invented in Pawlet by Philo Stewart, and this village became famous for its stove manufacturing.

Route 30E leads to Manchester Center. Route 30W goes to Route 149 and Route 4.

A beautiful day trip from the Rutland area can be made by combining Route 133 with Route 30 to Fair Haven, followed by Route 4A back to West Rutland.

ROUTE 4:
Vermont's East-West Highway

t is only sixty-three miles from the New Hampshire border at White River Junction to the New York border along this major east-west highway. Route 4 connects I-89 from southern New Hampshire and Massachusetts, and I-91 in eastern Vermont, with Route I-87 in New York. Also connecting primary north-south Routes 100 and 7, it is also a major tourist highway, with the villages of Quechee, Woodstock, and Killington on the eastern side of the state and access to Lake George, New York, on the western side. There's lots of traffic on sections of this road, especially from the interstate access to Woodstock and from Route 100 over Mendon Mountain to Rutland. From Rutland to the New York border you can travel on Route 4A (the old Route 4) or take the faster, interstate-style, new Route 4.

Portions of this highway are beautiful, but I recommend using it only for access to Woodstock, Route 12, Route 100, Rutland, or New York.

(For more on White River Junction see Route 14, page 142.)

0.0   Route 4 winds into the village of White River Junction from West Lebanon, New Hampshire, and intersects Routes 14 and 5 by the bridge. **Turn onto combined Routes 4 and 5 and cross the bridge** over the railroad tracks and the White River. **At the traffic light (.2 mile) turn right and continue up the hill** staying in the right-hand lane. **Take the second turn on the right (.5 mile)**, directly across from the 25,000 Gifts shop, to continue west on Route 4. *Route 5S continues up the hill leading to the access onto Routes I-89 and I-91.*

0.5   Route 4W goes under the I-91 bridge. You can see the railroad freight yard and tracks below to the right and the White River beyond them. Route 4 continues to climb as it travels along the ridge following the White River Valley. For the next three miles the road continues uphill with occasional glimpses of the receding river below.

3.4   The first access onto I-89S (Exit 1) is on the left.

3.7   The highway finally crests the ridge and turns west away from the White River Valley. From White River to Bridgewater Corners, Route 4 is part of what is known as the Calvin Coolidge Memorial Highway.

4.0   The access onto I-89N (Exit 1) is on the left. From here the road gets narrower and the traffic heavier. This is one of Vermont's primary tourist roads as well as a major commercial east-west highway, so be prepared for turning traffic.

6.0   Timber Village, the antiques mall on the left, marks the beginning of an area that relies heavily on tourism. Traffic on this stretch of highway can get heavy during some summer weekends and during foliage season.

6.6   The bridge over the 165-foot-deep Quechee Gorge was first built as a railroad trestle in 1875. The Quechee Gorge Gifts and Snack Bar is on the right, just before the bridge. If you choose to view the gorge or walk down one of the paths leading along it, park in the gift shop parking lot. There are trails that begin at the shop and others on the opposite side of the bridge. On the far side of the bridge are two gravel parking lots, one on either side of the highway, with picnic tables and access to more trails.

7.4   The turn to the village of Quechee is on the right next to a small shopping mall with an antiques shop and restaurant.
    In mid-June Quechee hosts its annual Hot-Air Balloon Festival and Crafts Fair, while in late August there's the annual Scottish Festival. Both are worth attending.

10.1   Routes 12N and 4W merge here. Route 12 south is on the left while Routes 12N and 4W continue to Woodstock.

10.7   This is the village of Taftsville. Taftsville General Store is on the left and the covered bridge, built by Samuel Emmons in 1836, and a hydroelectric dam are on the right.

13.1   As you begin to enter into the village you pass the most reasonably priced motels in Woodstock.

13.7   Routes 12N and 4W divide at a very small green that's actually not much larger than a traffic island; Route 12 goes straight. **Bear left** on Route 4 and you will immediately find yourself on Central Street in downtown Woodstock. Specialty shops, antiques shops, art galleries, and eateries are tucked in and around each other in this highly desirable retail location. Part of the fun of Woodstock is finding places you didn't know existed.

13.8   On the right is a small residence with a Vermont historic site sign in the yard: "Justin Morgan: On this site the progenitor of the famous Morgan breed of horses owned by Sheriff William Rice about 1800. Justin Morgan took his name from that of the singing schoolmaster who originally brought him to Vermont but who later lost possession of the famous horse to Sheriff Rice in a payment of a debt." This horse, who sired the breed of horses bearing his name, is one of Vermont's sacred icons.

14.0   This is the center of downtown with the Woodstock Green only .1 mile farther on. Consider stopping at the Unicorn Shop and browsing its great selection of greeting cards. There are numerous fine restaurants in town. Try the Creamery on Central Street—great food and they make their own ice cream.

Woodstock

Woodstock is not, and has never been, a typical Vermont village. However, it has been home to many individuals who have shaped and influenced Vermont, the United States, and even the world. Charles Marsh, appointed U.S. attorney general by George Washington in 1797, and his son, George Perkins Marsh, are internationally recognized. As a congressman George Perkins Marsh championed the formation of the Smithsonian Institution; he was a minister to Turkey and was appointed minister to Italy by Abraham Lincoln in 1861. It was in 1864, while minister to Italy, that he wrote Man and Nature. *Marsh is considered to be the father of the American environmental movement.*

Frederick Billings moved to San Francisco in 1849 and became the first lawyer to practice there. He was one of the founders of the University of California at Berkeley, and as president of the Northern Pacific Railroad, supervised the construction of the transcontinental railway. Finally he came home to purchase Charles Marsh's farm (Billings Farm, now open to the public), where he advanced many of the ideas behind modern farming. Frederick Billings purchased Marsh's important library and donated it to the University of Vermont.

Jacob Collamer graduated from the University of Vermont and settled in Woodstock. He was a congressman, senator, U.S. postmaster-general, and advisor to President Lincoln during the Civil War. Alvin Adams founded the first express line in the United States between Windsor and Woodstock; the Adams Express Line became Railway Express. Vermont governors Julius Converse and Peter Washburne were born here. Also from this village are sculptor Hiram Powers and painter Benjamin Franklin Mason, whose work

*can be viewed in the Dana House, the former residence of Charles
L. Dana, President of the New York Academy of Medicine and a
world-renowned neurologist.*

14.1 The long, oval green on the left, faced by many beautiful
buildings in a variety of architectural styles, is one of the best places
in Vermont to view the variations in Federal architecture. On the
north end of the green you'll see the yellow-brick, columned Vermont National Bank that is adjacent to the fieldstone buildings and
the Romanesque-styled library, all of which blend together harmo-
niously. Just beyond the library is the northern end of Route 106 and
the famous Woodstock Inn. On the right is a covered bridge of modern construction, made in the traditional manner, that crosses the
Ottaquechee River. After that you'll find the Dana House.

14.3 As you leave the green, the brick town hall with its four pillars is on the right and Saint James Church, constructed of stone, is
on the left. Woodstock has a variety of beautiful buildings and many
can be seen along Route 4.

One of the popular sites to visit in Woodstock is the Vermont Institute of Natural Science, the Raptor Center. The VINS staff cares for
injured birds, and those that can be rehabilitated are released back
into the wild. Part of the educational program consists of several
dozen owls, hawks, eagles, vultures, and ravens which, because of
sustained injuries, cannot be returned to the wild. Viewing birds in
their large weirs (flight habitats) gives visitors an opportunity to become acquainted with these birds of prey, many of which are rarely
seen in the wild, even by the most ardent woodsman. *To visit the Raptor Center turn off Route 4 at the west end of the green in downtown Woodstock (at the large stone church) onto Church Hill Road. Go 1.9 miles on
this paved road to the VINS sign on the right at the large barn.*

14.5 As you cross the Ottaquechee River you'll see a beautiful
stone building on the left that has been converted from an old mill
into a local performing-arts theater.

15.4 The White Cottage Snack Bar on the left is a good place to
take a break. Stop, get a creemee, and walk down to the river to soak
your feet on a hot day.

Route 4 now follows the banks of the Ottaquechee River all the
way to Sherburne Center.

15.6 The Carriage House Inn of Woodstock is on the right. You'll
find plenty of lodging between here and the city of Rutland. This

portion of Route 4 houses some of the fancier inns, while the Mendon Mountain section has the tourist motels, and the city of Rutland the national motel chains.

17.4 The covered bridge crossing the river on the left is the Lincoln Bridge, built in 1865.

20.5 This is the village of Bridgewater. The Bridgewater Marketplace on the left was converted from the old woolen mill and contains a minibrewery, where Long Trail Ale is made (tours are held), craftshops, and antiques. Killington is the mountain visible directly ahead (west) as you enter the village.

22.5 This is Bridgewater Corners where Route 100A junctions on the left at the Junction Country Store. *Route 100A is a steep, winding road leading through the mountains, past the birthplace of Calvin Coolidge, and then down to Plymouth Union and Route 100. If you plan to ride south on Route 100, I recommendtaking this road.*

   Continue on Route 4W riding up the visibly narrowing valley that follows the river.

   It was here that the Vermont gold rush began in the late 1850s, when gold was discovered in Buffalo Brook. Soon discoveries of gold in Plymouth Five Corners and Bridgewater Center created a rush to Vermont's streams in search of the placer deposits. No one knows how much gold was discovered. As in all gold rushes, most people went away empty-handed, but a lucky few, like William Hanerson and F. W. Coolidge, found small fortunes. Although the mother lode was never found, various specimens of gold in quartz from this area exist in collections. It's interesting to note that if you draw a straight line on a map from the old mines in Bridgewater Center, due south to the upper reaches of Buffalo Brook, it will intersect all the places gold was discovered in this area. Gold is still panned in Vermont streams; however, I can tell you from experience that you'll work for a long time before you accumulate enough metal to make a piece of jewelry. Still, gold can be found in many streams emerging from the eastern side of the Green Mountains.

23.7 If you don't get stuck behind traffic, this wide road weaving up into the Green Mountains along the river is a great drive. The valley is so narrow and the mountains on both sides so steep that it feels like a gulf. It gives the illusion of climbing a steep grade for miles, and the rushing river adds to the sensation. In reality you're only climbing about 200 feet of elevation—from 885 feet above sea level in Bridgewater Corners to 1,065 feet in West Bridgewater.

On the rugged slopes to the right (north) there are numerous abandoned gold mines.

27.8 As you continue to climb you'll see a restaurant built in a notch on the side of the mountain on the left. Ahead you're looking up at Killington and Bear Mountains. This short stretch of Route 4 reminds me of traveling through the Appalachian Mountains of West Virginia.

28.3 In West Bridgewater you join Route 100 and continue on combined Routes 4W and 100N. From West Bridgewater to Sherburne you climb about two hundred feet, as you did from Bridgewater Corners to West Bridgewater, but here the illusion is opposite; you don't have the sensation of climbing along this straight, glacier-gouged valley.

29.4 Bear Mountain and the base lodge for the gondolas going up Killington are on the left. The gondolas are often operating during summer weekend months and offer a opportune break from driving.

33.5 If you choose not to take a gondola but still want to see Killington, you can take the shortcut, West Hill Road on the left, next to the Killington maintenance garage.

34.7 The main access road to Killington is on the left just before the division of Routes 4 and 100. The Killington ski area is now a village with its own post office, gas stations, lodging, and many fine restaurants and shops.

34.8 The division of Routes 4W and 100N is here at the base of Mendon Mountain. Route 100N turns to the right and Route 4W continues straight. About .1 mile farther on, traffic is entering from Route 100S onto Route 4W.

Gifford Woods State Park is .25 mile north on Route 100. From this campground you have the option of hiking in one of Vermont's virgin stands of forest, climbing the various trails that lead up the mountainside to the Long Trail, or exploring the numerous caves in the vicinity.

I've broken Route 4W into two sections. Many people use Route 4 to gain access to Woodstock and to Route 100; more people use Route 100 to access Route 4 over Mendon Mountain to Rutland and to New York. By resetting the trip odometer to 0.0 at the base of the mountain, the mileage of Route 4W as listed becomes usable to more people than just those traveling from White River Junction to Fair Haven.

0.0   From the junction of Routes 100S and 4W, the road climbs Mendon Mountain, a steep but straight climb that seems pretty tame in the summer, but during a winter snowstorm can be extremely tense. From here to the village of Mendon, all the land on the north side of Route 4 is part of the Green Mountain National Forest.

0.3   The motel on the left is just one of many on this road built to cater to winter skiers. During the summer you'll find plenty of places to stay; during foliage season every room is filled.

1.5   The Inn at Long Trail, on the right, at the crest of Mendon Mountain and built on the Long Trail, is a welcome luxury after many after days of hiking along the high peaks of the Green Mountains. If you'd like to spend a day or an afternoon hiking on the Long Trail, this is one of the better access points. The Appalachian Trail, wending from Georgia to Maine, and the Long Trail, following the Green Mountains the entire length of the state, have combined as a single trail following the backbone of the southern Green Mountains. About .25 miles north of the inn, these two world-famous hiking trails divide, with the Appalachian Trail going east through virgin forest, Gifford Woods, and along Kent Pond before continuing to Maine; the Long Trail continues north, providing majestic views at various overlooks. If you plan to spend a day or even an afternoon of hiking, this is one of the best places to do it provided you're in good physical shape.

From here the road goes downhill for the next 7.5 miles, all the way to the city of Rutland.

2.0   The access to the Pico ski area is on the left. In the summer this ski area offers not only a scenic chair lift, but also an alpine slide. You don't have to hike steep trails to enjoy these mountains.

3.3   This is the beginning of a concentrated stretch of lodging. In another .5 miles you'll begin to encounter numerous motels for about 1.5 miles, followed by a long stretch without development until you reach the village of Mendon.

6.8   The Sugar and Spice Restaurant is on the right. Out in the grove of maples, at the base of the hill near the old sugar shack, is a large boulder inscribed: The grave of Gen. Edw. H. Ripleys OLD JOHN A Gallant War Horse of the Great Civil War 1861–1865.

7.2   In Mendon you encounter more motels, shops, and other services as you enter the outskirts of Rutland. Directly ahead (west) you can see as far as the Adirondack Mountains in New York, while the Green Mountains slope down on either side of the highway toward Rutland. Here is the western boundary of the Green Mountains. Rutland sits in the widest part of the Valley of Vermont, with the Taconic Mountains rising on the other side of the city.

9.1   You finally stop descending Mendon Mountain when you reach the traffic lights. Now you are entering the city of Rutland with its fast-food restaurants and other tourist-oriented businesses. A short distance ahead you'll find a Taco Bell on the left and a McDonald's on the right, and that's just the beginning.

Rutland, with a population of just over eighteen thousand, has an interesting layout with a central downtown, local shopping malls on the south side of town, tourist businesses on the east, and light manufacturing and wholesale on the western side of the city.

10.5   Route 4W merges with Route 7S. **Position yourself in the center lane as you approach the light; turn left.** Once you make the turn, you want to be in the right-hand lane to continue on Route 4A. If you want to continue on the alternate route, the modern superhighway Route 4, you want to be in the left lane as you will travel on Route 7S for two miles. *If you plan to travel on Route 7N, position yourself in the right lane at the light.*

ALTERNATE ROUTE:
7S to 4W

Driving Route 4 is 2.2 miles longer than following Route 4A through downtown Rutland, but on a busy day it is much quicker despite the traffic lights. Also, if you are looking for lodging, this is the route to take. If you wish to take the side trip to Proctor, I suggest you not take this alternate route, but stay on the primary one, Route 4A.

10.6   Position yourself in the center or the left-hand lane. After turning left at the traffic light, immediately position yourself in the right-hand lane before the next traffic light and the beginning of Route 4A.

10.7   At the traffic light **continue straight**, with the green on the right. You'll go through a series of traffic lights. Almost any of the streets to the right will take you into downtown Rutland.

11.2   The Midway Diner is set back on the left at the bottom of the hill.

11.4   Strong Avenue, from downtown Rutland, merges on the right.

11.5   As you crest the next small rise and cross the railroad tracks, the Rutland Fair Grounds are on the right. The Rutland Fair, held during Labor Day week, is a county fair featuring livestock, poultry, and commercial vendors. Of course, most people come for the midway with its rides or for the evening events that range from stock car racing to country-western music stars.

There are plenty of places to eat and stay along this 1.5-mile stretch of Route 7. Dunkin Donuts, KFC, The Comfort Inn, McDonald's, Sirloin Saloon, Bagel Cafe, Sunset Motel, Lum's, Day's Inn, car dealerships, and gas stations line this four-lane highway. As you approach the junction of the modern Route 4W, you will see Denny's, Howard Johnson's Inn and restaurant, Holiday Inn, Ponderosa, and the Green Mountain Plaza.

12.7   The access onto Route 4W is on the right just past the shopping plaza. *Route 7S continues straight. From here it's twenty-nine miles to Manchester and fifty-four miles to Bennington.*

As you begin to travel on this section of Route 4, you're presented with beautiful views of farmlands on the outskirts of Rutland and the Taconic Mountains directly ahead.

16.5   At the exit to West Rutland you have the option of rejoining the original highway at 14.3 miles or continuing on this interstate-like highway all the way to the New York border, 14.5 miles.

West on Route 4A

10.7   Turn right at the light. The green is now to the left. Traffic is very heavy in this area as you go down the hill into the north end of downtown Rutland on West Street.

11.8   After crossing the railroad tracks, bear left continuing on Route 4A. For the next two miles you'll see light industry, wholesale services, and a few of the surviving marble, granite, and slate finishing sheds.

12.8   The junction of Route 3 is on the right leading to Proctor. *(See Alternate Route 3 in Route 7S, page 52.)* The second right, West

Proctor Road, leads to Wilson Castle, the folly of an Englishman who wished to entice his wife to stay in Vermont.

14.3 On the right is the access to Route 4, the modern highway connecting Rutland with New York. Much faster than Route 4A, it also offers beautiful scenic views; however, it does not give one a sense of the history of this part of the state provided by the old highway. *It is 14.5 miles to the Welcome Center where Routes 4 and 4A merge.*
I recommend continuing straight on Route 4A into West Rutland.

14.6 The junction of Route 133S is in the village of West Rutland. *Route 133 goes south through the heart of the Taconic Mountains to Route 30 in Pawlet.* Route 4 actually makes a loop around the southern edge of the village of West Rutland.

This town is world famous for its marble. At one time the West Rutland area, including Proctor, Pittsford, and Brandon, had as many as twenty-three marble quarries. However, the number of active and inactive quarries varies from year to year depending upon demand for particular types of stone. The famous West Rutland quarries lie on the northern edge of town, where the Vermont Marble Company is still mining the pavanazzo marble.

15.4 In the outskirts of West Rutland, you enter into the Taconic Mountains through the gap along the Castleton River.

The Taconic Mountain Range is believed to have been the top of the southern Green Mountains until a cataclysmic event sheared them from their base and pushed them westward to their current position. The rocks that form the Taconic Mountains are older than the sedimentary rocks on which they sit! When older rocks are forced over younger rocks, it is known as a klippe, and the Taconic klippe is world famous in the field of geology. The intense heat generated by the older rock being forced westward over the younger sedimentary limestones was what metamorphosed (cooked) the limestones into marble. All the marble mined in Vermont is located along the edges of the klippe, underneath the mountains, as in the Imperial Quarry under Dorset Mountain, or in the valley which lies between the Green Mountains and the Taconics.

21.7 As you enter the historic village of Castleton you find yourself on a broad avenue with beautiful homes set back from the road. Here there are footpaths along the highway instead of sidewalks and you get a sense of stepping back in time. The Federated Church of Castleton, designed and built by noted architect Thomas Dake, is on the right next to the old cemetery as you enter the village. The

The Manse House in Castleton is unusual in that it is a duplicate of the Wilcox–Cotts house in Orwell, but it was built to two-thirds scale.

Manse House, circa 1846, is but one of many classic homes built in the days of prosperity when the slate from this area was in demand as a building material.

The Hubbarton Battlefield, on the outskirts of town, is the site of the only battle of the Revolutionary War fought on Vermont soil on July 7, 1777. Seth Warner and a thousand Green Mountain Boys attempted to stop the advance of eight thousand British regulars commanded by General Burgoyne. Although the Green Mountain Boys were forced to retreat from the superior force of the Hessian divisions, they were successful in delaying the British force long enough for John Stark to assemble his troops. Five weeks later, John Stark, aided by Seth Warner and the Green Mountain Boys, defeated General Burgoyne and the advancing British in the Battle of Bennington, considered to be the turning point in the Revolutionary War.

21.8 Castleton College, Vermont's first college, eighteenth in the nation, was chartered by the General Assembly of the Republic of Vermont on October 15, 1787. It also has the distinction of having housed Vermont's first medical school, established in 1818. The public library now stands on the site; the campus of Castleton College moved to its present location, across the street, in 1833.

The first wind-powered, alternating-current electric turbine in the nation, the Putnam Wind Generator, was erected and operated at

Grandpa's Knob in 1941. If I remember correctly, this giant turbine had two wooden propeller blades, each ninety feet long and weighing eight tons. In 1945, after enduring two days of intense wind and generating vast amounts of electricity, one of the blades came off and tumbled down the mountain. Although the turbine successfully produced electricity for the grid, it was not considered to be economically viable enough to rebuild during wartime.

To many fishing enthusiasts Castleton is known as the home of Jules Buel who invented the fishing spoon lure in 1830.

23.5 The intersection of Route 30 is in Castleton Corners. *Route 30S leads to Route 100 in Manchester Center, while Route 30N leads to Middlebury. Route 30N also leads to the eastern side of Lake Bomoseen while Point of Pines Road—the second right after Route 4A passes the southern end of the lake—leads to the western side, including Avalon Beach.*

26.7 The merging of Routes 22A and 4W is at the beautiful green in the village of Fair Haven. Route 22A going north is on the right.

The Vermont Marble Inn is located on the back side of the green and numerous churches face this gentle park with its maple trees. The two marble buildings on the green are recognized as being two of the finest marble Federal-style homes in the entire country.

Continuing straight you go through the business district, a holdover from the 1950s.

(For information on Fair Haven and its founder, Matthew Lyon, see Route 22A, page 203.)

27.0 Route 22A turns to the left and continues south. Route 4A continues straight. The highway passes through the property of a slate mill where the gray, green, and red slate of the region is shaped into roofing slate, building blocks, tile, and other building products. The slate industry in this area began just north of town in 1839.

28.5 Route 4A joins Route 4 at the New York border. The Vermont Welcome Center, made of the green and red slate of the region, is a good place to stop and get information on what is happening in Vermont for services, events, places to see, and more.

Route 4W continues on to Whitehall, New York, located on the southern end of Lake Champlain. From Whitehall you can turn north on Route 22 to Ticonderoga and the western side of the lake, or continue on Route 4W until you're following the Hudson River south to Albany. Route 4W also leads you to Route 149, which leads to Route 9 on the southern end of Lake George. You can continue north on Route 9 along Lake George through Ticonderoga and then cross the lake back to Vermont on one of the three ferries, or by the Crown Point Bridge.

Central Vermont
Route 4
to Route 2

ROUTE 14:
The Old Central Corridor

Route 14, once the major highway leading from the Connecticut River to central and north-central Vermont before the building of the interstate highway, now caters to local traffic, as most people—locals and tourists—favor the faster interstate highways to get from one place to another.

The White River is an extremely popular river for fishing, swimming, and tubing. Between Hartford and Sharon there are numerous turnoffs along the highway, providing easy access to the river. From Bethel to Williamstown the highway is a narrow, twisting touring road. The only congested section of this highway is in Barre, but this also provides access to lodging and a side trip to the granite quarries. The road is rural from East Montpelier to Newport, except for the village of Hardwick. If you're traveling from White River Junction to Montpelier or Burlington, I recommend Route 14 and one of the bypass routes around Barre.

White River Junction: Railroads in Vermont

In 1847 there was a single farmhouse located where the White and Connecticut Rivers met. By the middle of the 1850s there were five railway lines running through the boomtown of White River Junction.

While growing up I played with trains. Real trains. My favorite engine had eight drive wheels, each taller than I was, and weighed over a hundred tons; it was one of the largest steam engines ever built and was used to pull entire trains—engines and all—over the Continental Divide. The trains I played with weren't mine, of course; they were in a millionaire's private collection that was stored in the rail yard at the base of Fall Mountain, before Steamtown U.S.A. became a reality. Although it wasn't encouraged, a couple of my friends and I used to clamber through, over, and under these engines, Pullmans, and dining cars, playing out our Wild West and military fantasies in a world of stage props a Hollywood producer would envy.

I wasn't the first Vermonter to be fascinated by the iron horse. The first steam train pulled into Bellows Falls in January 1849. Twelve months later you could ride from Boston to Burlington, and more importantly, ship products south to the population centers of coastal New England. Vermonters learned much in building these railways and went beyond the borders of the state to build the railways of the West. Famous railroads such as the Canadian Pacific, the Union Pacific, the Northern Pacific, the Erie, and the Chicago and Northwestern were built by Vermonters. The Baltimore and Ohio, the Illinois Central, the Fort Worth and Rio Grande, the Fort Wayne and Chicago, and the Grand Trunk Railway were among the famous lines run by Vermonters. The Atchison, Topeka, and Santa Fe Railroad was run by no less than six different Vermonters. John Converse was the president of the Baldwin Locomotive Works; Elisha Harris designed the hospital railcar; William Chandler invented the refrigeration car; and Benjamin Field was partners with George Pullman. One Vermonter designed the layout for Grand Central Station in New York City, while another built the New York elevated train. Thomas Davenport of Brandon invented the electric train, but it was Charles B. Holmes of Springfield who became the Street Railway King of America.

The railroads that opened the West also allowed people to emigrate from the stony Vermont hills to the rich prairies and the promised lands of California and Oregon. Trains moved Vermonters and their sheep to Kansas and allowed lumber, marble, and granite to be shipped economically to markets outside the Green Mountain State. Of course, these same railroads allowed dairy products, meat, and manufactured good from the Midwest to compete effectively with Vermont products in the markets of the eastern cities.

0.0   This route begins in the village of White River Junction at the intersection of Routes 4, 5, and 14 (see map on page 275). The village center is actually across the bridge and down the hill, but this intersection may be the busiest part of town.

1.2 The Hartford Diner is on the left. I've eaten breakfast here several times and recommend it to those who like a hearty meal on a cold day.

1.4 An interesting piece of architecture, the House of Seven Gables is on the right. This yellow-brick house with its turrets has been converted to a bed and breakfast.

As soon as you leave the village of Hartford you can enjoy the views of the White River on the left. Hartford and Hartland are two adjoining towns, with White River Junction on their boundary.

6.8 In West Hartford, on the left, is the turn going over to Pomfret and Queechee. The road on the other side of the iron bridge follows the river to the village of Royalton before joining Route 14 at the junction of Route 110. This road has less traffic than Route 14, so it's ideal for bicyclists.

This stretch of the White River is a popular fishing area for brook and rainbow trout. The brook trout is the only species indigenous to Vermont; brown and rainbow were introduced into the state's rivers in the 1800s.

12.7 The junction of Route 132 is on the right, and the access onto I-89 (Exit 2) is here in the village of Sharon. Brooksie's Restaurant and the Sharon Trading Post are on the right as you pass the junction. Route 132 leads to the village of Norwich and Route 5.

16.6 On the left is the road leading to Mormon prophet Joseph Smith's birthplace, a short ride up the mountain. Watch for a Vermont historic site marker on Route 14.

SIDE TRIP *Joseph Smith Birthplace*

Watch for the Vermont historic site marker at the junction, but the birthplace of the founder of the Mormon Church is another two miles up the hill. Climb the steep hill to its crest; the pavement ends at the gates to the Mormon chapel and the paved road to the memorial. Turn right and continue up the drive with the chapel on the left. The granite monolith, which rests on the site of the house where the Mormon prophet was born, is behind two modern stone buildings, one of which contains historical information on Joseph Smith, born here on December 23, 1805, on his grandfather Mack's farm.

Imagine the amazing feat to haul this granite monolith—

the largest single block of finished granite in the world—up this muddy road by oxen and manpower.

Another interesting story is the discovery of what may be an ancient (or ancient-style) calendar site located adjacent to the Mormon property. This structure, called Calendar I, was built in the same fashion as those scattered throughout Great Britain and western Europe. Beehive-shaped stone chambers and standing stones are precisely oriented to midwinter, spring-equinox, and midsummer sunrises and sunsets. Another major calendar site is located in nearby South Woodstock. I've always wondered what, if any, relationship exists between the Calendar I site and the alleged relics of the Mormon church. A controversy has raged over the origins of these Vermont calendar sites and the question of whether or not they are pre-Colonial.

As you ride back down the hill to Route 14, notice the magnificent views of the mountains directly ahead (west).

17.6   On the right is the junction of Route 110, *a top-quality touring road along a narrow valley through Tunbridge and Chelsea to East Barre, is an alternative to following Route 14 to Barre.*

On the left is the bridge leading over the White River and into the village of South Royalton, the location of the Vermont Law School, specializing in environmental law. The main college building is the restored schoolhouse, 1893, but there are other wonderful buildings to be seen here. The village is built around a long rectangular green with the old depot, now a bank, on one side. The old Royalton Inn on the south side of the green, the raised gazebo in its center, and even the row of commercial buildings on its north side are all of interest. This is one of Vermont's classic village centers.

When you pass through the small village of Royalton you may notice a Vermont historic site marker commemorating the Royalton Raid in 1780, the last Indian raid in Vermont, years after the conclusion of the French and Indian Wars. Although it was called an Indian raid, a third of the party was white, led by British officers from Quebec.

Caution: In the next three miles Route 14 passes under the railway tracks twice. Both underpasses are narrow with S-corners, but the second underpass, only one lane wide, is a blind curve and usually has sand on it.

After passing through the last underpass you'll see the Fox Stand Inn on the left. This brick Georgian-style house with ten fireplaces was built as a private residence in 1818.

21.0   The junction of Route 107 is on the left and leads to an access onto I-89 (Exit 3). *Route 107 leads to Routes 12 and 100 and is part* *of the major east-west route across Vermont.* Here you leave the White River and follow the Second Branch White River all the way through the Williamstown Gulf. This narrow valley supports numerous family dairy farms and several small rural villages.

25.0   After crossing the brook and the sweeping S-turn, you find yourself in the small village of East Bethel. The community library, one of the state's few octagonal buildings, is on the left and was once a schoolhouse. Route 14 from East Bethel to Williamstown is an excellent road for bicycling.

25.5   On the left in a small cleared field next to the covered bridge is a public picnic table. The sign on the bridge is the only indication that you are now in South Randolph.

30.0   The junction of Route 66 to Randolph Center is on your left in the village of East Randolph. Route 66 leads to Randolph, I-89, and Route 12. As you continue winding up Route 14, you'll pass through the small village of North Randolph and then the village of East Brookfield. This is a pleasant road with plenty of corners and rises.

36.4   On the north side of the village of East Brookfield is the junction of Route 65 on the left leading up to Brookfield and the floating bridge on Sunset Lake. *Route 65 is paved all the way up the mountain, but when you reach the village of Brookfield it becomes dirt. Sunset Lake and this very small village are extremely scenic and often photographed. The floating wooden pontoon bridge, usually covered with a few inches of water, is very slippery, and Route 65 is a fairly rough dirt road all the way to Route 14. I don't recommend crossing the bridge on a motorcycle unless you're an experienced rider.*

38.2   Here on the left is a turnoff with drinking water coming out of a plastic pipe from the spring above. Just around the next corner is a picnic table on the left. This is the beginning of the Williamstown Gulf, where the road twists and turns its way between the steep mountain shoulders and climbs to the higher level of central Vermont. At the top of the gulf on the left is Staples Pond, the source of the Second Branch White River.

After Staples Pond is Cutter Pond and the Lotus Lake summer day camp for boys and girls. Although the waters of Staples and Cutter Ponds are separated by only about a hundred yards, the water from Staples Pond flows south to Long Island Sound, while the water in Cutter Pond flows north into Lake Champlain and eventually into the St. Lawrence Bay.

42.2 On the left is the entrance to the Limehurst Lake Campground, central Vermont's most popular RV campground, but tenters will find a few spots by the pond that are separated from the big rigs.

From the Williamstown Gulf north to Barre you'll see numerous sand and gravel pits. The rolling hills of this area are primarily the result of the giant lake that existed in central Vermont after the last ice age and was connected with Lake Champlain by the vast water-filled valley of what is now the Winooski River. The major drainage of this lake was through this gulf, hence the deposits of sand.

42.8 The Chelsea Road is on the right. Because part of this is dirt I don't recommend it, but this road connects with Route 110 just north of Chelsea.

43.5 The Pump & Pantry on the right is as good a place to stop if you need fuel, a snack, or a deli meal.

44.0 This is Williamstown village. *On the left is Route 64 that provides access to Exit 5 of I-89 that follows the top of the ridge. Route 64 also joins Route 12 in Northfield (5.7 miles).* The commemorative bronze plaque on the boulder in front of the library at this junction is in memory of Thomas Davenport, who was born in Williamstown and invented the electric motor and other electric devices. Although his inventions changed the world as we know it, he was born ahead of his time and died a pauper.

On the right is the brick hardware store, and downstairs is a small restaurant.

44.0 As you leave the village of Williamstown on Route 14N, you'll go through the S-turn immediately after the cemetery and continue for almost 2.5 miles into the village of South Barre.

47.9 The traffic light at the junction of Route 63 is in South Barre. Route 14 used to be one of the primary routes from White River to central Vermont before the interstate highway was built and, although I-89 makes bypassing the twin cities easy, all the services are still located on Route 14 and Route 302 between this junction and Montpelier.

The Texaco gas station on the left contains a deli owned by R. Lefebvre & Sons. Since they are one of Vermont's noted smokehouses for meats, the sandwiches ordered here are the best in this entire region. There are two nice places to stay on Route 14 within the next two miles.

If you're planning to connect with Route 2 going northwest to Burling-
ton, with Route 12 to Morrisville, or riding to Montpelier for any reason,
the following two bypass routes should be considered instead of going
through Barre. There's a Comfort Inn at Exit 7 of I-89 and a local motel at
the intersection of Route 62 and Airport Road just one mile from Exit 7.

Access to I-89:

This is the longest access road to I-89 in the state.

0.0 Turn left onto Route 63 and climb the hill on this three-lane
highway. Two miles up the hill is the turn to Montpelier. This is
probably the best place to stop and get a look at, or take a picture of,
the granite quarries. Looking east you'll see the quarries on Millstone
Hill. Route 110 runs behind Millstone Hill and the ridge with the
tower on it. You can also see Spruce Mountain, the cone-shaped
peak, in Plainfield from this vantage point.

Continue straight, climbing the hill all of the way to its crest.

3.6 The access onto I-89 (Exit 6) is the end of Route 63. *The right-*
hand lane is north to Montpelier and Burlington, the left lane, south to
White River Junction.

Bypass: Barre to Montpelier via Airport Road

This is not only a way in which to avoid the congestion of Barre
and miles of strip development, it's also breathtakingly beautiful. An
avid photographer can spend hours on the next few miles of road.

0.0 Starting from Route 14 in South Barre at the traffic light: For
a side trip to the granite quarries turn right; to bypass Barre, turn left
onto Route 63 and climb the hill on the three-lane highway. As you
climb the hill—or make the turn at mile 2.0—you can look back
(east) to view the granite quarries on Millstone Hill. This is the best
spot from which to photograph the quarries.

2.0 At this intersection (the only one on the hill) **turn right** and
continue on this delightful road with beautiful views and scenic
farms. Off to the right you can see the granite quarries on Millstone
Hill, and the cone-shaped mountain is Spruce Mountain in Plainfield.

3.5 Here, with fields on three sides, Miller Road junctions with
Airport Road. In the fall be on the lookout for wild turkeys and
Canada geese in these fields. *Going straight will take you down into*

Barre. **Turn left.** As you crest the first rise you may see the model-plane-club members out flying their radio-controlled planes on the right. The view is stupendous from this vantage point, with Camel's Hump, Hunger Mountain, and Mount Mansfield visible ahead. You'll pass the Edward Knapp Airport on the left.

6.9 The intersection of Route 62 is at the traffic lights in Berlin. On the right is a local motel and restaurant. *To access I-89 (Exit 7), the Comfort Inn, or Shoney's, turn left and travel one mile. To the right leads to Route 302 in Barre or between Barre and Montpelier.* **Continue straight.** The Central Vermont Hospital is on the right and the Berlin Mall is on the left.

7.4 **Turn right onto Berlin Road.** *Turning left will take you to the I-89 access (Exit 7), the Comfort Inn, and Shoney's Restaurant.* The ponds on the right are the water supply for Montpelier. As you enter the city limits and ride down the hill, you have a view of downtown Montpelier. The gold dome of the state house (State Street), the clock tower (City Hall, Main Street), and the twin white towers (Vermont College, East State Street) are all clearly visible on the far side of the Winooski River and serve as landmarks for visitors.

9.6 Berlin Street junctions with Routes 302 and 2 at the traffic light. **Continue straight,** with the Winooski River on the right. The next traffic light is the intersection of Routes 12, 302, and 2. **Turn right to enter downtown Montpelier.**

SIDE TRIP *To the granite quarries*
(from Route 14N in South Barre)

0.0 At the traffic light at the junction of Route 63, turn right and climb Quarry Hill on Middle Road.

1.4 The Lazy Lion's campground is on the left at the top of the hill.

1.5 The Rock of Ages manufacturing plant is on the left. Graniteville Road, on the left, leads down into Barre. **Continue straight.**

1.7 **At the stop sign bear left** and ride into the village of Graniteville in the town of Barre. Huge piles of granite the size of small hills dot the landscape, and houses are built around them. I've been told that there are over eighty quarries, most of them abandoned, on this hill. On the left you'll see the massive derricks built of Douglas fir that are used in one of the active quarries.

2.3   Donahue Road, on the left, leads to Route 302 and Route 110 in East Barre. **Continue straight.**

2.5   The Rock of Ages sheds and administrative offices are on the left, the visitor's center and parking are on the right; tours are available. Park at the visitor's center and walk up to the largest, deepest granite quarry in the world.

From the visitor's center you can go back down the hill the way you came, take the road to East Barre where you can 1) take Route 302W down to Barre City, 2) take Route 302E to Wells River, or 3) take Route 110S to Chelsea and Route 113 to the Connecticut River Valley.

47.9   **Continue through the traffic light** on Route 14N in South Barre. After another .5 mile you'll dip down into Jockey Hollow with Jockey Hollow Pizza on the left at the bottom. There's a motel located on the right after climbing out of the hollow; another is ahead on the left.

Continue down the short hill on South Main Street and you're in the beginning of the traffic congestion. There's a shortcut to reach Route 302E directly ahead, branching away from Route 14 on the right. Just ahead on the left is The Tip of the Cone, a favorite local spot in the summer.

49.4   You are in the city of Barre at the green. Route 302E is on the right and merges with Route 14 at the light. Routes 14N and 302W continue left through downtown Barre.

Barre developed around the green where two early stage roads, including the important Boston to Montreal route, joined. The churches and the old hotel face the green. On the left is the U.S. Post Office built of Barre granite and the Barre Opera House (1899) of granite and yellow brick, which has been restored and has once again become the focal spot for the city's cultural entertainment. Ahead on the right is the brick and granite Aldrich Public Library, which houses the Barre Museum and its rich history of the town's granite industry. The bandstand on the green is still used for its original purpose, and the granite statue is a striking example of the granite sculptors' art.

Turn left at the traffic light and continue through downtown Barre.

Caution: The traffic coming from Elm Street (directly ahead) has the right-of-way. (See the close-up map of Barre-Montpelier on page 265.) If you plan to continue on Route 14N and wish to escape the worst of this downtown traffic, continue straight through the traffic light onto Elm Street for one block. Turn left onto Summer Street (don't go up the hill) and follow this street for several blocks until it ends. Turn right onto Maple Avenue; you're now on Route 14N.

Downtown Barre has many examples of granite work applied to architecture. The Aldrich Library incorporates what were, at the time, experimental techniques in granite work, while the Granite Bank features two types of granite finishing in its facade. If you walk along North Main Street you'll see cornices, medallions, quoin, sashes, and other ornamental devices of granite used in conjunction with brick. If you're interested in architecture, ask directions to the old Spaulding Grade School (Washington Street) and the Italian Baptist Church (Seminary Street).

50.2   At the traffic light is the intersection of Routes 14, 302, and the access road to I-89 (Exit 7) and the Central Vermont Hospital. The Pierre Motel is on the left and Mr. Z's pizza (specializing in Vermont brewed beers) is on the right at this intersection. On the far right corner is a granite statue commemorating the immigrants who came to work the Barre stone.
Turn right onto Maple Avenue.

51.0   After coming up the hill you'll see Hope Cemetery on the left. Unless your interest is genealogy or U.S. history, you probably wouldn't consider stopping and looking at tombstones. If, however, you have an interest in sculpture, this world-famous cemetery is worth a visit. Here you'll find some of the best twentieth-century sculpture north of the Boston Museum of Fine Art and some of the world's best memorial art. Classic busts and contemporary images such as a soccer ball, an airplane, and even a stock car are carved in Barre's famous granite; many of these monuments were sculpted by local artists for themselves and their families, making this a unique collection of personal art.

53.0   The scenic view to the northwest is the Northfield Range of the Green Mountains with the highest peak, Camel's Hump, in the Presidential Range beyond.

55.2   Route 14 joins Route 2 as you cross the Winooski River on the concrete bridge. **Turn right** here in East Montpelier.

55.4   Dudley's General Store and gas station and the post office are on the left just before the routes divide. This is the best place to fill up for many miles; gasoline will get more expensive north of here.

55.5 **Route 14N forks left** at the blinking light; *Route 2E forks right leading to Plainfield and St. Johnsbury.*

58.6 In the village of North Montpelier, on the right at the bottom of the hill, is the junction of Route 214 leading to Goddard College and Route 2 in Plainfield (two miles). Ahead on the right is North Montpelier Pond that used to provide the power for the local mills. For those interested in water power, look under the steel bridge just before the junction.

63.2 The village of East Calais is typical of many you find in the northeastern corner of the state. There are only a few homes in the village plus a retail establishment selling groceries, gas, beer, and other incidentals needed by the folks living in the hills here.

65.7 On the left is Sabin Pond, generally known as Woodbury Pond, a popular summer-camp location. There are many such small ponds in this area, and most are accessible only by gravel roads.

65.7 Woodbury village sits in the middle of moose country. To the left as you enter the village and to the left and right as you leave it, you will see prime moose territory—beaver ponds, dense brush, and deep woods.

On top of the mountain to the left are old granite quarries. These were the quarries that made Hardwick the Granite Capital of the World in the middle of the 1800s. The quarries are also at a higher elevation than any others in the state and, until the railroad was built, the stone had to be hauled downhill by teams of oxen or mules to the finishing sheds in Hardwick. Granite quarried here was used to build the Pennsylvania and Kentucky state capitol buildings, the Cook County Courthouse in Chicago, and the Carnegie Library. This is a dark granite. References to "Hardwick white" are misleading, as the light-colored stone is quarried in the town of Bethel, but in a quarry that was previously owned by the Hardwick Granite Company.

70.8 Route 14 makes the descent down two miles of winding road. Think what it must have been like getting twenty-ton blocks of stone down this grade before the railroad was built. About .5 mile down the hill is a turnoff to the right with clean drinking water in the concrete watering basin. Opposite the large turnoff for the drinking water is a smaller one with two picnic tables nestled in against the slope of the mountain.

73.8   In the village of Hardwick, you enter into what is locally known as The Northeast Kingdom.

Hardwick

In the middle to late 1800s Hardwick was the Granite Capital of the World, but as the industry declined in this area that mantle was acquired in the late 1890s by the booming granite town of Barre. Economically, and even socially isolated, Hardwick was the butt of Vermont jokes for decades. Fortunately, the image of the town is changing, but it remains in contrast to the elite summer resort town of Greensboro just a few miles away on the shores of Caspian Lake.

Hardwick might be called the gateway to the Northeast Kingdom, the vaguely defined rural area of Vermont stretching from the eastern side of the Green Mountains to the Connecticut River and from Route 15 north to the Canadian border. From Hardwick Route 14 leads south to Barre and Montpelier or north to the city of Newport; Route 15 takes you east to Route 2 in West Danville, just a few miles from St. Johnsbury, or west to Morrisville (Routes 12S and 100) and eventually to Burlington; Route 16 goes from Hardwick into the very heart of the Northeast Kingdom and ends at Lake Willoughby.

74.7   You must stop at the blinking red light where Route 14 merges with Route 15 in the center of the village. *If you continue straight through downtown, you'll be on Route 15E leading to Route 16 and finally to Route 2 in West Danville.* **Turn left.**

75.9   Here Routes 14N and 15W divide. *Continuing straight you'll travel Route 15W to Morrisville and Route 12S and Route 100.* **Turn right.**

This is an enjoyable stretch of highway, with beaver ponds and small lakes along the roadside. For the next couple of miles Hardwick Lake will be on the right; Elligo Pond is a long, narrow lake just a couple of miles farther north.

For many years there have been unconfirmed sightings of cougars in Vermont. Until recently, these mountain lions, known in the East as catamounts, had not been "officially" recognized as living in the state since Alexander Crowell shot the "last" one in 1881. Many years ago, a friend of mine found one that had been killed by a car in Castleton, and some residents of Stowe tell stories of these big cats coming down from the mountain in the winter. But, it was here, on Elligo Pond in 1994, that the mountain lion was confirmed by the Vermont Fish and Wildlife Department as residing in the state.

82.8   The turn right at the northern end of Elligo Pond leads to Craftsbury. *You can take this road as a simple alternate, returning to the main highway at mile 88.4. Or, by going to East Craftsbury, then Greensboro, you can go back to Hardwick or to Route 16 in Greensboro Bend. Caspian Lake is located only about 1.5 miles due east of the southern end of Elligo Pond, but to get there you have to go to the four corners in East Craftsbury and take the road on the right.* I consider Craftsbury to have some of the finest fall foliage color in northern Vermont.

Alfred Hitchcock's classic movie *The Trouble with Harry* was filmed here in Craftsbury.

87.6   Route 14 becomes a wonderful touring road that travels through farm country and is burdened with little of the traffic that often plagues Route 100 to the west.

88.4   The northern road from Craftsbury is on the right.

92.1   This is the village of Albany—not to be confused with Albany, New York. The transcript taken from my tape recorder after a recent visit to the area on a late September day reads: *A beautiful stretch of highway. The fields are as green as can be, and there's corn— acres and acres of corn—rippling in the wind, its green and gold colors in motion. The hills are peaking in color—the vivid reds of the sugar maples and red maples, the oranges and yellows, and the green yellows of the willows and ash. Some of the green, on the lower levels, hasn't begun to turn yet. The incredibly vivid colors on the rolling hills are combined with this wonderful, rich green. Even in the pastures that aren't mown, there is a wonderful beige hay, with purple flowers and yellow goldenrod running through the fields. The sumac is turning red along the highway. There is blue sky with small clouds overhead, and the air is extremely comfortable. Just a gorgeous touring road. This is a lot of fun.*

99.4   Irasburg is one of three Vermont towns named after Ira Allen. On the right along the spacious village green, Route 58 merges with Route 14N. *Route 58E on the right leads over to Orleans and Route 5, then onto to Route 5A near Lake Willoughby.*

100.6   Here is the division of Routes 58W and 14N. *Route 58W on the left leads to Route 100 in Lowell and offers outstanding scenic views of the northern Green Mountains.*

104.1   Route 14N now briefly merges with Route 5N. **Turn left onto Routes 14N and 5N.**

104.7 Routes 14N and 5N divide. *If you want to go into Newport, I suggest continuing straight on Route 5N. If you wish to connect up with Route 100 and go south or Route 105W and travel to St. Albans or Swanton, turn left onto Routes 14N and 105W (truck route).*

There is a rest area on the left (the west side of the highway) behind a hedge of cedar that makes a nice place to regroup if you are touring with others.

To Newport Via Route 5N

104.7 **At the division of Routes 14N and 5N, continue straight on Route 5N,** an enchanting stretch of road that winds its way along the Black River to the right. There are plenty of turnoffs for the next five miles.

109.2 The road forks here. **Continue straight going up a slight hill on Pleasant Street.** There are no signs to indicate this is Route 5N. *If you continue on Coventry Road, to the right, you will still end up in downtown Newport.*

109.6 The Motel Bayview on the right is one of only a few motels in Newport.

109.8 Route 5N merges with Route 105E. **Turn right and continue on Pleasant Street** (Routes 5N and 105E).

110.2 Pleasant Street ends; **turn left onto Third Street; go one block (.1 mile), then turn right onto West Main Street.** This is downtown Newport.

110.5 The gas station, on the left and next to the park and the bridge over the lake, is the spot where I have begun, or ended, all of my mileage measurements on tours and routes that pass through Newport.

ALTERNATE ROUTE:
Route 14N to Routes 100S or 105W or Newport

104.7 Turn left onto Route 14N.

109.3 This large traffic island with a barn in its center is the northern end of Route 14. The triangular-shaped traffic island is about .2 mile wide. *Continuing straight will place you on Route 100S.* **Bear right on Route 100N.**

110.2 This is the northern end of Route 100. Route 105W is on the left. Route 105E continues straight and leads to Newport. Approaching the city from the west enables you to see a couple of gorgeous vistas of Lake Memphremagog from the ridge.

114.0 **Bear left** at the merging of Route 5N with Route 105E. You are now on Pleasant Street in Newport.

114.7 **When Pleasant Street ends, turn left onto Third Street.** Downtown Newport and the lake are directly ahead of you. **Travel one block (.1 mile) and turn right onto Main Street.**

ROUTE 110:
Royalton to East Barre

Route 110 is one of Vermont's best motorcycle touring roads. Running roughly parallel with Route 14, it's not the quickest route from Royalton to Barre, but with its twisted, narrow pavement leading you up the ever narrowing valley, it certainly is the most enjoyable.

0.0 The southern end of Route 110 begins at Route 14 on the edge of the village of Royalton. On the other side of the White River, lie the village and the Vermont Law School.

The road follows First Brook north, gaining elevation almost imperceptibly. You can sense the valley narrowing as you wind ever deeper into it. The abrupt rounded hills of this section of the Vermont Piedmont create a twisting, turning valley that can be plainly seen as you continue toward Tunbridge.

5.0 Entering Tunbridge you'll notice the fairgrounds on the left. The Tunbridge World's Fair, held on a mid-September weekend since 1867, is an exhibition begun by the Union Agricultural Society.

Chelsea Cheese, one of America's famous cheddars, is still being made in Tunbridge. A hundred years ago many farmers produced cheeses that were different from those in neighboring communities. Until the development of refrigerated railcars, the milk produced by Vermont's dairy industry had to be converted into cheeses and butter in order to be shipped to the markets to the south. When it became profitable to ship milk to the Boston, Hartford, and New York markets, many specialty cheeses stopped being produced. Today Vermont's Department of Agriculture encourages, assists, and promotes many of the specialty foods produced in the state.

5.3   The Village Store is on the right and the access to the fairgrounds is just beyond, across the covered bridge on the left.

As you leave Tunbridge the road on the right at the bridge takes you over to Strafford. You cross First Brook and wind your way for two miles to North Tunbridge. The road gets even narrower and more snaky as it continues on to Chelsea. The yellow warning signs along the highway are a motorcyclist's or performance driver's dream: "Narrow Road," "Narrow Bridge," and wiggly arrows indicating lots of tight curves.

13.1   In the village of Chelsea, at the second green, is the junction of Route 113E. *Route 113E goes over to Vershire and Thetford to Route 5.*

The shire town, or county seat, of Chelsea is located where the valley briefly widens. For the first 120 years Chelsea's existence, like that of most of Vermont's villages, was primarily dependent upon what could be produced by agriculture or by use of water power. Transportation was by foot, horseback, and ox-driven wagon. Most goods were transported along the valleys until they reached a river on which they could be shipped. Transporting goods over distances was time-consuming, and over the mountains it was difficult to impossible except where nature provided a gap or a gulf between the high ridges. Just north of Chelsea is a narrow divide that twists through the mountains and then descends to Williamstown, and while the climb was steep and arduous, the relatively short route over the mountain to the copper mines of Vershire (along what is now Route 113) made Chelsea an important crossroads.

As you leave Chelsea the valley gets even narrower and the road twists more. Now you can feel the constant increase in altitude. It's a wonder that anyone was able to make a living farming these steep hillsides. It's no wonder the sheep pastures took over the subsistence farms in the early 1800s.

17.4   To the left you can see the gap in the hills that leads to Williamstown. This is a dirt road for several miles so I don't recommend it; I use it all the time, however, since it leads directly home. At this point the valley ends, and you begin climbing through a narrow gap or gulf that runs between two ridges. Route 110 becomes a narrow, twisting, constantly climbing road with very few houses. During the summer the trees overhanging the road provide a cool, comfortable drive.

21.1   You are now cresting the top of Washington Heights with beautiful views of the mountains ahead. Spruce Mountain in Plainfield is the 3,037-foot cone-shaped peak. Not to be confused with Spruce Peak in Stowe, this mountain is a monadnock like Mount Ascutney. The smooth cone shape is the result of glaciers wearing away the rock that used to surround and cover this peak. Most of the mountain peaks you see are about three thousand feet above sea level. The highway immediately begins to descend rapidly, with tight curves for the next 1.5 miles.

22.8   This is the village of Washington. After leaving the village, the highway flattens out for the next 4.5 miles and travels straight toward East Barre. You're on a high plateau, with the mountains to the right (east).

As you begin to enter East Barre you'll see the flood-control dam and Route 302 to the right. The flood-control dam was built in the early 1930s by the Civilian Conservation Corps in the aftermath of the disastrous 1927 flood and, fortunately, prior to the terrible flood of 1936.

One of Barre's famous granite quarries can be seen on the summit of the hill to the left. This is Millstone Hill, where the vein of granite is two to four miles wide and eight to ten miles deep. Known geologically as the Barre pluton, it was formed about 200 million years ago deep within the earth's crust. Since that time erosion and four periods of glaciation have removed miles of rock, leaving this plateau and granite pluton exposed.

26.5   The center of the village of East Barre is in the township of Barre, which stretches from the hilltop villages of Upper and Lower Websterville, Upper and Lower Graniteville, and East Barre to the cutting and finishing sheds in the city of Barre. Collectively, these settlements are known as the Granite Capitol of the World.

26.9   This is the junction of Route 110 at Route 302. *To the right Route 302 goes east to Wells River, Route 5, and the White Mountains of New Hampshire. To the left Route 302 descends the hill to the city of Barre where, in 3.8 miles, it merges with Route 14N at the green.*

ROUTE 113E:
Chelsea to East Thetford or Norwich

It's thirty minutes and twenty-two miles from Chelsea to East Thetford, a shortcut over the mountains used since colonial times. You can combine Routes 14, 110, 113, and 132 to create an enjoyable day tour of the central portion of the piedmont.

0.0　This route begins in the shire town of Chelsea, the county seat for Orange, at the green and the junction of Routes 113E and 110. At the end of the green on the left is the Greek Revival–style courthouse built in 1847.

The village of Chelsea is located where the valley briefly widens. For the first 120 years Chelsea's existence was dependent primarily upon what could be produced by agriculture or by use of water power. Transportation was by foot, horseback, and ox-drawn wagon, and most goods were transported along the valleys until reaching a river on which the goods could be shipped. Transporting goods over distances was time-consuming and over the mountains difficult to impossible except where nature provided a gap or a gulf between the high ridges. Just north of Chelsea is a narrow divide that twists through the mountains and then descends to Williamstown, and beyond that is another to the village of Washington.

Just past the courthouse you begin to snake uphill for four miles until cresting Judgment Ridge. Think about what it must have been like hauling a load of supplies up this hill with a team of horses or oxen.

4.2　On the left is the junction of the road leading over to Goose Green and Route 25, and on the right is the Vershire Garage. You'll now be descending along a relatively straight highway and will see some farmland, homes, and some nice open views as you ride down into the valley.

This was Vermont's copper region in the 1800s. Many portions of the land around here are still damaged ecologically due to mining and the process used to extract the copper salts from the ore. Fish still can't live in the upper reaches of the Ompompanoosuc River because of the high degree of acidity leaching from the old mine tailings.

6.9   This is the village of Vershire with a population of just over five hundred people—the same today as it was in the 1790s. During the early part of the nineteenth century this rugged terrain was deforested to meet the demands for timber and charcoal used in copper mining. The opening up of this land made this prime pasture for sheep. In 1837, during one of the peaks in the Vermont wool boom, there were 4,558 sheep registered with the town clerk.

The road twists and turns more frequently as you continue to slowly descend into the valley. You can see the mountains closing in ahead and how the highway will have to twist and turn around the shoulders of various ridges to follow the Ompompanoosuc River.

The road then flattens out after another 4.5 miles.

13.0   In the village of West Fairlee there is a turn right leading to South Vershire or Strafford. The ghost town of Copperfield and the old Ely copper mine are located about 1.5 miles up this road.

Historically these towns grew around the copper mines of Vershire and Strafford after copper was discovered in these mountains in the late 1700s. The first copper mine in the United States was in Strafford in 1793, and in the mid-1830s more than 60 percent of the copper produced in the United States was mined in this area. The copper salts produced here were of critical importance during the Civil War and played a part in Vermont's growing role in America's Industrial Revolution. Production from these mines peaked in 1880, and the towns from Vershire to the Connecticut River grew and prospered until mismanagement caused the workers to stage an armed insurrection in 1884. The mines never recovered. Copper was produced at a lower cost-per-ton in Michigan and other states farther west; and the railroads provided inexpensive transportation for this ore.

There have been attempts to reopen the mines in Vermont, the last being the operation of the Elizabeth Mine from 1942 to 1958. But the cost of extracting the copper from local ores just can't compare with the price of metal mined in other states, so they will probably remain closed.

13.9   The left turn is a shortcut over to Lake Fairlee and Route 244.

14.7   The junction of Route 244E is on the left in the village of Post Mills. *Route 244, a beautiful ride, leads over to Lake Fairlee, Ely, and Route 5.*

Continue to follow Route 113 down the narrow Ompompanoosuc Valley that will begin to widen and open up as you approach Thetford.

18.7 Thetford Center is one of those collections of homes you might not recognize as being a village if you aren't familiar this area.

20.0 This is the village of Thetford Hill, with its green on the right. This is a beautiful village, a classic image of Vermont, where Colonial and Victorian homes line the highway and surround the green. The Congregational Church was built in 1787. More recently the novels of Archer Mayor use Thetford Hill as the family home of Brattleboro police detective Joe Gunther.

Among the numerous men of fame who have come from this now small village were philanthropist George Peabody, after whom the Peabody Museum in Cambridge, Massachusetts, is named, and Henry Wells, founder of Wells Fargo. I find it interesting that Wells Fargo, American Express, and Railway Express all originated in Vermont. Even the Pony Express was founded by a Vermonter!

Here you have a choice whether to continue straight on Route 113 to East Thetford or to travel the alternate route to Norwich. I prefer the alternate route if going south to Hanover or White River Junction.

Continue straight on Route 113. A few yards from the green the highway begins a rapid, twisting descent down the hill. In places you get views of the White Mountains of New Hampshire as you approach the Connecticut River.

20.8 Here's an access onto I-91 (Exit 14).

22.3 The junction of Route 113 at Route 5 is in East Thetford. *If you plan to go south to Hanover, New Hampshire, I suggest going south on Route 5 for about 0.1 miles then turning left to go to Lyme, New Hampshire.*

ALTERNATE ROUTE
From Thetford Hill to Norwich

20.0 At the green in Thetford Hill **turn right onto Academy Road.** Continue through this part of the village with the green to the right.

20.3 Thetford Academy, established in 1819, is on the right. As you begin to descend the hill, there are spectacular views to the left. You're traveling through an area where many people commute to work in Hanover, New Hampshire. Besides beautifully restored Vermont farmhouses you'll see many interesting examples of modern architecture. This is one of the best of Vermont's touring roads. The trees provide shade on a hot summer day or spectacular color during foliage, coupled with open vistas and interesting sites. The road is smooth, narrow, and twisting as you go downhill for a couple of miles.

22.7   In Union Village make the S-turn through the covered bridge, built in 1867, over the Ompompanoosuc River and through the village.

Caution: The wood flooring of these covered bridges become quite slippery when wet.

23.2   This is the junction of Academy Road with Route 132. *If you turn right you will go over to Strafford and eventually to Sharon on Route 14.*
Continue straight onto Route 132 toward Norwich.

This road is magnificent, with ups and downs over ridges as you wind the way toward Norwich. At times the branches of the trees create a canopy over the road, while at others vistas of the mountains to the east open across farmland. You'll pass a couple of roads on the left, both of which lead to Route 5, so continue straight.

As you enter into the village of Norwich, you'll see Dan & Whitt's store and the Norwich Inn on the right. Beautiful Victorian homes line this wide street.

Norwich, known as the site for Vermont's first country grammar school, 1785, and as the original home of Norwich University, now located in Northfield, is now home to the corporate headquarters of King Arthur Flour.

29.1   Route 132 junctions of Route at Route 5 in Norwich at the green. Route 5S is straight ahead. Route 5N is on the left.

ROUTE 302E:
Montpelier to Wells River

Route 302, linking central Vermont with the Connecticut River Valley, is probably the best route to the White Mountains of New Hampshire from central Vermont. The portion that connects Routes 12 and 14 and the twin cities of Montpelier and Barre is known as the Barre-Montpelier Road.

(See Map on page 270 in the appendix.)

0.0   Technically, Route 302 begins as Exit 8 of I-89 and leads to where I begin the mileage, the intersection of Routes 2 and 12 at the Main Street bridge in Montpelier. **Follow River Street**, Routes 2E and 302E, with the Winooski River on the left.

0.5   At this traffic light you can go right and up the hill on Berlin Street to: 1) access Exit 7 of Route I-89; 2) reach the hospital, the La Gue Inn or Comfort Inns, and the Berlin Mall; and 3) use the bypass around Barre to reach Route 14S in South Barre.

1.3   At the third traffic light, counting the one at the junction of Routes 12 and 302, **continue straight** and then stay in the right-hand lane.

1.8   The division of Routes 2E and 302E is at the fourth traffic light. Bearing **left (straight)** will take you to St. Johnsbury on Route 2E. **Continue right,** as River Street becomes the Barre-Montpelier Road.

2.2   AAA of Vermont is located on the right just after the curve. The Wayside Restaurant on the right is one the area's most popular restaurants.

2.8   The access to I-89 is on the right at the fifth traffic light.

This is the junction of Route 63 leading up the hill to the hospital and to the interstate highway. You'll find a motel and restaurant on the left at the first traffic light and another motel and restaurant at the third light.

On the left is a restaurant and behind it is a motel, the Vermonter. The Twin City Motel is on the right just .1 mile beyond the traffic light. This portion of the Barre-Montpelier Road is all strip development. There are numerous restaurants and fast-food franchises in the next .75 mile.

Barre-Montpelier: The Twin Cities

Montpelier is the capital of Vermont and Barre is the Granite Capital of the World. Each is quite different from the other and yet, like fraternal twins, the two are tied by geography and economics. Barre-Montpelier is actually comprised of two cities and one town, Berlin, which is sandwiched between them. The towns of Middlesex, Worcester, East Montpelier, Plainfield, Marshfield, Barre Town, Orange, Washington, Williamstown, and Northfield are also part of the demographic region that centers on the twin cities.

The twin cities lie in an ancient basin that was a giant lake at the end of the last glacial period. Routes 2, 14, 12, and 302 follow Vermont's valleys and lead into this basin. The Winooski River Valley cuts through the most mountainous section of the Green Mountains, providing easy access to Vermont's largest city and Lake Champlain. The geography certainly was a factor that lead to Montpelier being chosen the capital in 1805—decades before cars, railroads, or even decent roads were built in the state.

Although the granite business in Barre began just after the War of 1812, it didn't become of major importance until the coming of the railroad in the 1880s. Before the railroads, the blocks of granite had to be laboriously sledded down Millstone Hill by oxen. When the present State House was built in 1859, it became the first major building to use Barre granite. It took teams of thirty oxen eighteen hours to haul each load of granite blocks from the quarries to the building site. Once the railroads were built, the granite quarries and the marble and slate quarries in western Vermont were able to ship their heavy product to markets outside the state. The Rock of Ages manufacturing plant and its quarry, the largest and deepest in the world, is a popular tourist attraction. Granite finishing sheds are scattered throughout Barre and remain the principal industry in the city.

Today the major employers of the area are the State of Vermont, National Life of Vermont, one of the oldest insurance companies in the United States, the Central Vermont Hospital, and Blue Cross and Blue Shield of Vermont. Most of the business growth and expansion in the area is taking place in the centrally located town of Berlin.

4.6   The Knoll Motel is on the left. The access road from Barre to the hospital and I-89 can be seen climbing the hill to the right.

As you enter the city of Barre you'll notice numerous granite finishing sheds located to the right just off Route 302 for the next mile.

6.1   At the traffic light the access road to I-89 in Barre is on the right, and Route 14N is on the left. This is the point where the Barre-Montpelier Road becomes North Main Street. On the left is a granite statue commemorating the granite workers of Barre. Another motel is on the right after the light and a pizza place is on the left.

Continue straight heading into downtown Barre on combined Routes 14S and 302E.

As you drive down North Main Street notice the architectural enhancements made of granite: pillars, facades, casements, quoin (the decorative stonework on the corners of buildings), steps, and even plaques. I haven't seen another main street in America that has as much architectural detailing utilizing granite.

6.6 The division of Routes 14S and 302E is at the green in downtown Barre. **Bear left in the right lane so the green is on the right.** *Bearing right on Route 14S, you continue through Williamstown, to the Bethel access, or on to White River Junction. Follow Route 14S for a side trip to the granite quarries.*

The Aldrich Public Library in Barre was built of beige brick and granite, both originating in Vermont. Many of the techniques used to produce these building materials were experimental in 1907.

Barre developed around the green, as did most Vermont towns. The churches and old hotel face the green. On the far right is the U.S. Post Office, constructed of Barre granite. The Barre Opera House, built in 1899 of granite and imported yellow brick, has been restored and has again become the focal spot for the city's cultural entertainment. On the left is the brick-and-granite Aldrich Public Library, which houses the Barre Museum, featuring the rich history of the

Barre granite was widely used in sculptural and building applications. The statue (foreground) is part of the veterans' memorial on the green in Barre; City Hall (background) was constructed of local granite and yellow brick.

town's granite industry. The bandstand on the green is still used for its original purpose, and the granite statue, commemorating Barre's war veterans, is a striking example of the granite sculptors' art.

Continue straight through the lights and follow Route 302 up the hill.

10.4   The junction of Route 110S is on the right in East Barre. *Route 110 leads south to Chelsea, Route 113, and Tunbridge.*

One of Barre's famous granite quarries can be seen on the left on the summit of Millstone Hill, where the vein of granite is two to four miles wide and eight to ten miles deep. Known geologically as the Barre pluton, it was formed about 200 million years ago deep in the earth's crust. Since that time erosion and four periods of glaciation have removed miles of rock, leaving this plateau and granite pluton exposed.

The small flood-control dam on the right was built after the disastrous flood of 1927. Although it doesn't look like much, this dam can hold a tremendous amount of run-off from the mountains to the east, and it saved Barre from the ravages of the 1936 flood.

You're now in the town of Orange traveling on the William Scott Memorial Highway.

17.1   The junction of Route 25 is on the right. *Route 25 goes southeast to junction at Route 5 in Bradford. If you're planning on traveling south on Route 5, this will save you many miles.*

23.1   As you're going down the hill there's a turnoff to the right with the granite commemorative marker for William Scott, the sleeping sentinel. On August 30, 1861, he took a friend's turn at picket duty on the Chain Bridge at Georgetown and fell asleep while on duty, as did all the sentries. Court-martialed, found guilty, and sentenced to be shot, William Scott was subject of newspaper stories throughout the country. Pardoned by Abraham Lincoln on September 9, Scott died in the battle of Lees Mills on April 16, 1862. The farm where he grew up is just beyond the granite marker.

The road gets very snaky as it follows the South Branch of the Wells River down the mountain.

25.5   The junction of Route 232N leading to Groton State Forest and to Route 2 is on the left as soon as you finish descending the hill. Route 302 now becomes wider, smoother, and flatter all the way to Wells River.

26.2   This is the village of Groton. *The turn right by the church is*

Powder Spring Road that goes over the mountain through Topsham to Route 25.

27.4 *If you turn left and go up this steep hill, this town road will take you to Harvey's Lake, to Barnet, Peacham, and onto Danville and Route 2.*

33.9 The P&H Truck Stop is on the left at the entrance (exit 17) to I-91. This is the only truck stop in Vermont that resembles those found in other parts of the country. It's open twenty-four hours a day, seven days a week, the food is good, and folks travel miles for their pies.

The Wells River, Route 302. Like many other Vermont rivers, this one has been used to provide power since the arrival of the first settlers. The remains of an old mill dam can be seen here; a small, active hydroelectric dam is located just downstream.

36.8   The merging of Route 302 and Route 5 is in downtown Wells River. *Route 5N, to the left, leads to St. Johnsbury and through the northeast kingdom to Canada.*

The village of Wells River in the town of Newbury was the starting point of the Bayley-Hazen military road built in 1776 and was the northernmost port on the Connecticut River. In later years the village was the junction of the Canadian Pacific, the Montpelier and Wells River, and the Boston & Maine railway lines. (Don't confuse Wells River, on the eastern border of the state, with the town of Wells, on Route 30 along the New York border.)

36.9   Turn left at the stoplight if you plan to continue on to Woodsville, New Hampshire. *This leads to the Kancamangus Highway through the White Mountains, one of the best touring roads in the Northeast. Continuing straight on Route 5S will lead you to Fairlee, Norwich, and White River Junction.*

ROUTE 232:
Groton to Marshfield

Route 232 is a popular touring road for Vermont motorcyclists. This twisting, turning road doesn't offer mountain vistas; in fact, during the summer the dense leaves screen any view except the winding highway. Only in the early spring or late fall can the broken, rocky mountains of this area be glimpsed through the leafless trees. However, if you like touring roads that twist, snake, and follow the contours of the land you'll love this short stretch of road.

0.0   The junction of Route 232 at Route 302 is just west of the village of Groton. As you turn onto Route 232 and begin to head north, the area to the right is filled with beaver dams and lodges.

0.2   There is a small turnoff on the right next to a small waterfall that cascades down into the beaver ponds. ***Caution:*** *This shoulder is gravel and is sloped; pull off the pavement cautiously.*

1.6   The southern end of Ricker Pond can be seen ahead on the right. You can pull off into a small parking area and view this diminutive lake. The old railway bed of the Montpelier and Wells River Railroad is quite visible. This railroad once connected the Central Vermont Railway in Montpelier with the Canadian Pacific in Wells River and the Boston & Maine in Woodsville.

The road now begins to twist and turn as it slowly climbs in elevation. For the next eight miles you'll be traveling on a beautiful woodland road with only an occasional house to be seen.

2.2   You are entering Groton State Forest. In an old photo taken in the late 1800s, the hills of this area are clearcut, and the lake is filled with logs for Hazen's Mill. A hundred years ago, 75 percent of Vermont was open (unforested) land; today, the opposite is true.

5.2   On the right is the entrance to Groton Lake, the state beach where the locals come in the hot summer months for a swim and a picnic. The two campsites, Deer Run and Stillwater, are quickly reserved for the summer and filled by Vermonters and others in-the-know long before the heat of summer arrives. Most of this access road is loose gravel, so be careful.

The road continues to twist and roll as you keep heading north. You'll see a posted turn for Owl's Head on the right. The road climbs on loose gravel to a parking area from which you'll have an easy, short hike to the granite cliffs and the lovely vistas overlooking the wildlife areas in the park and Kettle Pond.

9.2   Once you leave the state forest you'll begin descending and will be back in cultivated and settled land. Drew Mountain is the rocky hill on the right.

13.4   The junction of Route 232 at Route 2 is just east of Marshfield. *Turn right to travel toward St. Johnsbury. Turn left to go toward Montpelier.*

ROUTE 12:
Woodstock to Morrisville

R oute 12 originates in Norwich, Connecticut, and meanders northwestward through Massachusetts and New Hampshire until it enters Vermont at Ascutney. From Woodstock, Route 12 follows the eastern side of the Green Mountains north, passing through Montpelier and ending at Route 100 in Morrisville. Like most highways in the state it's rarely traveled from one end to another, but instead is used as a connector highway, especially the segments from Woodstock to Bethel, from Northfield to Montpelier, and from Montpelier to Morrisville. I'm especially fond of the Brookfield Gulf stretch and the Worcester to Morrisville section.

It's twenty-one miles from Ascutney to Woodstock, all but seven and a half of which is shared by Routes 5 and 4. Although the segment from Hartland to Route 4W is an enjoyable road, most people planning to take Route 12 north will begin in Woodstock. For those coming into Vermont from Claremont, New Hampshire, I'd suggest taking either Route 131W or Routes 5N and 44W to Route 106N into Woodstock. By doing such you'll have a more enjoyable drive, better roads, and far less traffic.

For those traveling north on Route 100, take Route 100A through Plymouth Notch and then Route 4E into downtown Woodstock. Those coming east on Route 4 should consider going north on Route 100; those coming into White River Junction from New Hampshire would be advised to go north on Route 14 and then Route 107W to Bethel.

From the Woodstock Green, where Route 106 junctions with Route 4, it's only .1 mile to downtown and .4 mile to the wrought-iron bridge. Route 4E continues straight along Central Street, but **take a left onto Elm Street.** Pleasant Street, Route 12S, is the first street on the right; **continue straight on Route 12N.**

Traveling on Routes 4W and 12N from Quechee you can either go into downtown Woodstock to sightsee and get something to eat, or take a right onto Pleasant Street and avoid the traffic congestion. If you're touring Vermont, I'd suggest going through downtown and making a circuit of the oval-shaped green before continuing. The best parking spaces are along the perimeter of the green, and you can stretch your legs or take a break on one of the benches situated on the green.

I suggest stopping to eat at the Creamery, a small restaurant on Central Street that makes its own ice cream, or choose one of the other good places to have lunch or dinner. *(For more information about Woodstock, see Route 4, page 132.)*

0.0   I begin the odometer at the wrought-iron bridge that crosses the Ottauquechee River. The road makes a tight ninety-degree turn right and then immediately curves to the left. The estate on the left, as well as much of the prime real estate in town, belongs to the Rockefellers. On the right you'll find Billings Farm, an agricultural museum open to the public.

The road is posted for 25 MPH and it is enforced, so beware.

0.5   At the fork in the road is Thompson's Garage. Route 12N curves away to the left *and the road to the right leads to South Pomfret.*

1.8   The steep hill on the right is the site of the first ski tow in the United States. Built in 1931, this simple rope tow powered by a modified Ford engine changed the nature of this winter sport forever and created an industry that has made Vermont famous throughout the world. This is the south side of Hurricane Hill, on the northern slopes is the modern ski resort called Suicide Six.

9.6   You enter Barnard going down a long hill into the center of this small village. At the bottom of the hill the road makes a hard turn left. The Bernard General Store is on the right just before the turn. The eastern end of Silver Lake, with its public swimming area, is just across from the store. You can stop and take a swim or get something cold to drink at the store and sit on the porch and watch other people swimming.

Instead of making the turn and continuing on Route 12, you have the option of taking the alternate route on North Road. North Road leads you to Bethel following the ridge, while Route 12 follows the valley. The mileage is the same.

ALTERNATE ROUTE:
North Road

0.0   North Road begins as Hill Road at Route 12. Silver Lake is on the left and then you begin to climb Hill Road.

0.2   The entrance to the Silver Lake State Park is on the right.

1.0   You'll begin to get nice scenic views as you reach the ridge. Ancient sugar maples and stone walls still line portions of this road. As you ride north you'll see the Green Mountains and the White River valley.

When the road begins its descent you're only a mile from Bethel.

6.8   North Road junctions with Route 12 next to the Greenhurst Inn in Bethel.

15.7 At the stop sign, Route 12N merges with Route 107E. *If you turn left and follow Route 107W for 8.3 miles you'll reach Route 100.* For those who are fishing enthusiasts, the White River National Fish Hatchery is only .3 mile west on Route 107. Tens of thousands of salmon are hatched here each year and then are reintroduced into Vermont streams; tours are available.

Turn right. The highway runs along the banks of the White River, while on the right the hills rise steeply from the shoulder of the pavement. You might see people tubing or fishing in the fast, shallow water.

17.1 The Greenhurst Inn is the white Queen Anne-style house on the right. North Road junctions with Route 12A adjacent to the inn just as you're entering the left-hand corner. You'll cross the iron-truss bridge over the White River, go through the railway underpass, and stop at the Y.

17.7 Route 12 divides from Route 107E just a few yards beyond the underpass. *If you turn right, Route 107E brings you to I-89 (Exit 3) in 2.7 miles and to Route 14 in 3.4 miles.*

Turn left and ride through the village of Bethel. As you ride along the narrow main street you can't help but notice that most of the commercial buildings date from the late nineteenth century. Downtown districts with wooden buildings are becoming increasingly uncommon. Prosperous villages usually built their commercial buildings of brick, especially when replacing the old wooden structures destroyed by the all-too-common fires of those times. When you make the ninety-degree turn left and arch over the bridge, you'll see why these wooden buildings have never been replaced. The Third Branch White River runs through a deep gorge that parallels the downtown district.

Route 12 makes another turn right, goes past the plastic-molding plant and the school, and then follows the valley to Randolph.

20.8 Onion Flats is on the left. If you like deep-fried food, this is a good place to stop.

After passing Onion Flats, the highway gets more exciting, but only if you don't get stuck behind traffic. There is only one safe place to pass between Onion Flats and Randolph because the twisting, turning road offers limited visibility. It becomes obvious that you're entering another village when you go past the outlying stores and the posted speed limit is reduced. When you pass by the Gifford Medical Center you're on South Main Street in Randolph.

Just beyond the hospital, at the bottom of the small hill, is downtown Randolph. There are a limited number of places to eat in the depot square area. On the right, on the corner of Main Street and Merchants Row, you'll find a restaurant, or you can get a cup of Green Mountain Coffee Roasters' coffee in the brick depot building or find a full-dinner menu at the August Lion located farther down Main Street. The Chandler Music Hall is farther along Main Street.

25.6   The junction of Routes 12 and 12A is just across the concrete bridge. Route 12A is on the left and Route 12 continues on the right. There's a Cumberland Farms store on the right. *Route 12A is an alternate route north and joins Route 12 in Northfield.*

25.7   Stop at the blinking red traffic light. Route 12 bears to the left. *Route 66 junctions directly ahead. Route 66 heads west to Randolph Center and then to Route 14 in East Randolph. It also leads to Exit 4 of I-89 in 2.7 miles.*

It's 20.9 miles from Randolph to Northfield on Route 12A, while it's only sixteen miles on Route 12. Route 12A is an open road following the broad valley of the Third Branch White River in the midst of the Northfield Mountains. Route 12 follows the narrower valleys and goes through the Brookfield Gulf. Route 12A is favored by bicyclists, while Route 12 is a dream-come-true for sport-touring motorcycles.

ALTERNATE ROUTE:
Route 12A from Randolph to Northfield

25.6   Turn left onto Route 12A, Park Street. After leaving the village you'll be riding in a broad valley through farm country.

27.5   Route 12A makes a sweeping turn, and Camp Brook Road is on the left. *This is the road through Rochester Gap that leads to Route 100 in the village of Rochester.*

40.3   In the village of Roxbury, across from the school and next to the grange, is the Roxbury Gap Road that leads over the Northfield Mountains and into Warren. This road is used extensively by local residents, but the top portion is gravel and can be a bit rough after a hard rainstorm. During July and August the summer camp becomes the main activity in this small village.

North of Roxbury the road follows the narrow, twisting valley of the Dog River. This is the best part of Route 12A.

51.0 Route 12A junctions at Route 12 on the south side of the village of Northfield.

25.7 From the blinking traffic light and the junction of Route 66, Route 12 passes the union school, crosses Ayers Brook, and quickly leaves Randolph behind. It doesn't take you long to realize that you're on a great touring road, as it twists back and forth along the brook following the contours of the land. Most farms are located close to Randolph, because as you travel north, the valley narrows and the mountains become steeper and more rugged.

30.1 As you approach the small village of East Braintree you'll descend a hill and then will enter an S-turn in the center of the village. *(Caution: This S-curve often has gravel on it.)* The Snowville General Store is located on the right as you exit the curve.

Looking ahead you can see that the valley begins to narrow, and you can even glimpse where it ends.

31.3 You're now entering a very intense stretch of highway where the road snakes upward from the valley through the Brookfield Gulf. Forested and cool in the summer, this is one of those places where you have to focus on the pavement and not on sightseeing.

Caution: When the pavement is fractured and broken by Vermont's winter weather this becomes a treacherous stretch of road where potholes and frost heaves can bring down a motorcycle or break a strut on a car.

34.5 When you leave the Brookfield Gulf you've stopped climbing in elevation. Most of the land to the right is Allis State Park. Route 12 remains a premium touring road as it follows this new valley northward.

35.4 The junction of Route 65 is on the right. Baker Pond is on the left. *Route 65 is the only state-maintained highway that is a gravel road. It leads over the hill past Allis State Park and into Brookfield, crossing the floating pontoon bridge on Sunset Lake.*

From Baker Pond flows Sunny Brook, which you'll follow along the base of Shaw Mountain and into South Northfield.

39.9 The junction of Route 64 is on the right in South Northfield. *Route 64 leads up the mountain to I-89 (Exit 5) or over to Williamstown and Route 14.*

41.9 The junction of Route 12A is on the left on the south side of the village of Northfield.

After you pass this junction you'll see the buildings of Norwich University on the left. A Vermont historic site marker commemorates it as the first private military academy in the United States. The university became a coed college only a few years ago; even more recently, it purchased Vermont College in Montpelier and moved that institution's undergraduate programs to Northfield.

This town was known for producing roofing slate. The hard, brittle stone of the Northfield Formation is different from the slates of Poultney. As you ride down South Main Street, after passing the university but prior to entering downtown, notice the home on the left, which is made of the local stone.

43.0   The square, or common, is on the left. A restaurant, a cafe, and a pizza parlor are all located facing the common. The area just beyond used to be the center of downtown, but a massive fire destroyed everything up to the banks of the Dog River.

After passing through the traffic light and past more businesses you'll encounter a long, wide, straight stretch of highway. Beware! This is a speed trap and runs past the police station to boot. The village of Northfield merges into the village of Northfield Falls after the curve at the end of this straightaway.

44.7   The Falls General Store is on the left. This village grew in the days when the flowing water from the Dog River provided the power necessary to run the mills.

Between Northfield Falls and Riverton is Ellie's, which during the summer appears to be a typical roadside produce stand, but come Halloween, the hill behind the stand is filled with hundreds of carved jack-o-lanterns lighted by candles. The sight is so fantastic that I've seen the Amtrak *Montrealer* passenger train stop on the track to allow its riders to view the scene.

47.2   You cross the Dog River on the iron bridge in Riverton. The Riverton General Store and Deli is located on the right. This next four miles of Route 12 is an enjoyable approach to Montpelier.

51.7   Leaving the Dog River valley the road climbs the hill, goes under the I-89 bridge, and enters the city of Montpelier as you crest the ridge. Off to the left you can see the National Life of Vermont insurance company—a principal employer in the capital city.

52.6   You are on Northfield Street, and as you make the descent down the hill you'll see a classic American Gothic–styled gingerbread house on the left, and immediately behind and above it, a second one. This was the home of the famous American painter Thomas Waterman Wood, and the second house was his studio. Many of his famous paintings were done in this studio, and the building is now listed on the National Historical Sites' registry.

52.8 The intersection of Routes 2 and 12 and the junction of Route 302 is at the traffic lights. Downtown Montpelier is directly ahead on the other side of the Winooski River. (See Map 270 in the appendix.)

This is generally a point where one connects up with Route 2 or I-89 going north to Burlington and Canada. I-89 *(Exit 8) is reached by turning left and continuing straight through all of the traffic lights and onto the interstate highway.* The Capitol Plaza hotel can be seen across the Winooski River to the left. There are three bed and breakfasts, the Capitol Plaza, a very exclusive inn on Main Street, and the motel at the top of Northfield Street for lodging in the state capital. *Those planning to stay in Montpelier should refer to Route 302, page 162.*

When you cross the Winooski River, you are on Main Street, with the Grand Union supermarket on the left and Sarducci's Italian restaurant on the right.

The New England Culinary Institute is based in Montpelier, so it's not surprising that this city is the place to find a good meal. My recommendations are all on Main Street: Sarducci's across from the Grand Union for dinner; Julio's across from City Hall for lunch or local atmosphere; and the Coffee Corner at the traffic light just beyond city hall for breakfast anytime. However, these are not the only restaurants in town. The famous Horn of the Moon Cafe is located on Langdon Street. Fiddleheads is on State Street. The New England Culinary Institute owns two local eateries as part of its renowned training programs: LaBrioche is their cafe, and The Main Street Bar and Grill their restaurant.

53.0 At the traffic light (the only one downtown) **continue straight**; *turn left to continue on Route 2W.*

53.3 **Turn left by using the minirotary in front of the Masonic Temple**; this is Spring Street and you immediately cross the North Branch of the Winooski. After only one block, .1 mile, **stop, then turn right, and continue on Elm Street**, Route 12. On Elm Street you'll pass by the Montpelier Recreational Area, and after a couple of miles will find yourself in relatively open country following the North Branch of the Winooski River. The mountains of the Worcester Range are ahead of you as you travel north. You'll see the Wrightsville Reservoir on the right after about four miles.

57.7   The entrance to the boat launch is on the right. The Wrightsville Reservoir was built in the 1930s by the Civilian Conservation Corps. Barre and Montpelier, like many Vermont towns, were devastated by the great floods of 1927 and 1932. The C.C.C. built two dams to help protect the twin cities. These completed flood-control projects were justified when Vermont was again subjected to floods in 1936.

58.4   The entrance to the picnic area is on the right. The road is loose gravel leading down to the reservoir.

59.2   This is the village of Putnamville. The villages of the town of Middlesex are scattered from here across the mountain to the Winooski River and Route 2. The physical layout of Vermont's townships are not based upon terrain; up until about fifty years ago the village of Putnamville was geographically isolated from the village of Middlesex for six months of the year. These are the Worcester Mountains, essentially an extension of the Northfield Range and part of the Green Mountains.

61.2   You're entering into the village of Worcester.

61.9   As you are leaving Worcester you cross Minister Brook. I often go panning for gold and have always found "color" in every pan taken from this brook. Vermont is the only New England state to have had a gold rush, and Worcester was briefly famous for the alluvial gold recovered from Minister Brook. Only two miles separates the source of Minister Brook from that of Gold Brook that flows into Stowe. Somewhere along this ridge running from Morrisville through Plymouth and into southern Vermont is a seam of gold. Many of the brooks flowing from this ridge contain small flakes of nearly pure gold, but to this day the mother lode remains hidden.

From Worcester to Morrisville is one of my favorite stretches of road. The rugged terrain through this softwood forest is beautiful, there's very little traffic, and I've seen more moose along this portion of Route 12 than anywhere else in the state.

66.0   On the left you might glimpse the Winooski Falls. The turnoff is just .1 mile ahead on the left. You can park and walk down to the river where you can wade and swim in the pools or lie in the fast current and let the water massage your tired muscles. As you ride north you'll notice beaver dams, small gorges, and other waterfalls along the highway. Many of the turnoffs are great places to stop and rest. Since this river is well stocked with trout, you can count on any turnoff leading to an interesting pool or white water to fish.

The highway steadily increases in elevation for the next 5.5 miles. If you're driving in the evening or at night, be very aware that this is moose territory.

74.1 You have a great view of Lake Elmore as you descend toward this cold mountain lake.

74.9 The population of the village of Elmore increases during the summer. A surprising number of people who have summer camps in Elmore live in nearby towns like Montpelier.

75.2 On the left is the entrance to Lake Elmore State Park, one of the best state parks in the north country—except during black-fly season.

75.6 As you travel around the northern end of Elmore Mountain, you have a 160-degree panorama of mountains: Sterling Mountain and the northern end of the Presidential Range is on the left (west); Jay Peak, identified by its ski slopes, can be seen directly ahead at the northern end of the Green Mountains; and ahead to the right is the center of the Northeast Kingdom.

77.5 Going down the hill into Morrisville you can look into the upper Stowe Valley on the left. This thriving village is situated along the Lamoille River and the northern end of both the Stowe and Worcester valleys.

78.8 Park Street, on the left by the elementary school and the triangular green, is Route 15A that leads to Route 15E. *Route 15W leads to Wolcott and Hardwick.*

78.9 Route 12 ends at Route 100 at the traffic light in downtown Morrisville. *At the blinking red light and four-way intersection, turn right to continue on Route 100N or to reach Route 15W; continue straight on Route 100S to Stowe. Most facilities are located near the merging of Routes 100 and 15W.*

For day touring you can make a loop back to Montpelier by going east or west. Route 15W goes to Hardwick and Route 14; Route 14S takes you to East Montpelier and Route 2W, the last few miles back to the Capitol City. Route 100S goes through Stowe to Waterbury; Route 2E then returns you to Montpelier.

ROUTE 73E:

Brandon to Route 100

R oute 73 actually begins at the ferry crossing from Fort Ticonderoga to Larabee's Point, but these three sections—the lake to Route 22A, Route 22A to 30, and Route 30 to Brandon—are not usually used contiguously; the portion known as the Brandon Gap is the most popular.

Brandon was the home of Thomas Davenport, the inventor who built the first electric motor in 1834, the electric printing press, the electric piano, and the electric railway. The editor of the first electrical journal, Davenport was a man born before his time. Considered to be an eccentric, he never profited from the inventions that changed the course of the modern world.

Stephen Douglas, the great American orator, was born and grew up in Brandon before emigrating to Illinois where he gained national fame. Despite his origins, Vermonters voted for Abraham Lincoln, who opposed Douglas in the election of 1860, perhaps due to Douglas's slur in a speech in which he referred to Vermont as being a good state to be *from*, provided you emigrated early.

0.0   Route 73E leaves Brandon at Park Street. This tree-lined street with its beautiful homes is often photographed. Two of this village's excellent bed and breakfasts are located here. At the end of Park Street, Route 73E turns to the left and continues to the village of Forestdale on Marble Street.

3.4   On the left is Route 53 that follows the eastern side of Lake Dunmore. Leaving Forestdale you immediately begin ascending the mountain, twisting up and into the Green Mountain National Forest. As you make the climb along the gorge of the Neshobe River, watch for the Vermont historic site marker on the left side of the road. John Conant built one of this country's first stove factories near this site, harnessing power from the river and using the ore for which this region was known. The famous Conant stove was the first of the modern cast-iron stoves. Vermont was a leader in the development of heating stoves and is still the world's leading manufacturer of cast-iron stoves, which now takes place about twenty miles due east in the town of Bethel.

7.7   The crest of Brandon Gap is at 2,170 feet and situated between Mount Horrid to the north and Goshen Mountain to the south. The gap is over 1,700 feet higher than Brandon, or an ascent of over 400 feet per mile, which in the days of horses and oxen pulling wagons was quite an arduous route. From here you have beautiful views of the Taconic Range and the Adirondacks to the west (behind), while to the east are the Green Mountains. The Long Trail crosses the highway on this ridge.

As you begin down the mountain there's a turnoff on the left. From this vantage point, peregrine falcons can often be seen during the early and late hours of the day. Common ravens also nest on the cliffs above. You may even see a moose in the mud pond below.

For the next five miles the highway continuously descends, following the Brandon Brook until it reaches the valley floor.

13.0 *Caution: This is a ninety-degree turn onto a narrow concrete bridge, and gravel is often scattered across the pavement.* This area is known as Robinson, but to call it a village or settlement would be misleading. After the turn, the road follows the narrow valley and the West Branch of the White River.

16.9 The bridge crosses the White River at the junction of Route 73 at Route 100, which was known as Talcville, after the mineral that was once mined here.

Route 100N goes to Rochester and on to Waitsfield and Warren. Three more gap roads—Route 125W, Lincoln Gap, and Route 17W—junction with Route 100N, and each will bring you back to the Champlain Valley. Route 100S reaches the junction of Route 107 in Stockbridge and continues to Route 4 in Killington.

ROUTE 125W:
The Middlebury Gap

lso known as Robert Frost Memorial Drive, this road goes over the Green Mountains and across the Champlain Valley to Chimney Point on Lake Champlain. It's the lowest gap through this part of the Green Mountains and certainly the best road for trucks, RVs, and trailers.

0.0   The junction of Route 125 is at Route 100 in Hancock. The Old Hancock Hotel, no longer an inn, is located at the junction, and it houses an excellent restaurant, a bakery, and a small bookstore. This is an convenient place to regroup a tour before beginning over the mountain.

3.0   The turn to Texas Falls is on the right. This national park scenic area is less than a mile up the road and is a wonderful place to visit and photograph.

Texas Falls is a couple of waterfalls, a short, deep gorge with potholes, and a series of cascades on the lower side. Rail fences, stone steps, and picnic tables line the course of the stream.

4.4   The highway begins to ascend the mountain. This is the lowest of the four gaps in this section of the Green Mountains. Not only is the road wider and the degree of slope less, the length of ascent is shorter than the other three gaps. For these reasons you'll see more bicyclists and trucks on this route than on any of the other three. As you near the top, the ski lifts you see on the left are part of the Middlebury College Snow Bowl ski area.

6.2   Cresting the mountain in the Middlebury Gap you are 2,149 feet above sea level. Here the highway intersects the Long Trail, the most popular hiking trail in the Northeast. The rocky ledges above to the right are the top of Hat Crown, which at 2,580 feet high is the lowest peak in this part of the Green Mountains. A map of the Long Trail shows all but one peak exceeding 3,000 feet in this area. For the next four miles the highway is relatively straight and the downgrade is gentle.

6.8   Access to the Middlebury College Snow Bowl is on the left.

9.2   This is the Breadloaf Inn and the Breadloaf Campus of Middlebury College, site of the famous writers' conference workshops and summer writers' school. The yellow buildings with their green trim are the symbol of this famous Middlebury College program with which Robert Frost was once associated.

9.5   In the picnic area on the right, under the pines, is a historic site marker that reads: *Robert Frost, 1874 to 1963. A distinguished American poet by recognition and a Vermonter by preference, Robert Frost was poet laureate of Vermont and for many years first citizen of the town of Ripton. He was long associated with Middlebury College's school of Eng-*

lish and its writers' conference. Robert Frost is buried in the cemetery by the Old First Church in Bennington.

Just beyond the picnic area, on the opposite side of the highway, you'll find the Robert Frost Interpretive Trail, a boardwalk that runs through the scrub brush with his poems posted at varying intervals.

10.7   Access to the Green Mountain National Forest campground is on the left. The highway gets more interesting from this point to East Middlebury as it twists and turns in its descent.

11.7   This is the village of Ripton, with the Chipman Inn on the right and the Ripton Country Store on the left. The road soon begins to follow the south bank of the Middlebury Gorge and the combined flow of the North Branch and the South Branch brooks.

14.2   Ahead you glimpse views of the Champlain Valley and the Adirondack Mountains.

14.5   The beginning of East Middlebury is at the end of the Middlebury Gorge and the base of the Green Mountains. You've descended 1,675 feet in the last 8.25 miles and can physically see where the mountains end and the Chaplain Valley begins. As you enter East Middlebury, an inn and restaurant are on the right. Two bed and breakfasts are located on the right as you continue through the village.

15.3   The fork to the left leads you through more of the village and past commercial service businesses for another .5 mile to junction with Route 7S.

15.4   The intersection of Routes 116 and 125 is at the blinking traffic light. A store/gas station is on the right and the post office is on the far right. *Route 116 is a pleasant alternative to Route 7 if you're going to Burlington. It doesn't have as much traffic and follows the base of the Green Mountains for most of the way.*

16.0   Route 125 merges with Route 7N. **Turn right** to continue on Routes 125W and 7N.

It's 3.9 miles from here to the green in Middlebury. The three motels on the south side of Middlebury are about the only convenient lodging in the area, but there are several good restaurants in the village. From the green, Route 125 continues through downtown Middlebury and the Middlebury College campus before going across the valley to the Crown Point Bridge.

ROUTE 17W:
The Appalachian Gap to the Adirondacks

Leaving Route 100 in Waitsfield, the highway climbs over the Green Mountains and then crosses the Champlain Valley to New York. Route 17, that winds through the Appalachian Gap, is also known as the McCullough Highway. The location and importance of the Appalachian Gap can only be appreciated from a vantage point on the mountains opposite it, particularly from Roxbury Gap to the east. From such a vantage point the gap looks like the notch in the rear sights of a gun, with the mountains to the south rising over four thousand feet high. This is a popular road for local touring clubs.

0.0   The junction of Route 17W at Route 100N is in the town of Waitsfield. One of the most popular touring roads in the state, it is well maintained because it leads to a major ski resort. The road twists and turns climbing the backbone of the Green Mountains. After about four miles you need to be cautious of the curves because a couple of them are much tighter than they appear as you enter them.

4.7   On the left is the Mad River Glen ski area; on the right, the road makes a broad sweep around the parking lot. Immediately after the ski area you will encounter some very tight turns a couple turn out to be unmarked S-turns!

6.2   The top of the Appalachian Gap is at 2,365 feet. Here there is a rest stop where one can take in the view to the west—the peaks of the Adirondacks are plainly visible. The Long Trail crosses the highway at this point. You are in Buel's Gore (population, 2) with an area of 3,520 acres. This portion of Route 17 is the McCullough Highway and was built by the Civilian Conservation Corps in the mid-1930s. Many of the best touring roads in the East, including the Blue Ridge Parkway, were built by the C.C.C. during this era.

The several tight turns in the first three miles of the descent from the gap are indicated by yellow signs with arrows and should not be taken at more than 30 MPH because they may contain gravel. The road soon straightens out and you can move right along. At about 13.9 miles you enter the gulf following Baldwin Creek, where the road twists and turns following the creek for about two miles.

15.7 At the stop sign Route 17 meets Route 116 *to the right, which leads north to Hinesburg and into Burlington.* **Turn left** and ride on the combined routes toward Bristol.

Driving along this beautiful valley you are actually on top of the Hinesburg Fault, often considered to be the western boundary of the Green Mountains.

17.4 A concrete bridge spans the New Haven River and the northwestern end of the New Haven Gorge. Directly ahead is the road to Lincoln. If you'd like to take a swim, see a great waterfall, or take the gravel road over Lincoln Gap and back to Route 100 in Warren, this is the road to take, unless you're on a motorcycle or driving an RV. If you just want a glimpse of the gorge or to see the geological evidence of an overthrust, cross the bridge and immediately turn left and park along the gravel road.

If you are parked anywhere near the gorge you'll be able to see how the mountains to the east were pushed over the rocks to the west by the distinct angle of the rock layers visible on the cliffs of the southern end of the Hogback Mountains. This gorge is the southern end of the Hinesburg fault that runs all the way to Canada. In the gorge you can see how the layers of rock are horizontal on the eastern side, then begin to slant upward on the western side. This is called an overthrust and is one of the predominate geological features of the Champlain Valley.

SIDE TRIP

Turn left before crossing the bridge, travel no more than .2 mile, park in any of the turnoffs to the right, or turn onto the shoulder of the road. In the summer this location, always crowded with cars, is one of the most popular swimming holes in Vermont. This is New Haven Gorge and New Haven Falls, sometimes misidentified as Bristol Falls. A swimmer can climb onto the rock ledge on the other side of the river and walk behind the waterfall!

Continuing toward Bristol you'll see a white restaurant, The Squirrel's Nest, on the right that offers fried clams, French fries, burgers, and creemees.

18.3 On the left you'll see the Bristol Boulder into which the Lord's Prayer was inscribed in 1891. Since then, the highway has had to move around the boulder. The story is that Dr. Joseph C. Greene of Buffalo, New York, had the prayer inscribed on this rock because of his childhood experiences growing up in Bristol and working as a driver of oxen or horses. It seems that the wagons traveling this road had to pass through a mud bog, and the cursing and cussing that took place as the wagons with their loads of logs and other products sank in the quagmire made a profound impression on the young man.

19.0 In the center of the village of Bristol, (population, 1,800), the green is a good place to stop and rest. The gazebo will give you some shelter if it is raining and you need a break. Pick up a snack or deli meal at the gas station/deli or, if you prefer to sit down, you'll find two good restaurants on Main Street. Downtown Bristol's quaint look dates from 1987–1988 when the film *The Wizard of Loneliness* was shot on location here in fictitious Stebbinsville.

Bristol is built on an ancient delta formed at the end of the last Ice Age by the New Haven River as it entered Lake Vermont—475 feet higher than the present shores of Lake Champlain and twenty-one miles away. As you begin to leave the village you may wish to stop at the small creemee stand on the left. From here you can look back over the lumberyard and see the gap in the mountains carved by the New Haven River and the narrow valley. The river has now worn a narrow channel through the ancient sediment on the south side of the village. At the end of the village the road winds down the hill that marks the end of this ancient delta.

21.1 Stop at the intersection and division of Routes 116S and 17W. *Route 116 continues to East Middlebury where it meets with Route 125. Visitors to the state often use the gap roads, Routes 73, 125, and 17, to zigzag up or down the central portion of the Green Mountains.*

Continue straight on Route 17W, which goes up and down gentle hills as you head due west. The numerous small hills running through the Champlain Valley make for a great drive.

23.0 This is the village of New Haven, centered around the green, as in most villages.

24.4 Route 17W briefly merges with Route 7N in New Haven Junction. **Turn right.** The routes merge for only .1 mile. **Turn left** immediately after crossing the railroad tracks.

Even though this is the Champlain Valley, you'd never know it from the terrain this highway follows. After leaving New Haven Junction, Route 17 follows the base of Buck Mountain then, after crossing the intersection of Route 23, runs along the northern end of Snake Mountain. These mountains are on the Champlain fault and are overthrusts (older, harder metamorphic rock forced up and over

On the green in Fair Haven stands one of the finest examples of an American residential home built of marble.

younger softer sedimentary rock), the same as the Hinesburg fault. As the glaciers scraped the Champlain basin, this harder rock didn't wear as quickly or as easily, so more sedimentary material was removed, and these overthrusts remained as mountains.

31.9 The intersection of Routes 17W and 22A is in West Addison. This is the last height of land before reaching the lake. From this slight rise you get a magnificent view of the Champlain basin and the Adirondack Mountains of New York. If you'd like to get a picture of this panoramic view, pull into the fire station and park.

Going across this flat stretch of land, you pass through the Dead Creek Wildlife Management Area, a major stopover in the fall for snow geese, Canada geese, and other migrating waterfowl. This area also abounds with wild turkey, great horned owls, screech owls, and hawks.

38.6 The D.A.R. State Park on the right is a great place to take a break, to go for a swim, to generally unwind—or to look for trilobites, fossils of a marine creature that lived from 550 to 375 million years ago and are believed to be the ancestors of our modern crustaceans and insects. The limestone rocks of the Champlain Valley provide us with the record of when life first began on our planet. Fossil imprints ranging from corals to that of a whale have been discovered along the shores of this inland lake.

39.8 Route 125 junctions with Route 17W by the snack bar just before the bridge. Lake Champlain lies in the states of New York, Vermont, and the province of Quebec; Vermont lays claim to 172,800 acres of this glacial lake. Lake Champlain is only ninety-five feet above sea level, about .5 mile lower than the Appalachian Gap you rode through thirty-four miles past. This is the narrowest part of the lake and has played a strategic and historical role in the development of North America since Samuel Champlain first discovered it in 1609. The Vermont side is known as Chimney Point, while the New York side is Crown Point.

40.0 This area was settled as early as 1731 when the French built a fort here. On the left, just before the bridge, is a state historic site, the Museum of Native American and French Heritage, in what was once a colonial tavern. On the New York side are the remains of Fort St. Frederick and Fort Amherst. During the Revolutionary War a pontoon bridge was maintained at this strategic site. This was also the western end of the Crown Point Military Road that cut through the Green Mountains from Fort Number 4 on the Connecticut River at Charlestown.

The twenty-two-hundred-foot Crown Point Bridge, built in 1929, replaced the old ferry that operated here for generations. I've always wondered why this bridge was built so high, and only recently came upon an old photo of the great steam paddle wheeler *Vermont III* passing under the bridge on its route to the port of Whitehall, its smokestacks just clearing the underside of the bridge.

On the New York side is the Champlain Light House memorial, with a bronze sculpture by Auguste Rodin adorning its peak.

If you continue past the museum, you can drive down to the fishing access under the bridge. Park and walk under the bridge along the shore. Here you'll find black limestone rocks with fossils of shells, ammonites (they look like nautilus shells), corals, and, once in a while, a trilobite.

After crossing the Crown Point Bridge into New York, you'll travel to combined Routes 9 and 22. Turning left will take you south to Ticonderoga and along Lake George; turning right will take you north along the lake to Plattsburgh. If you go north you can cross the lake to Vermont by ferry at Essex (to Charlotte), Port Kent (to Burlington), and Plattsburgh (to Grand Isle).

ROUTE 116:
East Middlebury to Burlington

This is a pleasant alternative to heavily traveled Route 7. Forty-one miles in length, it follows the western edge of the Green Mountains until a few miles south of Burlington. If it's a hot day you should consider stopping at Bartlett Falls in Bristol to swim.

0.0 The junction of Route 116 is a few miles south of Middlebury on Route 7. For the first .5 mile you'll ride past commercial businesses and residential homes in East Middlebury.

0.5 The intersection of Routes 116 and 125 is at the blinking light. On the far right is a gas station and variety store and on the far left the post office. *If you turn right you go east on Route 125 over the Middlebury Gap and down into Hancock on Route 100.* **Continue straight.**

East Middlebury is a bedroom community for Middlebury, and the takeover of farmland by residential homes reflects this. A couple of roads are shortcuts to Middlebury in the 3.5 miles.

4.7 You begin to move into more open country—the Green Mountains rise abruptly on the right while farmland rolls westward. To the right is Robert Frost Mountain, with its western slopes a mass of rocky landslides. As you approach Bristol you'll see a massive sand and gravel pit on the left and, a little farther, the gap in the mountains through which you'll be traveling. This deposit of sand and gravel was once the delta of a mighty river that carried the debris from the melting glaciers in the mountains, through the gap, and into the Lake of Vermont.

10.8 Route 116 merges with Route 17E at the four-way-stop intersection. *If you turn right and travel west on Route 17 you can reconnect with Route 7 or continue to New York.* **Turn right** and snake up the hill into the village of Bristol. This hill, now used as a sand and gravel pit, was also part of this ancient delta. From this approach it's easy to see where the river flowed through the gap and into the great Lake of Vermont at this level, 475 feet higher than the present shores of Lake Champlain. In the last ten thousand years, the New Haven River, although diminished in size, has continued to flow from the mountains to the lake, cutting through the old glacial delta and forming a deep valley on the edge of the village. Driving down West Street in

Bristol you can see ahead to the gap; the mountain on the right is South Mountain, the tall mountain directly ahead is Lincoln Mountain, and the mountain to the left is the south end of Hogback.

12.3 In the center of the village of Bristol, the green, with its gazebo, park benches, and canon, is a good place to take a break. Pick up a snack or deli meal at the convenience store across the street or, if you prefer, there are two good restaurants located in the next block. Continue through the traffic light and downtown Bristol.

13.6 The Lord's Prayer boulder protrudes into the road on the right. Turn off the highway on the other side of it to see the engraved inscription. Dr. Joseph C. Greene of Buffalo, New York, had the Lord's Prayer inscribed on this rock in 1891 because of his childhood experiences growing up in Bristol and working as a driver of oxen or horses. It seems that wagons traveling this road had to pass through a mud bog, and the cursing and cussing that took place as they and their heavy loads sank in the quagmire made a profound impression on him—or so the story goes.

14.2 The Squirrel's Nest Restaurant on the left is a popular local summer spot for creemees, French fries, hot-dogs, and the like.

14.5 The concrete bridge crosses the New Haven River at the end of the New Haven Gorge. **The road on the right becomes gravel after passing the town of Lincoln, and then climbs to the lofty Lincoln Gap and plunges to Route 100 in Warren.** *Do NOT take an RV, a motorcycle, or a trailer over this gap unless you are experienced in traveling on mountain roads.*

The southern end of the Hogback Mountain rises to the left, the exposed cliff showing the layers of rocks angling westward, pushed over the sedimentary rocks of the Champlain Valley. Even the layers of rocks in the gorge are slightly angled. This is the southern end of the Hinesburg fault, and what you see is a classic example of a geological overthrust. From the vantage point of the dirt road next to the bridge, you can see the metamorphic rock of Lincoln Mountain beginning to tilt upward in the middle of the gorge at the fault line.

 SIDE TRIP *To Bartlett Falls*

This is the place to stop for a swim or take photos. Turn right as if you were going to Lincoln, travel no more than .2 mile, park in any of the turnoffs to the right or on the shoulder of the road. Always crowded with cars in the summer, and one of the most popular swimming holes in Vermont, this is New Haven Gorge and Bartlett's Falls—also known as New Haven Falls and sometimes misidentified as Bristol Falls. A swimmer can climb onto the rock on the other side of the river and walk behind the waterfall! Above the falls the sculpted rocks provide small pools and fast water—a natural Jacuzzi.

Continue on Route 116 as it turns left.

As you drive up the narrow valley you are following the Hinesburg fault, often considered to be the western boundary of the Green Mountains. This fault continues all the way to Canada, and Route 116 follows it to just north of Hinesburg.

16.2 This is the division of Route 116N and Route 17E. *Route 17 turns right and goes over the Appalachian Gap, then down to Waitsfield and Route 100 (15.7 miles).* **Continue straight on Route 116N.** You'll find a restaurant and an inn just ahead on the right. Beaver Brook is the stream you'll see on the left for the first couple of miles; however, when the highway crosses a stream it will be Lewis Creek, the principal watershed in the valley.

21.6 This is the center of Starksboro with the Starksboro Country Store on the left. This valley seems filled with small family dairy farms. This landscape doesn't show much evidence of the rapid urban growth of the Burlington area, but more and more people are commuting from these small towns to city jobs.

26.1 The junction of a road leading over to Richmond is on the left. Approaching Hinesburg you get glimpses of the Adirondack Mountains.

29.2 Hinesburg is one of towns experiencing rapid growth from the growing urban Burlington area. Towns such as Williston and Hinesburg have been hard pressed, balancing the rural village feeling with the demands for new residential housing. Lake Iroquois, one of Vermont's small lakes encircled by small summer cottages, is in the process of being transformed into an enclave of expensive year-round homes.

29.7 The center of Hinesburg is one of my favorite villages.

30.0 On the right is a road that leads over to Lake Iroquois and Richmond.

30.6 Stop **at the traffic light and intersection.** A minimart is located just down the road on the left. The road on the right leads to Richmond; the previous turn to Richmond joins it. **Continue straight.** Route 116 begins to move away from the Green Mountains, angling toward the city of Burlington.

32.7 The junction of Route 2A is on the right in St. George. On the left is a country club. St. George is a unincorporated village that has discouraged the residential growth found in the surrounding communities due to its tax structure. Most of the residents live along Route 2A, while the large farms are situated along Route 116. *Route 2A goes to Tafts Corners in Williston where it intersects Route 2; it continues and intersects Route 15 in Essex Center and junctions in Colchester at combined Routes 2N and 7.*

35.2 As you sweep through these S-turns, notice Shelburne Pond off to the left.

36.2 Large farms spread their acreage across the town lines of Hinesburg, Shelburne, Williston, and South Burlington, but where their boundaries end, development begins. The next three miles exemplify the conflicts between Burlington's rapid growth and the aesthetics of Vermont's landscape. This used to be one of the most beautiful areas of Vermont, as well as New England, with unspoiled views of the Adirondacks and Lake Champlain to the west (left) and Mount Mansfield and the Green Mountains to the east (right). In the early 1970s this was farmland. Now you see housing developments and light industry as you continue on Route 116 (Hinesburg Road) into South Burlington.

38.8 Hinesburg Road crosses I-89.

39.4 Hinesburg Road intersects with Kennedy Road in South Burlington at the traffic light. You now have three options, depending upon where you want to go in Burlington or on which route you wish to continue. (See Map on page 268 in the appendix.)

To get to Route 2W, access to I-89N, the University of Vermont, or downtown Burlington, go straight.

40.4 The end of Route 116 is at Route 2, Williston Road, at the traffic light.

Turn left and position yourself in the right-hand lane of this four-lane road.

40.9 This is Exit 14 of I-89 and the quickest way to Winooski. It's also the easiest way to pick up Route 15E (Exit 15) or Routes 7N and 2W (Exits 16 and 17). I recommend taking the interstate highway instead of East Avenue.

41.2 East Avenue, on the right just past the large Sheraton Inn Conference Center, takes you directly to combined Routes 2W, 7N, and 15E.

41.7 University Place and the UVM green on the right are the center of the University of Vermont Campus. **Continue straight** through the traffic lights and down the hill to reach downtown Burlington and the Champlain ferry dock.

To get to Route 2E and Williston Road turn right.

39.9 At the junction of Kennedy Drive and Route 2, Williston Road, turn right to go to Williston or Waterbury.

To reach Route 7S, Shelburne Road, or downtown Burlington, turn left.

40.0 The Dorset Street intersection is at this light. *If you turn right you pass the school, the University Mall, the Dorset Street Mall, to Williston Road (Route 2) and Exit 14 of I-89.*

Continue straight, which leads onto Route I-189W. As you travel on this connector you'll have a fantastic view of the Adirondacks and Lake Champlain.

41.6 The junction of I-189 is at Route 7, Shelburne Road. **Stay in the right-hand lane to go north into Burlington. The left-hand lanes go south on Route 7 to Shelburne and Vergennes.**

ROUTE 30S:
The Seth Warner Memorial Highway

've broken Route 30 into two sections: west from Brattleboro to Route 100 in West Jamaica, and south from Middlebury to West Jamaica. While technically listed as an east-west highway, Route 30 runs north and south from Middlebury to Manchester Center, and then east and west from Manchester to Brattleboro. Route 30S parallels Route 22A, but the differences between the two roads is striking. While Route 22A rolls across the open farmland of the lower Champlain Valley, Route 30 skirts the western edge of the Taconic Mountains until it cuts through them along the Mettawee River. Route 22A is a faster highway, but it's an extremely hot drive on a summer day; Route 30 is slower, but the shade from the trees and the mountains makes it much cooler. The scenery is diverse along Route 30; you pass through a summer lake area, the slate region, the Taconic Mountains, the village of Manchester, and finally over the Green Mountains to Route 100.

(For more on Middlebury see Route 7S, page 49.)

0.0   In the village of Middlebury Routes 7, 125, and 30 meet. Route 30 junctions at, and Route 125 merges with, Route 7 at the green in the center of the village. If you're traveling south on Route 7, turn right at the green and drive into the downtown area.

The downtown area is a historic district and of special interest to those who are fascinated by architecture. You'll find the Emma Willard house, the John Warren house, the Congregational Church, and literally hundreds of other buildings worth seeing. The Episcopal Church on the green is made of the local stone quarried in Weybridge. This town is known for education, but the mills on the second falls of the Otter Creek were the source of its prosperity. The old mills on Maple and Mill Streets have been converted to retail shops, but the structures remain, giving the visitor a sense of the industry that used to be centered here.

Mill Street is on the right immediately after crossing the small concrete bridge in the center of downtown. Frog Hollow Craft Center is located in one of the restored mill buildings on this street. Just beyond is the Sheldon Museum, a glimpse into life in Middlebury during the late 1800s. In front of the museum is a Vermont historic site marker commemorating a journeyman blacksmith by the name of John Deere.

0.3   The division of Route 125W to the right is College Street, which goes through the Middlebury College campus before continuing west to the shore of Lake Champlain at Chimney Point. **Continue straight** on Route 30S, South Main Street, to Route 74. Route 30S leads through Middlebury College, with the art center and the field house on the left and the main campus on the right. Middlebury College was chartered in 1800 as a counter to the University of Vermont.

South of the college campus is a couple of miles of residential settlement and then open farmland, with views of the Green Mountains to the left and the Adirondack Mountains of New York to the right.

4.3   The junction of Route 74W is on the right in Cornwall. *Route 74 leads over to Route 22A in Shoreham.*

As you ride south, Route 30 becomes more rural. The vistas of the mountains are not as dramatic or as constant as on Route 22A a few miles to the west, but they are beautiful nevertheless. The road twists and turns, and magnificent views of the Green Mountains are constantly opening up. To the left (east) are farms and the Cornwall Swamp Wildlife Management Area, over thirteen hundred acres providing refuge for deer and waterfowl. The extensive marshlands between Routes 7 and 30 run from Middlebury to Brandon. Recognized as important nesting areas for waterfowl, many wildlife management areas have been established in this region.

10.8   This is the village of Whiting. Here county roads intersect Route 30. *The road to the right leads to Route 22A in Shoreham, the one on the left to Brandon.* Don't be afraid to do a little exploring if you have the time. It's difficult to get lost on these county roads because you can always use the mountains as reference points.

13.8   The junction of Route 73E on the left goes to Brandon and Route 7. *Route 73E leads from Brandon over the Green Mountains through Brandon Gap to Route 100. For photographers, especially during the migrations of geese, this is the only easy access into Brandon Swamp.* Route 73W merges with Route 30 here in the middle of nowhere.

15.9   Route 73W divides and turns right just north of the village of Sudbury. Like all the other routes that turn west from Route 30, this one also goes to Route 22A. **Continue straight on Route 30S.**

18.2   On the right is the junction of Route 144 , which leads west past Lake Hortonia, through the village of Hortonia, and along the Hubbardton River to Route 22A. This is rugged country, and these local roads lead to some of the best hunting and fishing areas in western Vermont.

18.4   Lake Hortonia is on the right. Burr Pond, Hinkum Pond, Echo Lake, and Beebe Pond are also located in this immediate area that abounds in wildlife and game fish. Lake Hortonia is known for rainbow and lake trout and for bass.

20.5   Beebe Pond is on the right, then, about .5 mile farther, you descend through the Hubbardton Gulf.

22.3   At the northern end of Lake Bomoseen there is a well-marked left turn that leads to the Hubbardton Battlefield. The northern end of Lake Bomoseen, on the right, is a large wetland area.

The Battle of Hubbardton

On July 7, 1777 the only battle of the Revolutionary War fought on Vermont soil took place here. Seth Warner and one thousand Green Mountain Boys attempted to stop the advance of eight thousand British troops commanded by General Burgoyne. Although the Green Mountain Boys were forced to retreat from the superior force of the Hessian troops, they were successful in delaying the British force long enough for John Stark to assemble his men. Five weeks later, John Stark, aided by Seth Warner and the Green Mountain Boys, defeated the advancing British in the Battle of Bennington, considered to be the turning point in the Revolutionary War.

26.8   The population of the small village of Bomoseen swells during the hot summer months. The hundreds of small summer camps perched on the edge of this beautiful lake can make this village busier than downtown Montpelier on a hot day. This area is extremely crowded in the summer and requires slow, cautious driving. After passing through the village, the highway parts from the lake, which continues southward for almost another three miles.

As you drive along the shore of Lake Bomoseen, notice a small island—Neshobe. This lake was a thriving summer resort at the turn of the last century. During the 1930s and 1940s Neshobe was a popular retreat for many Hollywood celebrities.

There is a story firmly embedded in local lore about how one local resident successfully discouraged autograph seekers from trespassing on the island. One day, when a group of them disembarked, Harpo Marx was lying in ambush. When the celebrity hounds were close enough, he charged from the underbrush screaming, his body naked and painted blue. This solved the problem for that season.

Another local story involves area resident Jules Buel, who was fishing from his boat when he dropped the spoon with which he was eating. Seeing a fish lunge for the spoon as it twisted into the depths, he was inspired to invent the fishing lure now known by the same name as the eating utensil. This tale may or may not be true, but Buel did patent this item, and the J.T. Buel Company manufactures fishing lures to this day.

28.8   The access onto Route 4—the modern, interstate-like Route 4—provides a fast highway west to New York's Route 9 or east to Rutland. This is the best route on a rainy day or if you're riding at night. Otherwise Route 4A is preferable.

29.7   The intersection of Route 30 with Route 4A is in Castleton Corners. *The village of Castleton is about 1.5 miles east on Route 4A; Fair Haven is about three miles west.*

Route 30S is often used as a connector when people are traveling from New York to southern Vermont. Once again I've broken the mileage into two segments. If you reset the trip odometers to 0.0, the following mileage will agree. Otherwise just add thirty miles and subtract .3 mile, and you'll be accurate.

0.0   The intersection of Route 30 and Route 4A in Castleton Corners is where we reset the odometer to 0.0.

I believe that the barn on the left, just a few yards from Route 4A, was the first building in Vermont to be shingled with slate. The next couple of miles of the Seth Warner Memorial Highway are residential, but it quickly opens up into farmland.

3.3   For the next .5 mile you get your first glimpses of the slate quarries for which this area is famous. Off to the right (west) you can see the slate dumps and the high derrick towers which are used to lift the stone out of the quarries. The slate region is west of the Taconics and extends into New York; the red stone comes from New York, while the green and purple come from Vermont. The deposits were discovered in 1839, but the quarries didn't become profitable until after the railroads arrived in the early 1850s. Very little of the slate quarried today is used in roofing, but the stone is still used for tile, landscaping, billiard tables, and blackboards.

7.3   The intersection of Route 140 is on the left in the village of Poultney.

To the right, at the end of the broad avenue, is Green Mountain College, established in 1834 as the Troy Conference Academy. A Methodist academy, it became a state college in 1931. The Federal-style brick buildings and mature maple trees makes this an attractive campus. Downtown Poultney is different from most; the buildings are plain and widely spaced along a very broad avenue. This village grew along with the development of the slate industry.

The vital center of town during the colonial era was the village of East Poultney on Route 140. The library, 1790, was one of the earliest in the state; the Eagle Tavern, 1790, still stands as do many other early buildings. Horace Greeley, founder of the Republican Party and of the *New York Herald Tribune*, served his apprenticeship working for the *Northern Spectator*. From New Haven (eleven miles to the west in New York), he lodged at the Eagle Tavern for his four-year apprenticeship. It was Horace Greeley who, in one of his famous editorials, wrote the words "Go west young man" and encouraged the emigration of Vermonters to the lands of the Midwest. Interestingly enough, he worked with another apprentice, George Jones, who went on to cofound the *New York Times*. Francis Ruggles, also of Poultney, helped established this newspaper.

Continue straight as Route 31 merges with Route 30. **At the stop sign, turn left** to follow Route 30. *Route 31 continues straight leading to Granville, New York.*

After winding through the rest of the village, this becomes a wonderful twisting rural road following the contours of the land and the whims of colonial property boundaries. About two miles beyond Poultney you'll see Lily Pond, the northernmost portion of Lake St. Catherine, on the right followed by Lake St. Catherine State Park on the left.

11.8 The road finally approaches the lake and follows the eastern shore.

Across the lake in South Poultney you can see the derricks and dump piles of slate quarries. For the next mile Route 30 is cut between the steep slope of St. Catherine Mountain and Lake St. Catherine. The low-grade slate that lines the left side of the road is not what is quarried on the other side of the lake. The commercial slate of this area is purple and green, and the geological formation from which they are mined is known as the Cambrian St. Catherine Formation. Before the building of the railroads, the slate used to be ferried down the lake and then transported on sleds pulled by oxen during the winter to the canal in New York. From the canal the slate was shipped south to New York City and the New England coast.

The small private summer camps are precariously perched on the narrow, steep bank between the water and the road. You have to travel slowly and cautiously along this stretch of highway in the summer, but it's cool and comfortable on a hot summer day.

13.1 This is the southern end of Lake St. Catherine. Little Pond to the south is connected to the lake by a narrow waterway and can be seen on the right just before entering the village of Wells.

15.6 You're in the village of Wells and the green is on the right. A country store is located just before the green.

16.9 The Wells Trading Post is on the right just outside of the village.

17.3 On the right is the junction *of Route 149, which leads to Granville, New York, Route 22, Route 22A, and Route 31.* You can see another slate dump on the right across the highway.

18.3 On the right is the junction *of Route 153, which goes to the border town of West Pawlet and then follows the Vermont-New York border south to West Rupert and Salem, New York.* From here you have a spectacular view of the Taconic Mountains ahead.

You enter into the Taconic Mountains in North Pawlet, passing between Burt Hill (1,180 feet) on the left and Indian Hill (1,007 feet) on the right. These low, beautiful mountains are extremely steep and rocky and are made of rock that is older than the base rock on which they sit. When older rocks are forced over younger rocks, the overthrust is known as a klippe. The Taconic klippe is world famous in geological circles, and these mountains are believed to have been the top of the southern Green Mountains that were sheared off and moved miles westward during the Acadian mountain building period 350 million years ago.

22.6 The junction of Route 133 is on the left here in Pawlet, a beautiful, small village in which the road dips down, along, and out of a narrow little gorge along Flower Brook. *Route 133 goes north to West Rutland. The combination of Routes 4, 30, and 133 make a nice day trip for those visiting the Rutland area.*

25.5 This is a fantastic fast-paced road through extremely lush farmland with fields of corn on either side. This spectacular landscape is the Mettawee Valley with the Taconics on both sides; Spruce Top and Rupert Mountain are on the immediate right followed by the peaks of Bear Mountain and Equinox. On the left are the higher mountains: Woodlawn Mountain, Dorset Peak, and Green Peak.

28.8 The junction of Route 315 is on the right in East Rupert, which is known for the mint of Reuben Harmon, Jr. These copper pennies (Harmon cents) were minted for the independent Republic of Vermont from 1785–1788 and are now highly sought after by numismatists.

Also located at the junction is the Dorset West Road that runs parallel to Route 30 for almost five miles. The majority of Dorset's beautiful homes and estates are located along this local road, but generally Route 30 is just as scenic.

30.8 You are now in the beautiful village of Dorset. The Dorset Inn and the long, narrow green are on the right. The Dovetail Inn is on the left across from the Dorset Inn. Pellitier's Market faces the green on the right, and the famous Dorset Playhouse is at the far end. Dorset is now known for its beautiful homes and antiques shops. Another inn is on the left as you leave the village.

Not far from the Dorset Inn, there was once a much smaller establishment known as Kent's Tavern. It was here, in this town of radical politics, during the summer of 1775, that the beginning of Vermont as a independent republic took place. Later, in September 1776, representatives from forty-four towns in what was then known as The Grants met and endorsed the Articles of Association. The next

This early, unusually ornate grave marker in Bennington's "Old Burying Ground" was hand chiseled from marble quarried on Dorset Mountain. It was there in 1785 that marble was first mined in Vermont. Initially, the stone was used for grave markers, hitching posts, and door lentils.

meeting was on the eastern side of the state in the village of Westminster in January 1777 where The Grants declared their independence. This was followed by the drafting of the Vermont constitution in Windsor during July 1777. The first commercial marble quarry in America was opened here by 1785. The New York Public Library, the Harvard Medical School building, and the U.S. Bank building in Erie, Pennsylvania, are built from the marble mined in Dorset Mountain.

36.8 The intersection of Route 30 with Route 7 is in Manchester Center and is locally called Malfunction Junction because there are no stoplights, the traffic is heavy, and there are many pedestrians. If you want to stop in this village I suggest taking the first parking space available to you along Route 30 before reaching Route 7. Manchester Center is filled with factory outlet stores, specialty shops, gourmet foods suppliers, restaurants, and up-scale shopping plazas. If you're looking for a wristwatch, browse in the Movado company store, or get outfitted by Ralph Lauren, Calvin Klein, Anne Klein, Saville, or Orvis at their respective factory stores. (To be fair, the Orvis facility is the original store, not a factory outlet.)

There are so many places to stay in this area that I suggest checking with the local Chamber of Commerce (.2 mile north on Route 7A on the right on the small green).

Turn right and in .1 mile, turn left to continue on Route 30S. *Caution: This is a dangerous intersection with heavy traffic and many pedestrians.*

36.9 Now on combined Routes 30S and 11E, you slowly drive past shops, plazas, and factory outlet stores.

37.6 You've now passed the heaviest concentration of commercial shopping, although there are factory outlet stores for another .5 mile.

38.3 This is the access onto Route 7, the modern highway built to replace old Route 7, the fastest way to go south to Bennington from Manchester.

39.0 There are numerous motels and restaurants in this area because of the access to the ski areas from Route 7. As you leave the town of Manchester you enter into the town of Winhall. The township of Winhall is primarily forest and mountains with the one village of Bondville located on Route 30 in the southeastern corner.

39.2 The ranger station on the right is the place to stop and ask questions about any portion of the Green Mountain National Forest or camping in it. This is the main public station for the southern section of the national forest. From here the road begins to ascend the foot of Bromley Mountain.

41.4   The road makes a turn and then begins to climb the steep grade of the south shoulder of Bromley Mountain.

43.2   The road now crests the ridge and The Lodge At Trout Pond is on the left where Routes 11E and 30S divide. *Route 11E goes straight, passing Bromley ski area and intersecting Route 100 in Londonderry.* **Turn right** to continue on Route 30S.

In exactly .5 mile, the highway crests another ridge, and you begin to descend down the eastern side of the mountain. In the summer the views are limited, but in the early spring and late fall the view is fantastic.

45.7   The view of Bromley Mountain is behind you to the left. About two miles farther you can see another ski area to the right, the world famous Stratton Mountain ski area.

50.5   Stratton Road, the access to Stratton Mountain ski area, is on the right in the village of Bondville. In the summer Stratton Mountain hosts not only World Cup tennis, but also a summer concert series every weekend featuring well-known artists.

52.1   Route 30 merges with Route 100 in Rawsonville. **Continue straight** on combined Routes 30S and 100s.

You are now in the West River Valley with rolling hills on either side of the highway. **Continue through the village of Jamaica.**

60.2   **The dividing of Route 100S with Route 30 is in East Jamaica—but don't look for a village!**

Just a few yards down Route 100S from Route 30 is the bridge over the West River, a good place to watch kayakers and canoeists run the rapids on the West River. The bridge re-enforcement beams make perfect seats from which to watch the frequent kayak races.

This is where Route 30W, the section from Brattleboro to East Jamaica, meets with this one. It's another 22.4 miles to downtown Brattleboro.

ROUTE 22A :
Fair Haven to Vergennes

This is my favorite road on the western side of the state. Route 22A rolls across the ancient basin of the Champlain Valley through open farmland. The Adirondacks to the west and the Green Mountains to the east provide an aesthetic backdrop to the beautiful farms of this region.

Fair Haven

Although the town was chartered in 1779 to Ebenezer Allen, it was settled by Matthew Lyon four years later. The early village was known for its industries, most of which were established by Lyon, and especially for its ironworks and the first forge in Vermont. Vermont's slate industry began just north of the village in 1839, and much of the wealth of Fair Haven is derived from this industry. Fair Haven was an important stop on the Underground Railroad in the 1850s and later was the home of the Vermont Clock Company.

Matthew Lyon

There have been a number of famous people from Fair Haven, but the most famous, or in some eyes infamous, was Matthew Lyon, an opportunist, the kind of self-made man who was attracted to the possibilities present in the frontier known as The Grants. He became part of the correct political movement, married the niece of Ethan Allen—and later the daughter of Thomas Chittenden—and served as an officer in the Revolutionary War. He moved from Wallingford to establish the town of Fair Haven in 1783, where he established an iron furnace, forges, a nail factory, a gristmill, a paper mill, a printing office, and numerous other local businesses. He then ran for public office and was elected to the United States Congress.

Matthew Lyon became the infamous anti-Federalist representative from Vermont known for his outrageous temper and actions on the floor of the United States Congress. The foremost opponent of the U.S. sedition laws, he was finally convicted of sedition and jailed. While in jail he was reelected to Congress, and when released, he returned to Washington in time to cast the deciding vote in the deadlocked election of Thomas Jefferson for president of the United States.

Bankrupt in Vermont, he moved to Kentucky where he again rebuilt his fortune, again was elected to Congress, and again went

bankrupt, this time in the financial upheavals after the War of
1812. You have to give this man credit for perseverance. He moved
to Arkansas where in 1822 he was elected to represent that state in
Congress. Matthew Lyon is the only man to have ever been elected
to Congress in three different states.

*Route 22A is an extension of Route 22N that runs along the eastern
border of New York from Millerton (just south of the Massachusetts-
Connecticut border) to just south of New Haven in Granville, New York.
Route 22A enters Vermont just south of New Haven and then briefly
merges with Route 4A as it goes through the village.*

0.0   The green in Fair Haven is exceptionally beautiful. Two of
America's finest examples of Federal-style homes built of marble face
the green, one of which is now the Marble Inn.

Route 22A provides a one-mile access to Route 4 from Route 4A
and the village. Traveling north through the broad Champlain Valley, Route 22A is a fast route, very open (and so hot on a summer afternoon), with very little traffic. You'll find truck traffic, especially
trailer trucks hauling milk and grain stock, on this highway, but it is
not crowded and there are many places to pass. Devil's Bowl, a small
dirt racetrack, is 5.5 miles from Fair Haven on the left.

9.2   The junction of Route 144 is on the right with beautiful
views of the Green Mountains above the low rolling hills to the east.
The road undulates up and down, following the gentle contours of
the rolling land. Cresting these gentle hills always affords magnificent views of the mountain ranges and the farmlands between.

15.2   In Orwell is the intersection of Route 73. *To the left Route 73
takes you to Larabee's Point, the southernmost ferry on Lake Champlain,
in about five miles.* Here are magnificent views of the Adirondack
Mountains to the left and the Green Mountains to the right.

21.4   In Shoreham the St. Guinevere Church is on the right at the
merging of Routes 74E and 22A. *To the left Route 74W goes to Larabee's
Point, Ticonderoga, New York, and the ferry.* **Continue straight.**

Shoreham is the birthplace of Levi P. Morton, vice-president of the
United States under Benjamin Harrison in 1888. Morton also served
in Congress, was minister to France, and later became governor of
New York. Also born here were Byron Sunderland, who served as
chaplain of the United States under Abraham Lincoln; Columbus De-
lano, secretary of the interior under President Grant; and Governor
Silas Jennison, the first native-born Vermont governor, in 1835.

21.8   This is the division of Routes 74E and 22A, with Route 74E, on the right, going to Middlebury.

28.0   Here Route 125W merges with Route 22A. *Route 125E is on the right and leads to Middlebury.*

28.4   The division of Route 22A and Route 125W is on the border of the Dead Creek Wildlife Management Area in the township of Bridport. *Route 125W, on the left, leads over to the Crown Point Bridge and into New York. A few miles after crossing the bridge you junction at Route 9. Route 9S leads to Ticonderoga and Lake George; Route 9N follows the western side of the lake north to Plattsburgh and Canada. You can cross back into Vermont on one of two ferries or the Rouse's Point Bridge on the Canadian border.*

This is a great vantage point to take a picture of the tall white silos of Addison County's numerous farms silhouetted against the purple-gray mountains of New York.

35.0   The intersection of Route 22A with Route 17 is in the village of Addison. *On the left Route 17W goes to the Crown Point Bridge; on the right Route 17E goes to Fair Haven Junction, Bristol, and over the Appalachian Gap to Waitsfield and Route 100.*

Addison is another great place to take a photo of the farmlands stretching to the west and northwest, because it sits on the last small rise before the lake. I think the best place to get a photo is a few yards down Route 17W at the fire station, where you get a great vista without telephone wires. Just outside the village to the west is the Dead Creek Wildlife Management Area. Addison, a major stopover for tens of thousands of snow geese and other migrating waterfowl, especially Canada geese, is also noted for its wild turkeys, great horned owls, screech owls, and hawks. If you're an avid nature photographer, this is one of Vermont's best areas to go hunting for that choice shot.

39.6   You'll see signs for the Basin Harbor Club as you enter the outskirts of the Vergennes. Turn left onto Panton Road to go to Basin Harbor and the maritime museum. Going down the hill into Vergennes you cross the bridge over the Otter Creek Falls and climb the hill into downtown.

Vergennes: The Smallest City

With a population of about twenty-five hundred this is the smallest, as well as the third oldest, city in the United States. First settled in 1766, it was incorporated as a city in 1788.

Here, at the foot of Otter Creek Falls, eight miles from Lake Champlain, were built the ships commanded by Benedict Arnold that fought the British fleet in 1776 and, although defeated, delayed the British advance for a crucial year. In 1814 another fleet was hastily built here that sailed north to defeat the British at Plattsburgh.

Vergennes may, at first, seem to be a strange place to build a fleet of ships, to say nothing of doing it twice, but in fact it was the ideal location. The power from the waterfalls ran a sawmill as early as 1764 and the first ironworks in 1786. The Otter Creek was navigable from the lake to the falls and provided transportation from the falls in Middlebury to the falls in Vergennes. The forests of the Champlain Valley and the western Green Mountains provided a ready supply of lumber and charcoal, while the iron ore came from local sources, eastern New York, and northwestern Vermont. While the safe harbor and large sawmill probably influenced Benedict Arnold's decision to build his fleet here, it was the ironworks that prompted the U.S. Navy to commission the building of Commodore Macdonough's ships at this location.

The blast furnaces and forges below the falls made this city prosperous in the middle of the nineteenth century. During the later half of the last century the iron industry shifted west, first to New York and then to Pennsylvania, and Vermont's famous ironworks closed down.

In 1902 the hydroelectric dam and generating station were built here, providing one of the early sources of electrification in Vermont.

41.4   At the traffic light the village green can be seen ahead on the left. There are several restaurants in downtown Vergennes.

After leaving downtown you'll see a gas station on the right at the traffic light. *You can turn right and travel down Monkton Road, past the school, to the junction of Route 7. At the junction there is a shopping center on the left.* **Continuing straight** you'll pass the Kennedy Brother's factory on the right, now a collection of crafts shops, and through the underpass to reach Route 7.

42.4   The junction with Route 7 is the end of Route 22A. *Route 7S leads to New Haven Junction and the intersection of Route 17; Route 7N leads to Shelburne and Burlington.*

ROUTE 2W:
The Connecticut River to Montpelier

This is the primary east-west highway from central Vermont to Bangor, Maine. Used in combination with the interstate highways, it becomes the main commercial artery for truckers moving freight between Toronto, Montreal, Plattsburgh, Burlington, and Maine. During the summer vacationers use it to go from Lake George and the Adirondacks to the White Mountains and the Maine coast. I don't care for the stretch of Route 2W running from the Connecticut River to St. Johnsbury. There's too much traffic, few places to pass, and no views of interest. Still, it's the only road going from Lancaster, New Hampshire to St. Johnsbury.

Route 2 between St. Johnsbury and Montpelier is an endangered highway like Route 9 in southern Vermont. Year by year, sections of the old twisting road are replaced by the new improved highway. For a taste of what Route 2 used to be like, try the short section of Route 2B on the west side of St. Johnsbury.

Route 2E from Alburg to Montpelier is covered as a north-to-south route (See Route 2E: The Champlain Islands to Central Vermont, page 218.)

0.0 Route 2W begins in Portland, Maine, and we pick it up on the Vermont–New Hampshire border by the bridge from Lancaster. This is also the junction of Route 102.

This part of Vermont is wilderness. The land to the right (north) has no villages or settlements and, except for access to Maidstone State Park, no roads. Geologically this is part of the White Mountains—solid granite that has been scraped and gouged by the glaciers of the last Ice Age—and the habitat is the southern boundary of the Northern Boreal Forest. The impermeable granite that holds the runoff from rain and snow in shallow depressions creates the vast bogs of this region. The soil is shallow and acidic, making this the worst agricultural land in the state.

18.6 It was in the village of Concord that the Reverend Samuel R. Hall established the first normal school (school for teachers) in America. He was also the inventor of the blackboard and author of the first American textbook on teaching. The originator of America's first advertising agency, George Rowell, was born in this village.

23.7 A motel and restaurant are located at the junction of Route 18. Route 2W (truck route) is to the right. On the left, Route 18S leads to Littleton, New Hampshire; I-93 to Littleton and I-93 to I-91 are accessed by bearing left on Route 18. Two of the three major accesses into the White Mountains merge at the junction of Routes 18 and 2.

The eastern side of St. Johnsbury is industrial, where the city's manufacturing base grew and still resides. The interstate highways and Route 2 provide easy access to points north, south, east, and west for shipping by truck.

St. Johnsbury Bypass:

This bypass is useful if you are planning to continue south on Route 5 or west on Route 2 and wish to avoid the village.

23.7 **Turn left onto Route 18S** and climb the hill. At the top of the hill (.4 mile) **take I-93 to the I-91 on ramp.** I-93 follows the St. Johnsbury–Waterford town line all the way to I-91. The first exit for Route 5 is just south of the village. *Take this exit to continue on Route 5 south.*

27.9 This is Exit I-93 onto I-91N that skirts the western side of the village. The next exit (two miles) is for Route 2W. The following exit is for St. Johnsbury Center, and it too joins Route 5N.

24.3 You'll pass by the Fairbanks Scale Company on the left. Much of the wealth and grand architecture of St. Johnsbury came from this company founded by Thaddeus Fairbanks in 1830. It was Fairbanks who invented the platform scale to weigh one of Vermont's big cash crops of the era, hemp. Fairbanks Scale grew to become one of the world's foremost companies. Today it produces electronic scales.

For the next mile the road pleasantly follows the Moose River and is free of commercial development.

25.6 The Maple Grove Museum and factory are on the left on Portland Street.

In many parts of the country the small bottles, rectangular metal cans, or plastic jugs of Vermont maple syrup offered for sale and used in restaurants have the Maple Grove label on them. Maple Grove is the world's largest producer of maple sugar candy. In this building they make three to five thousand pounds of those distinctive maple-leaf-shaped candies a day, and pack them all by hand. The machines used to make these candies date from the 1930s, illustrating that old reliable methods are sometimes best for producing a quality product. Actually, Maple Grove doesn't make maple syrup; they purchase it from Vermont farmers, then package and market it. Its successful marketing has made this product synonymous with Vermont, but only in the last century. Although the Indians, the early settlers, and the farmers of the nineteenth century made syrup and sugar for their own use, it wasn't a popular export. An enterprising salesman by the name of George Cary was successful in promoting maple sugar as a moisturizer and flavoring agent in tobacco in 1904. The production of maple candies was started by Katharine Ide Gray and her daughter Helen in 1915. It was so successful that by 1929 Maple Grove had merged with the Cary Company, and St. Johnsbury became the Maple Capital of the World.

26.1   At this traffic light, Route 2 (Portland Street) intersects Concord Avenue, which is a shortcut to Route 5N. It passes through the historical district of St. Johnsbury before joining Route 2W.

ALTERNATE ROUTE:
Concord Avenue and Main Street

Turn right onto Concord Avenue. On the left is a small park with numerous picnic tables on the grass alongside the Passumpsic River at the mouth of the Moose River. The small dams along the Passumpsic were used to power the mills of the last century.

Concord Avenue ends at Route 5 after .6 mile. Continue straight through the traffic lights and up Sand Hill to Main Street. From here at the park on the north end of Main Street it's only .4 mile to rejoin Route 2. (Main Street, as a side trip, is described traveling south to north after going through downtown.)

26.6   **Turn left** at the merging of Routes 2 and 5 onto Railroad Street in downtown St. Johnsbury.

27.1   Routes 5S and 2W divide in the downtown district, with Route 5S going straight and Route 2W turning right and up the hill as Eastern Avenue.

Turn right and climb the hill, Eastern Avenue, to Main Street.

SIDE TRIP *Historic Main Street*

0.0   The Athenaeum is located at the head of Eastern Avenue on Main Street. You can park anywhere along Main Street, but you'll probably find a space behind the fire station.

The Athenaeum, the public library, is a squat brick building crowded between the post office and the fire station. In a town of magnificent buildings it is often overlooked, but it's what's inside that captivates the eye. As you enter the building you're immediately struck by the Victorian fixtures, the spiral staircase, and the artwork in the niche under the stairs where you can read the daily newspapers. The interior is original nineteenth century with beautiful wood and ornately framed paintings on the walls.

Entering the reading room and the balconies, with their spiral staircases and whorled spindle banisters made of walnut and other hardwoods, the eye is lead past the original reading tables to the massive portrait of Horace Fairbanks in its gold-leafed frame hanging over the fireplace. Horace Fairbanks had the Athenaeum designed by John Davis Hatch, III, one of the first members of the American Institute of Architects, and built by Lambert Packard; when it was completed in 1871 Horace Fairbanks donated it to the town. One of

The frieze on the front of the Fairbanks Museum, St. Johnsbury. Representing the goddess Minerva with two students, a lion, a stork, and a crocodile, the carving was executed in Indiana limestone by F. Muer of Quincy, Massachusetts.

Vermont's great treasures lies at the far end of the reading room—the art gallery added by the Fairbanks family in 1873.

This is the oldest, unaltered, art gallery in the United States, and it was built to feature a particular painting, Albert Bierstadt's *The Domes of the Yosemite.* This dramatic landscape painting is considered by many to be the finest example of American landscape painting, My favorites are *The Views from South Mountain, in the Catskills* by Sanford Gifford, founder of Luminism, and the anonymous marble statues. Works by Thomas Waterman Wood of Montpelier, Asher Durand, the father American landscape painting, and other noted American artists crowd the walls illuminated by the central skylight. Park behind the building and take the time to make this journey into the intellectual and artistic life of the late nineteenth century.

There's more to see here: the cast-iron street clock on the corner of Main Street and Eastern Avenue once stood in Grand Central Station in New York City; in the green, on the opposite corner of Main Street and Eastern Avenue, is the Civil War monument designed by Larkin Mead and sculpted of Italian marble in Florence, Italy; in the South Congregational Church, next to the green, the stained-glass windows were made by Louis Comfort Tiffany.

0.1   The Fairbanks Museum is the red-sandstone building on the right and the North Congregational Church, made of limestone from

Inside the Fairbanks Museum, St. Johnsbury. The oak, barrel-vault ceiling of the main gallery is impressive from the vantage point of the upper balcony. The lighted cases on both the upper and lower level hold exhibits.

Isle La Mott, is on the left. Both of these buildings were built by Lambert Packard based on designs by H. H. Richardson—the North Congregational Church from a design for Trinity Church in New York.

The Fairbanks Museum of Natural History, 1896, is another gift from the Fairbanks family. When Col. Franklin Fairbanks's natural science and anthropological collections became too vast to house, he had the family architect build this beautiful museum with arched wood ceilings to showcase his exhibits in the classic style. The planetarium is impressive and intimate. This is a great place to be introduced to or reacquainted with the wonders of natural history.

0.3   The Jewett-Ide house, 1874, and the Ephraim Paddock House, 1820, are both on the right beyond the museum. The Estabrooks House, 1890, is only a couple of houses farther. These are only three of the numerous beautiful homes along this street, but they reflect three important and distinctive nineteenth-century styles.

The Jewett-Ide house is an Italianate style which, like so many of these large homes, has been altered from a one-family home to a du-

The Estabrooks House on Main Street in St. Johnsbury was designed and built by Lambert Packard.

plex. It's easy to confuse the French–Second Empire style with the Italianate style, but this house shows the starker lines and the slanted roof, two elements which distinguish it from the French style.

The Judge Ephraim Paddock's house, the first brick house built in St. Johnsbury, is a classic example of a Federal-style residence with its Palladian window over the front entrance, four chimneys, and a balustrade around the edge of the low hipped roof. The original wooden window shutters were built by a journeyman carpenter by the name of Thaddeus Fairbanks ten years before he founded the Fairbanks Scale Company.

The Estabrooks House was designed by Lambert Packard in the Queen Anne style. Notice the round turrets, fancy porch, hidden balconies, steeply pitched roof, and intriguing miniature dormer windows.

0.4 The fork in the road at Arnold Park was the site of the first frame building built in town. *The street to the right, Sand Hill, leads down to Route 5, Railroad Street, and Concord Street.*. Retrace the steps to Route 2.

The St. Johnsbury Academy is .2 mile past Eastern Avenue on the southern end of Main Street. *If you continue straight you'll pass through the St. Johnsbury Academy on South Main Street and then twist down between the hills to join Route 5S.* Thaddeus Fairbanks founded the academy in 1842. Today this private school also functions as the local high school (tuition is free to all St. J residents) and offers college preparatory and vocational courses.

Route 2W turns right and descends between the hills along Western Avenue. A motel is located on the left next to the Chamber of Commerce.

From Railroad Street to the interstate highway you travel on a ridge of sand and gravel called an esker, laid down as the last great continental glacier was melting. Eskers were formed by rivers that tunneled under the glacial ice while it was melting. This is the largest one in Vermont and New Hampshire and is twenty-four miles long. Not all of Vermont's hills are made of solid rock.

27.7 Route 2B, the old Route 2, junctions on the left. *Route 2B climbs the hill and for 3.4 miles winds and twists until it rejoins the new highway. The steep grades, sharp curves, and a narrow underpass make this a treacherous road for trucks and cars, especially in the winter.*

The modern interstate-like Route 2W continues straight. This is a fast, but boring highway. Route 2 between Montpelier and St. Johnsbury is gradually being improved, section by section, year by year. The old Route 2 was a dangerous stretch of highway and portions of it still are. Vermont's narrow twisting roads are fun, but they also demand caution.

28.3   This access onto I-91 (Exit 21) is where you would rejoin Route 2 if you used the interstate highway as a bypass around St. Johnsbury.

31.9   Route 2B joins Route 2W on the left. The mountain vistas and views into the piedmont to the south are beautiful, especially during foliage season. The mountains to the far left (southeast) are the White Mountains of New Hampshire.

34.8   The center of the village of Danville, with the beautiful green on the left, was the birthplace of the famous abolitionist Thaddeus Stevens and is now home to the American Society of Dowsers.

Dowsing—or water witching—is a technique used to find more than water. Advocates claim they can find lost articles, deposits of minerals and oil, and even answers to questions.

37.5   The junction of Route 15W is in West Danville on the edge of Joe's Pond. On the right, the Hasting General Store contains the post office in the true Vermont tradition. *To continue on Route 15W bear right. Route 15 is the major access route into the Northeast Kingdom and connects with Routes 16N, 14N-S, 12S, 100N-S, 108N-S, and finally, in Winooski, Route 2W.*

To continue on Route 2W, turn left and cross the small bridge; Joe's Pond, named after an Indian guide/scout of the Revolutionary War, will be on the right.

It's often forgotten that many Indians did not come in conflict with the white settlers who moved into the region. Joe was part of the Indian company that fought with the Green Mountain Boys against General Burgoyne. He lead the expeditions of Generals Bayley and Hazen and was highly regarded by General George Washington. He provided such valued assistance to the American cause that Vermont granted him a pension. Joe is buried in the cemetery in Newbury where his marble memorial still stands.

Between Joe's Pond and Marshfield two twisting sections of the old Route 2 are a delight but must be treated with caution.

44.0   The Marshfield reservoir is on the left. On maps you may see this listed as Molly's Falls Pond. Molly was the wife of Indian scout Joe. Interestingly enough, the waters that run into Joe's Pond flow east to the Connecticut River and Long Island Sound, but the water that runs into Molly's Pond flows north into Lake Champlain and the St. Lawrence River watershed.

45.7   On the left lies the junction of *Route 232S, which leads to Groton State Forest and Groton Lake.* From this point you descend the hill into the village of Marshfield and the Winooski River valley.

46.8 The Marshfield General Store is on the left opposite the junction *of Route 215 which leads to Cabot, where Vermont's famous premium cheddar cheese is produced.*

Just .2 mile ahead, over the rise and on the left, is Rainbow Sweets Cafe, a recommended stop for a coffee, a meal, or a pizza. You'll find several places to stay between Marshfield and Plainfield, including the Unique Cabins, the Winowaw Cabins, and the Marsh-Plain Motel.

53.7 The village of Plainfield is tucked into a narrow corner of the town of Plainfield; parts of the village are actually in the towns of North Montpelier and Marshfield. The Maple Valley Store and Deli, one of the best spots around for breakfast, is located in the town of Marshfield, on the left.

54.2 The junction of Route 214 is on the right as you're leaving Plainfield. *Route 214 from Plainfield to North Montpelier and Route 14 is two miles.* The foot path entrance to Goddard College is here; the car entrance is just up Route 214 on the left.

Goddard College was originally Goddard Seminary, 1870, located in Barre. Goddard's fame spread when it became a radical alternative college in the late 1960s, but it doesn't have many students now.

57.0 Route 14 briefly merges with Route 2 in East Montpelier at the blinking light.

Turn left, passing Dudley's General Store and the post office.

57.2 Route 14S divides from Route 2W on the left. *Route 14S leads to Barre and Route 302.* **Continue straight on Route 2W.**

After passing one of Vermont's largest RV dealerships, the road follows the river the rest of the way into Montpelier.

61.8 Route 302 merges with Route 2W at the traffic light on the outskirts of Montpelier. Route 302 is also known as the Barre-Montpelier Road and is four miles of commercial services joining the two cities. *(See Map on page 270 in the appendix.)*

Continue straight on Routes 2 and 302 to Montpelier, Exit 8 of I-89, or Route 12.

62.4 The next traffic light is at Barre Street, where a right turn will lead you to downtown Montpelier.

63.4 At the following traffic light is another steel-truss bridge, crossing the Winooski River on Granite Street. The truss bridges of Montpelier were built to replace the wooden ones washed away in the flood of 1927. During the three years following this flood, over sixteen hundred bridges were built in the state. The green-steel suspension and the concrete-span bridges are now showing the effects of almost seventy years of traffic and salt corrosion which their designers could not have conceived of. Although Vermont began to hard-surface and widen its roads for auto traffic in 1921, it was, ironically, the flood of 1927 that transformed the state's carriage tracks to highways.

Ahead you can see the gold dome of the state house.

63.7   At the third traffic light is the intersection of Route 12 and Main Street.

Turn left to go on Route 12S to Northfield.

Turn right to cross over the Winooski River and into downtown Montpelier and Route 12N to Morrisville.

Continue straight to bypass downtown on Route 2W or to access I-89.

To Bypass Downtown Montpelier

63.7   Continue straight through this and the next traffic light.

64.1   At this traffic light turn right onto Bailey Avenue. The high school will be on the left and the new Vermont Employee's Credit Union will be on the right. Cross the bridge over the Winooski River to the traffic light. **Route 2W continues on the left.**

If you continue straight, you will reach the on ramp to I-89 (Exit 8).

Downtown Montpelier

63.7   **When you cross the Winooski River,** you are on Main Street with the Grand Union supermarket on the left and Sarducci's Italian restaurant on the right.

Grab the first parking spot you find. There's public parking to the right behind the beige-brick and granite city hall and the fire department.

I recommend these Main Street restaurants: Sarducci's across from the Grand Union for dinner, Julio's across from City Hall for lunch or local atmosphere, and the Coffee Corner for breakfast anytime. However, these are not the only restaurants in town. The famous Horn of the Moon Cafe is located on Langdon Street. The New England Culinary Institute owns two local eateries as part of its renowned training programs: LaBrioche is their cafe and The Main Street Bar and Grill their restaurant.

64.3   At the traffic light (the only one downtown) **turn left to continue on Route 2W.** *Continue straight to go on Route 12N to Morrisville.* The county courthouse and the Federal building are located on the right as you drive up State Street. The Capitol Plaza Hotel and Conference Center is on the left.

From here State Street becomes the location of Vermont's government. The grand Pavilion Office Building on the right houses the governor's office, the department of taxes, the Vermont Historical Society Museum and Library, and the official state archives. Next is the small granite state library and State Supreme Court building set well back from the street. The green in front of the State House is a popular hangout on sunny days; stop here and stretch out on the grass if you've been traveling for too many hours or join in one of the numerous events, such as the Ice-Cream Social and Croquet held here during the summer. On the left is a fascinating brick building with turrets that originally housed National Life of Vermont, one of the oldest life insurance companies in the nation, founded by Julius Dewey, father of Admiral George Dewey. Also on the left is the marble building used by the Vermont Department of Transportation. The second house beyond the marble office building, a classic brick Queen–Anne-style home, was originally built for Edward Dewey in 1890 and remained in the family until sold to the State of Vermont in 1941. To make room for the marble office building, this brick house was moved 350 feet on railroad tracks and suffered only one cracked window in transit. There are plenty of other historic buildings in this city, especially along Main and Upper State Streets.

Vermont is known for its marble and granite, so it should be no surprise to see examples of this material in use along State Street. The Federal building facade is marble with green "verde antique" from Rochester. The State House, the State Library, and the Legislative Office Building are made of Barre granite. The modern office building opposite the State House is made of granite from Danville.

Before leaving the city, stop at the Vermont Department of Tourism, a small red-brick house located at 134 State Street, for any information you need.

64.8   At the traffic light, Bailey Avenue joins State Street on the left, where you would reconnect with Route 2W if you had bypassed downtown.

Route 2W continues to Burlington and on through the Champlain Islands to New York and Canada. "Route 2E: The Champlain Islands to Central Vermont" on page 218 covers the rest of Route 2 traveling from north to south and ending here, at Bailey Avenue.

ROUTE 2:

The Champlain Islands, Alburg to Burlington/ Burlington to Montpelier

Like most highways that transverse the state, Route 2 is rarely traveled end-to-end but is used sectionally. Although this is labeled as an east-west highway, in reality it has three sections: 1) Alburg to Burlington, a north-south route; 2) Burlington to Montpelier, northwest to southeast; and 3) Montpelier to New Hampshire, southwest to northeast.

I've chosen to travel Route 2 from Alburg to Burlington and from Burlington to Montpelier going from west to east, and from the Connecticut River to Montpelier in the opposite direction. Route 2 through the islands is a highway used primarily for local commerce and tourism, and many traveling cross-country enter into Vermont at Rouses Point. The highway from Burlington to Montpelier is heavily traveled by locals, tourists, and commercial traffic, but only on particular segments because the fastest way to get from Burlington to Montpelier is using I-89. Vermont's main east-west highway in the center of the state is Route 2 from Montpelier to New Hampshire and then Maine. Connecting the main highways on the eastern side of the state—Route 5 and I-91—with the network of roads in the central Vermont region—Routes 14, 12, and I-89—the traffic can often be heavy moving in either direction.

For those planning to take Route 2 to Route 7 and then down the western side of the state, or for those going from Alburg and then crossing the state on Route 15, I've indicated the mileage from Alburg to the UVM campus. For those coming across the lake on the Burlington ferry, for those who took the interstate south from Montreal, or for those who plan to spend time cruising around the Queen City, I began the second section of this highway beginning at the campus with an odometer reading of 0.0.

The Champlain Islands:Alburg to Burlington

The Champlain Islands are a summer paradise. This is a unique part of Vermont. Once primarily agricultural, it has become a summer refuge for Canadians and out-of-staters since the 1850s. The islands were a popular place to visit during Prohibition and, until the 1960s, remained the primary route into Canada. The year-round residents of the islands are on the increase again as Grand Isle becomes the outer edge of the urban expansion of Burlington.

Lake Champlain is the sixth-largest body of water in the United States. Not counting the shores of its seventy-five islands, Lake Champlain has just over 600 miles of shoreline along its 118-mile length. Besides pleasure sailing, scuba diving, sailboarding, and swimming, these waters are popular for sport fishing; salmon, lake trout, steelhead, rainbow trout, smelt, walleye pike, large and smallmouth bass, northern pike, chain pickerel, muskellunge, perch, catfish, panfish, carp, whitefish, cisco, burbot, gar, bowfin, mooneye, and the occasional sturgeon are among the fish found in the lake. There's also the lake's legendary Loch Ness monster known as Champ.

The United States Navy was founded on this lake, and famous battles of the Revolutionary War and the War of 1812 took place here. The cold dark waters of this lake have preserved many examples of early American shipbuilding including Benedict Arnold's flagship (now in the Smithsonian Institution), other warships, a horse ferry, commercial lake barges, and early steamships. Many of these are accessible to sport divers.

0.0   Route 78W junctions at Route 2 in Alburg Center. The town of Alburg is a peninsula, one of only two, that is not connected to land in the continental United States.

5.4   The junction of Route 129 is on the left in South Alburg. The town consists of one small store just before you cross the bridge over the Alburg Passage to the island of North Hero.

SIDE TRIP   *Isle La Motte—Vermont's first settlement*

Route 129 is a dead-end road leading across the peninsula and causeway onto Isle La Motte named after Captain LaMotte, who erected Fort Saint Anne at this strategic military spot in 1666, and which became the first European settlement in Vermont. The Jesuits built the Saint Anne Shrine on the site of the old fort. This was also the place where, in 1609, Samuel de Champlain first set foot on what was to become Vermont and here that vice-president Theodore Roosevelt, who spent much of his free time in Vermont, learned that President McKinley had been assassinated.

Here are found the oldest (petrified) coral reefs in the world. The dark gray "chazy" limestone of these reefs was used to build the stone houses of the islands, but was popular far from these shores. The Fisk Quarry was the first marble quarry in Vermont, and its location made shipping the limestone blocks easier than from any other quarry prior to the building of the railroads. The Brooklyn Bridge, the facade of Radio City Music Hall, and the facade of the United States Capitol were all built of stone from this island.

5.6   North Hero and all the islands are a summer paradise, with hundreds of small cabins and summer homes lining the lake. The summers are idyllic and many people come, by boat and by car, from Quebec to enjoy the cool breezes and pleasant waters. The winters are very different, when the winds sweep out of the Arctic and across Canada, unchecked by natural boundaries for thousands of miles. Notice how the top branches of the trees have been bent by the almost constant wind out of the northwest.

As you continue south, Route 2 reaches the eastern side of the island and follows the shore for miles. On the right (west) beautiful sheltered Carry Bay almost cuts the island in half, and you ride on a narrow natural causeway, then along City Bay (east) into the village of North Hero. This little strip of land was used by smugglers after the Embargo of 1807 and again during Prohibition to elude federal ships. The smugglers had small shallow boats that they would portage across on sleds or rollers, while the federal officers, in hot pursuit, had to sail south and round the end of the island. By that time the smugglers where already in St. Albans Bay.

You are now directly west of St. Albans on the mainland. Looking to the left across the lake, you see Butler, Dameas, and Knight Islands.

In late August the village of North Hero hosts the only North

American convention of bagpipe players and writers of traditional pipe music.

The islands have an eclectic mixture of small clapboard houses, limestone buildings, modern architecture, trailers, and camps. The beautiful stone buildings are made from the limestone of the region, known as chazy marble. The islands themselves are limestone, and the earliest coral reef in the world, the Chazgan Coral Reef, is exposed on Isle La Motte, where this dark gray limestone has been quarried since 1666.

13.0 The summer home of the Royal Lippizan Stallions of Austria is on the left. In July and August you can stop in to see a performance on selected days just before sunset and on weekends during the mid-afternoon. For more information check with the Chamber of Commerce.

Magnificent views of the Green Mountains are visible far across the lake.

13.7 To the left you can see Mount Mansfield, while getting occasional glimpses of the Adirondacks to the right.

14.4 Knight's Point State Park on the right at the southern end of the island of North Hero is open for picnicking and swimming only, no camping.

There's a lot of maritime history on this lake. The first American naval battle took place just to the west of here at Valcour Island in 1776, when Benedict Arnold's hastily built ships fought the advancing British fleet. Although outgunned, Arnold and his men damaged the British enough to hold off their invasion until the following year, thus gaining another winter's preparation for Vermont and the colonies.

In 1808–1809 the sidewheel steamship *Vermont,* launched for regular commercial service of freight and passengers, was the first steamship after Robert Fulton's *Clermont* to be in regular service. However, *Vermont* was far in advance of her predecessor's design and transported her passengers the length and breath of the lake in style. The last of these great steamships is the *Ticonderoga,* now exhibited in the Shelburne Museum.

In 1814 the last naval battle to be fought on this lake took place in Plattsburgh harbor, directly to the west. The United States won this extremely bloody and decisive encounter. Lake Champlain is where the U.S. Navy was born, and much of its early history was recorded here, in landlocked Vermont.

14.5 The drawbridge connecting North Hero to Grand Isle crosses a very narrow channel of water with the gut on the right (west) and the open lake on the left (east). The gut is an area between the two islands that is a double bay formed by the peninsulas of both islands. President Franklin D. Roosevelt often boasted that as a teenager he was one of only two civilians who could navigate one of the Champlain steamships through the gut. The waters moving through this small channel are fast and teem with salmon, lake trout, pike, and small and largemouth bass.

17.6   On the left is a log cabin built in 1783 and believed to be the oldest, still-standing log cabin in the United States. It remained in the Hyde family for over 150 years until it was given to the state as a historical site in the 1960s. Authentically furnished, this genuine article is a fascinating glimpse into the lifestyle of our ancestors.

19.1   On the right is the junction of Route 314 that leads west to the Grand Isle Ferry at Gordon Landing, which provides year-round service on its twelve-minute crossing to Cumberland Head, New York, and quick access to Plattsburgh, New York.

20.1   The Grand Isle State Park is located on the left. Unlike many state parks, this one is camping only.

22.2   The southern junction of Route 314 is on the right in the village of Keeler's Bay.

23.5   The village of South Hero, in the town of South Hero, is in Grand Isle County.

26.2   Apple Tree Bay is on the island side of the Sandbar Bridge and causeway. The Sandbar State Park is one of the most popular in the state for summer swimming and picnicking. The extremely shallow portion of the lake on the south side of the causeway is very popular with sailboard enthusiasts. Here the sailboards avoid boats and the choppy waters of the open lake while having plenty of maneuvering room.

After crossing the lake you enter the Sand Bar Wildlife Management Area located in the wetlands of the Lamoille River delta. The wild rice, arrowhead, and sedges in this delta attract migrating and nesting waterfowl. Wood duck, blue-winged teal, hooded merganser, great blue heron, mallards, and pintails nest in these wetlands. Virginia rail, osprey, owls, wild turkey, fox, coyotes, raccoons, porcupines, skunk, grouse, and deer all flourish in this management area.

You've now entered the township of Milton.

30.2 You're now crossing the Lamoille River. I've been lucky enough to find the multicolored hues of chalcopyrite crystals in the white rocks of the road-cut on the southwest side of the bridge.

32.1 The access to I-89 (Exit 17) is the fastest way to get to Burlington and the easiest way to bypass the congestion of Vermont's only major urban area. I frequently use this section of the interstate to bypass Burlington rather than following Route 2 through Winooski and Burlington. The interstate exits at Williston and Richmond will put you right back on Route 2.

32.4 Route 2 merges with Route 7 in Chimney Corner. *To the left Route 7N leads to the village of Milton and St. Albans.* **Turn right** and continue on Route 2E and Route 7S toward Burlington.

35.2 The junction of Route 2A is on the left. See Alternate Routes 2A-289-117 to Route 2E.

ALTERNATE ROUTE:

Route 2A to Route 289 to Route 117 to Route 2E in Richmond.

To bypass the cities of Burlington, South Burlington, Winooski, and the village of Essex Junction and access to Route 15E.

35.2 Turn left onto Route 2A at the Y. This is a very busy junction with traffic to and from the cities you're trying so hard to avoid.
Caution: You have about fifty yard's visibility looking south on Route 2 because of a small hollow. Be careful of vehicles heading north when you turn.

36.1 This is the center of the village of Colchester in the town of Colchester. Chittenden County is one of the fastest growing areas in Vermont, and in 1995 was the fourth fastest in the country. The farmland around Colchester is rapidly begin replaced by residential housing and service businesses.

38.6 Access onto Route 289S is on the left at the second set of traffic lights. **Turn left onto Route 289S.** *If you continue on Route 2A you'll enter into Essex Junction at the five corners, one of the busiest intersections in Vermont.*

Ahead on the left is Mount Mansfield and the high peak ahead on the right is Camel's Hump and in between is Bolton and Ricker Mountains.

40.4   This is the exit onto Route 15. *At the end of the exit ramp Route 15E to Jeffersonville is on the left. Essex Junction and Winooski are to the right on Route 15W.*

43.3   The junction of Route 289 is at Route 117, which is now the southern end of this bypass. The last stage to be completed will be from this point to Route 2 in Williston. **Turn left** onto Route 117 to Richmond. You're still in the town of Essex, and residential homes line the road.

44.3   Williston Road on the right leads to the village of Williston on Route 2. From here there are only a half-dozen homes and a couple of farms for the next four miles as Route 117 follows the Winooski River toward Route 2.

46.0   Barber Farm Road is a sharp Y-turn on the left that leads up to Jericho Center. On the right is a historic brick house built by the first governor of Vermont, Thomas Chittenden, in 1795.

48.5   The junction of Route 117 at Route 2 is 1.8 miles north of Richmond and just .1 mile north of the access onto I-89N (Exit 11). Camel's Hump can be seen directly ahead, beyond the interstate highway.

Route 2E: Through Winooski and Burlington

35.2   The junction of Route of 2A is on the left; **continue straight.**

36.9   This is the intersection of Route 127. *To the right leads to Malletts Bay and eventually into Burlington; to the left, Route 127 leads to Route 2A.*

38.2   You're now entering the commercial district in the town of Colchester. This area has grown in the last twenty-five years due to the easy access to I-89, the rapid growth of Chittenden County, and the increasingly important Canadian market.

38.6   You'll find a large inn and a restaurant on the left. Most of the lodging in the area is located on Williston Road, Route 2E, in

South Burlington and on Shelburne Road, Route 7S. Numerous fine restaurants are to be found from here to the south side of Burlington.

39.7 The I-89 access at Exit 16 is the last chance to opt out of the Route 2 traffic through the cities of Winooski, Burlington, and South Burlington. *You can take I-89 south to either the Williston or Richmond exits and get back on Route 2E. I-89S will also lead to I-189W to Route 7S.* You can see Mount Mansfield on the left above the suburban development. This section of road is filled with busy commercial traffic.

40.7 The intersection at the traffic light in downtown Winooski is where Routes 2E and 7S merge with Route 15. Route 15E is to the left. Routes 15W and 2S continue straight. The post office is ahead on the right and the Champlain Mill shopping complex is ahead on the left.

41.0 The Champlain Mill retail complex contains two fine restaurants, while on the right-hand side of the street you'll find a couple more.

Since the mid-1970s this old mill town has been revitalized with the growth of Chittenden County, and the old abandoned mills are being converted into offices and shops.

As you go through the series of traffic lights and cross the concrete bridge over the Winooski River **you need to position yourself in the left lane.** I recommend going up the hill to enter into Burlington, but you can take the right turn and enter Burlington on Riverside Drive also.

41.6 At the traffic light, East Avenue is on the left, and Trinity College is on the right. *East Avenue leads to Route 2E on Williston Road in .8 mile.*

To **continue on Route 2E to Route 100, Route 116, or Montpelier** without stopping in downtown Burlington, **turn left.**

To **go to downtown Burlington, to go to Route 7S, or to the ferry dock continue straight**; you'll ride past the Medical Center Hospital of Vermont and the Fleming Museum on the left.

42.0 This is the main UVM campus. On the left is the Ira Allen Chapel and next to it the gravesite of educator and philosopher John Dewey, a Burlington native who graduated from UVM before gaining worldwide acclaim and changing the nature of education in this country.

On the left is the UVM green—the heart of the UVM campus. Properly called the University of Verd Mont or University of the Green Mountains, but commonly called the University of Vermont, it was founded in 1791 by Ira Allen, who was also one of the original founders of Burlington in 1763 and who played a major role in the formation of the Republic of Vermont.

To continue on Route 2E without going downtown, turn left onto University Place, or at the traffic light on Prospect Street.

Whether you drive up University Place or Prospect Street, you will pass numerous historic buildings. The brick building next to Ira Allen Chapel is Billings Center (originally built as the UVM library), the last structure designed by Henry Hobson Richardson. The cornerstone of the fourth building on this street was laid by General Lafayette. Rarely will you see so many fine examples of the various architectural styles offered on this campus.

42.0 At the traffic light and intersection of Prospect Street with the UVM green on the left, Colchester Avenue becomes Pearl Street.

To go to Route 7S without going through downtown Burlington, turn left onto Prospect Street. *You can also go to downtown Burlington or the ferry docks by turning left onto Prospect Street.* See Route 7S, page 44 for further information on downtown Burlington, going to the ferry dock, or connecting on Route 7.

Route 2: Southwest to Montpelier

Route 2 is listed as Route 2E, but just as it is a north/south highway from Canada to Burlington, it's a northeast/southwest one from Burlington to Montpelier.

I-89 continues to parallel Route 2 all the way to Montpelier, which fortunately absorbs most of the commuter traffic. On this state highway you go through great villages, but it's much slower than the interstate.

Access to Route 2: From the King Street Ferry Dock—*for those arriving by ferry from New York.*

Leaving the ferry dock at King Street, **turn left** at the traffic light onto Battery Street. **At the next light, turn right** on Main Street and climb the hill. Three blocks, three traffic lights, and .3 mile from the ferry dock, you'll see City Hall Park on the left. The next street is Church Street, Burlington's downtown pedestrian mall. **Continue up the hill on Main Street.** At the top of the hill is the UVM campus (.7 mile). From here you can continue on Route 2E (straight), Route 2W or Route 7N (turn left), or Route 7S (turn right).

0.0 From the UVM campus to the intersection of Routes 2 and 2A in Williston is one of Vermont's largest strip developments; five miles of hotels, restaurants, fast-food eateries, business services, and commercial suppliers. The first major set of lights that you will encounter begins at East Avenue; Exit 14 of I-89 is just ahead. If you wish to avoid the next five miles of Route 2, position yourself in the middle lane, then after the next set of traffic lights by the Sheraton Conference Center, move into the right lane to enter the on-ramp for I-89S. *You can rejoin this route at either mile 5.1 (Exit 12) or 10.6 (Exit 11).*

5.1   The intersection of Routes 2 and 2A is known as Tafts Corners and is in the town of Williston, the fastest-developing area in the state of Vermont and the focus of much debate, litigation, and legislation on Vermont's development laws. *If you turn right you can gain access to I-89 (Exit 12) or follow Route 2A west to Route 116. If you turn left you will travel to Essex Junction and the five corners.*

7.3   Here you reach the center of the village of Williston. On the south side of town the highway drops down the hill and then runs across open farmland. After you cross the iron-truss bridge, be alert for turning traffic.

10.5   On the left is the junction of Route 117, the southern end of the recommended bypass around Burlington from the northern end of Route 2A in Colchester.

10.6   Exit 11 of I-89 is where most people heading south from the Champlain Islands would reconnect with Route 2. Burlington is a great place to visit, but for those who have come to Vermont to escape the urban onslaught, the stretch of I-89 from Chimney Corners to Richmond is a blessed alternative to riding through Vermont's only major city.

The gas station just beyond the I-89 on-ramp is a great place for touring groups to reorganize, especially for those coming south from the islands by the various routes through, and bypasses around, Burlington.

12.3   The only traffic light in the village of Richmond is at the four corners in the center of town. **Continue straight on Route 2.** *Turning right will lead you past the round church and over to Hinesburg and Route 116. If you should detour to visit the round church—actually it has sixteen sides—you can take the road behind the church that runs south to junction at Route 2 in Jonesville.*

> **Caution:** *Just after leaving the village and crossing over the interstate, you'll encounter a couple of very sharp downhill turns that are banked incorrectly.*

This stretch of highway, from Richmond to Jonesville, is known as Bolton Flats. Be on the lookout for moose, especially toward dusk during April and May.

Notice on the left the two very rare monitor-roofed barns—it appears that a second roof covers the ridgepole. Both barns received grants for restoration during 1997. People are beginning to acknowledge the historical significance of barns and the importance in preserving unusual styles.

15.7 You have entered Jonesville when the road passes beneath the interstate bridges.

Now the highway follows the edge of Stimson Mountain with the Winooski River on the right. From Jonesville to Waterbury you travel through the Winooski River Gap, 326 feet above sea level and by far the lowest gap crossing the Green Mountains. At the end of the Wisconsin glaciation, when Lake Champlain was over 700 feet deeper than it is now, this was a vast waterway connecting it to the interior lake of the Montpelier basin. After the glacial waters receded, it became the primary Indian route from Lake Champlain to the Connecticut River for thousands of years.

At the south end of the village of Bolton, the highway once again goes under I-89 and then cuts through the Presidential Range between Camel's Hump and Ricker Mountain. Under certain conditions the wind channeled between these mountains can attain gale force and above, a phenomenon known as a shirkshire that is sometimes seen here and in the Valley of Vermont on Route 7 near Danbury.

25.4 The merging of Route 2 and Route 100 is on the north end of the village of Waterbury. Access to I-89 (Exit 10) and Route 100N to Stowe are on the left. **Continue straight through Waterbury village.**

There's a nice inn on the right as you enter the village. Just beyond the inn is the traffic light at the corner of Stowe and Main Streets. There are several good places to eat or take a break within a few yards of the traffic light.

As you continue along Main Street you'll see a large complex of brick buildings that used to be the state mental hospital and now contains various agencies of the State of Vermont insurance company. Many of the old isolation cells used at the former state hospital still exist in the lower levels of many of these buildings. I've often wondered if they're still used occasionally to restrain stressed-out bureaucrats.

Waterbury was established by a royal charter granted by George III on June 7, 1763, but wasn't settled until James Marsh built a cabin here in 1783. It was in 1790 that the first organization of the town took place. Most towns in Vermont were established by royal charter, and most were not settled until after Vermont became an independent republic in 1776.

26.5 The division of Routes 100 and 2 takes place after crossing the Winooski River. A traditional fried-food restaurant is located on the left, and Route 100S makes a ninety-degree turn right. *Route 100S goes over the ridge and then follows the Mad River through the valley.*

You catch beautiful glimpses of the river through the trees on the left along this portion of the highway. Just before you reach Middlesex you cross an iron suspension bridge; slow down for this first corner, then restrain yourself from accelerating because you are about to pass the main barracks of the Vermont State Police.

30.5 The access to I-89 (Exit 9) is on the left.

Only .2 mile beyond the access, Camp Meade is on the right. Although it looks like a National Guard outpost, complete with tanks, a jet fighter, helicopter, and support vehicles, this motor court has become one of the most popular spots in Vermont for touring groups. One weekend the restaurant parking lot and the cabins may be filled with Gold Wings and on another with vintage Corvettes.

30.9 *Caution: The junction of Route 100B is on the right on a blind curve, the first curve past Camp Meade.*

After the S-curve you leave the village and are presented with the most pleasant five miles of road between Burlington and Montpelier. The interstate highway remains on the left and the Winooski River on the right.

The creemee stand on the right marks the beginning of the entry into Montpelier on State Street. Watch your speed, because local police with radar will often position themselves under the interstate bridge or in the cemetery.

36.8 At the first set of traffic lights in Montpelier, you need to decide whether to continue riding straight down State Street, or whether to turn right and cross the Bailey Bridge.

This is where Route 2E joins with Route 2W. *From Montpelier you can proceed south by Route 12 or Routes 302 and 14; you can go east on Routes 2 or 302; or loop back up north on Route 12 to Route 15.* See Map on page 270 in the appendix.

ROUTE 108:
Smugglers Notch

Route 108 through "The Notch" is undoubtedly Vermont's most popular road for motorcyclists. Route 108 goes from Route 100 in Stowe to Route 105 in Enosburg Falls, but the 17.5-mile portion connecting Route 100 with Route 15 in Jeffersonville is the most heavily traveled by both locals and tourists. *Caution: Don't attempt to drive your RV through this notch. The road is closed to all truck traffic. Do NOT attempt to tow a trailer through Smugglers Notch. Use Routes 100 and 15 to go around the north side of Sterling Mountain.*

If you see any snow on Mount Mansfield, please check with the tourist office or with the police to see what the road conditions are in the notch. Seasonal conditions determine when the highway is open to Jeffersonville.

0.0   In Stowe, the junction of Route 108 is in the center of the village across from the Green Mountain Inn, established in 1833. This junction has a complete stop for all traffic with each vehicle taking its turn in rotation. When it's your turn, go onto the Mountain Road.

The Mountain Road in Stowe is a commercial resort strip development filled with restaurants, motels, and shops. Some of Vermont's best restaurants and lodging will be found here. Stowe is known as the Ski Capital of the East and rightly so, but it's really a three-season resort area. Like Burlington, Stowe is a destination for Vermonters who want a night out on the town. My favorite restaurants are located on Route 108. With so many fine restaurants you'll have no trouble finding something that pleases you. Visit the Stowe Area Chamber of Commerce on Main Street to inquire about the many lodging facilities.

2.0   On the left is a turn that leads to the Trapp Family Lodge or to the village of Moscow and back to Route 100 (total, 3.8 miles) south of Stowe.

In the next mile you'll have views of the famous profile of Mount Mansfield with the nose being the predominate peak. The weather station and the summit of the Toll Road are at the base of the nose.

5.9   The Toll House is on the left. For five dollars you can take the road to the Mount Mansfield Summit Station, which is 4,062 feet above sea level and affords one of the most majestic views in all of

New England. The view from this vantage point brought visitors to Stowe in the mid-1800s—the very beginning of tourism in the state.

7.2   The Mount Mansfield State Park is on the right and the access to the Mount Mansfield ski area is on the left. This is the end of the commercial development of the Mountain Road. From here you begin to approach Smugglers Notch.

Caution: If the road barrier is in place, do not drive around it!

Smugglers Notch was believed to have started from stream erosion, but the vast glacier of the Wisconsin Ice Age forcing its way through the gap widened and deepened it. Apparently a mountain glacier remained in this bowl long after the ending of the last Ice Age, continuing to shape what is now an ideal formation for a ski resort.

Although a path lead through the notch in the late 1700s, it didn't receive much attention until it was used by smugglers during the War of 1812, hence its name. By 1894–1895, a carriage road had been built, and in 1918 it was widened to accept auto traffic; it wasn't until 1969 that the upper section of the road was paved.

In another .5 mile you begin to enter the notch. You'll see hikers' cars parked along the highway, while people climb the many trails on the mountain, including what is the most popular section of the Long Trail.

9.3   As you begin to climb the twisting corners to the top of the notch, you'll notice where rock slides from the cliffs have torn down the steep slopes in recent years. Some slides have left boulders so large that the road had to be rebuilt around them.

When you begin to move through the steep curves climbing into the notch, shift down into second gear. If the traffic on the road is heavy, shift into first and keep it there, even when you reach the top of the climb. The corners around the boulders are so sharp that the visibility in places is less than fifteen feet. Please be careful. Watch the road. Park and stroll around to look at the towering cliffs.

From the top of the notch Route 108 goes down the western side of the mountain, out of the Mount Mansfield State Forest, and past the Smugglers Notch ski area. The highway descends all the way from the notch to the village of Jeffersonville with only a couple of short, level stretches.

17.2   The center of the village of Jeffersonville, at the base of the mountain in the Lamoille Valley, in the town of Cambridge was named as a joke on Thomas Jefferson and his unpopular Embargo Act of 1807. Jeffersonville was one of the villages that actively took part in smuggling goods to Canada from 1807 to 1814. *Turn right to*

continue on Route 108, to connect to Route 109 or Route 15E (.3 mile);
continue straight to connect with Route 15W (.3 mile).

Turn right and ride down the main street of the village. There's a grocery store and bakery on this street.

I recommend going straight to Route 15 and stopping at Dana's Cupboard to pick up lunch and fuel. From there it's only .3 mile to the intersection of Routes 15 and 108.

17.5   The intersection of Routes 15 and 108 is at the Bell-Gates Lumber Company, on the left.

It seems appropriate to break Route 108 into two sections here at Jeffersonville and Route 15. Most people come through Smugglers Notch, and instead of continuing on Route 108 to Enosburg Falls ,choose one of the other routes. Route 15W leads to Route 104 (three miles) in Cambridge or on to the city of Burlington (twenty-eight miles). Route 15E leads around White Face Mountain to Route 100 (fourteen miles), or Route 12 in Morrisville and Route 14 (twenty-nine miles) in Hardwick. Route 109 leads to Route 118, which takes you either back to Route 100, north to Route 105, or over Jay Peak on Route 242. If you're going to the Burlington area, consider taking the Pleasant Valley Road that begins next to the Smugglers Notch Inn instead of Route 15W.

0.0   Continuing on Route 108 from the village of Jeffersonville at the intersection of Routes 108 and 15, you cross the bridge over the Lamoille River.

0.2   You'll find a great pull-off to the right that has picnic tables along the river. If you've picked up lunch at Dana's Cupboard, this is a good place to stop and enjoy it.

0.4   The junction of 109N is on the right. *This road goes to Montgomery Center.*

10.0   Here in the village of Bakersfield the junction of Route 36W is at the green. *Route 36W goes to Route 7 in the city of St. Albans.*

15.4   On the left is the gravel road leading to the birthplace of Chester A. Arthur, twenty-first president of the United States, from 1880 to 1884. Maintained by the Vermont Historical Society, this house is a replica of Arthur's birthplace.

17.0   This section of Route 108 is one of the best foliage routes in northern Vermont.

17.7 One of Vermont's classic round barns, in disrepair, is on the right. Round barns were popular in the late 1800s. The popular myth is that they were built in this shape so the devil couldn't get you in a corner; the reality is that they were briefly considered a modern idea in farming, but the efficiency in cleaning and feeding was offset by the cost of erecting and maintaining a structure with so much unusable space. In another twenty years, only three or four of these barns will remain, and one of them is already part of a fancy bed-and-breakfast inn.

19.1 After crossing the bridge over the Lamoille River, turn right immediately, and then it's one block, .1 mile, to the junction of Route 105.

19.2 The junction of Routes 108 and 105 is in Enosburg Falls, with the shopping area just ahead on the left on Route 105. *Continue straight on Route 105E to Route 108N and on into Canada, or turn left to travel to Lake Champlain. A great option for a day tour is to take Route 105E to Route 101, then south to Route 100S for a return to Stowe.*

ROUTE 15E:
Burlington to Jeffersonville

Burlington is due west of Danville as the crow flies. For those of us who have to follow Vermont's terrain from one side of the state to the other, it's a process of going around mountains and sort of zigzagging from west to east or vice versa. Route 15 leaves Burlington headed east, but soon has to swing north to circle around Mount Mansfield and Sterling Mountain before heading southeast along the Lamoille River Valley to Hardwick and then down to West Danville. This highway is often considered the southern boundary of the Northeast Kingdom, the rural northeastern portion of Vermont.

This highway also intersects or junctions with Routes 108, 100, 12, 14, 16, and 2. Because of the traffic patterns on this highway, I've broken this route into two sections: east from Burlington to Jeffersonville, and west from West Danville to Jeffersonville.

Access to Route 15 in Burlington

(See Map on page 268 in the appendix.)

From downtown Burlington you go up the hill on Main Street for about .7 mile. At the crest of the hill is a traffic light at the intersection of Main and South Prospect Streets. On the left is the UVM green. **Turn left** onto South Prospect Street and follow the green or take the second left onto University Place that runs parallel to it. (For more on the buildings of the UVM campus see Route 2E, page 225) Follow either street for the length of the green (.3 mile) to Colchester Avenue. **Turn right.**

0.0   The mileage begins at Colchester Avenue and University Place with the UVM green and the beautiful brick Ira Allen Chapel on the right. **Position yourself in the left-hand lane.** You'll pass the Fleming Museum and the Medical Center Hospital of Vermont on the right.

0.4   At the second traffic light, East Avenue enters from the right, and Trinity College is on the left. **Continue straight**, then down the hill to Winooski.

1.0   At the bottom of the hill the bridge goes over the falls on the Winooski River. The Champlain Mill retail complex on the right contains two fine restaurants. You'll find a jazz bar and restaurant on the left side of the street.

Ira Allen once owned all the land in this area and built a stockade fort where the bridge is located and a sawmill by the falls underneath it. Soon woolen mills were established, and Winooski became a mill town until the American Woolen Company went out of business in the 1960s. Since the mid-1970s, the old mills have been transformed into retail spaces and apartments, and the city has been revitalized as part of the growth of Chittenden County.

1.3   To continue on Route 15E, be in the right-hand lane as you approach the second set of lights past the bridge (the fourth since the foot of the hill), and turn right. To get to Routes 2W and 7N, move into the center lane as you approach the lights and then continue straight.

Continue riding through town.

1.9   The access onto I-89 is on the right; this is Exit 15, just one exit north of the Williston Road, Route 2, in Burlington. The highway now becomes four lanes.

2.2   Saint Michael's College is on the left. A few yards ahead Route 15 becomes a divided four-lane highway until entering Essex Junction.

3.4   This traffic light is for access to Vermont National Guard's Camp Johnson. Fort Ethan Allen, now UVM married housing, is on the left after the light and has never been part of Camp Johnson.

4.0   On the left is Suzie Wilson Road and a small shopping plaza.

5.0   The Champlain Valley Fairgrounds are on the left, and one of the best county fairs is held here every Labor Day. During the summer the annual hot-air balloon festival, a classic auto show, and other events are held here; check with the Chamber of Commerce or the listing of Vermont summer events published by the Vermont Department of Tourism for dates.

5.6   The five-corner intersection in downtown Essex Junction is one of the worst in the state.
Caution: As you approach it, position yourself according to the route you wish to take: the right-hand lane to turn right onto Route 2A leading to Route 2S and I-89 in Tafts Corners, Williston; the center lane to continue straight on Route 117 to the IBM plant or to Richmond and Route 2; **the left lane to continue on Route 15 ahead left** *or for a hard-left turn onto Route 2A to Milton and Route 2N.* **Continue on Route 15.**
Since the mid-1970s this town has grown, as the IBM plant has become the company's primary computer chip development facility.

7.2   This is the access onto Route 289, the bypass that connects Routes 2A, 15, and 117. Continue down this busy highway. Essex Way Shopping Center is on the right at the next set of traffic lights. The area also contains the Inn At Essex containing three of the New England Culinary Institute's eateries; the Birch Street Cafe, Butler's Restaurant, and a bakeshop.

8.7   Route 128 junctions at the traffic light; *it goes through Westford to Route 104 and is an alternate route to the village of Cambridge.* **Turn right to remain on Route 15.**
As you approach the village of Jericho you can see Mount Mansfield directly ahead and the peak of Camel's Hump on the right. This is the Presidential Range of the Green Mountains.

12.0   The Chittenden Mill—now a craft shop, gallery, and museum—is located on the left as you enter the village of Jericho. Just past the mill and the creemee stand, take a tight left-hand curve in the road. If you're a chocolate lover you might want to stop by Snowflake Chocolates and watch the process of making truffles by hand.

Wilson Bentley, also known as Snowflake Bentley, 1865 to 1931, lived on Nashville Road in Jericho. This impoverished farmer took over fifty-eight hundred photos of snowflakes using a large format camera and a homemade microscope. He proved that each snowflake is unique and symmetrical and received worldwide acclaim in the scientific community for his microphotographs.

As you leave the village, Mount Mansfield is on the right, but soon the highway heads directly toward the mountain. In the early 1970s from the small settlement of Essex Center to Underhill there were less than a dozen homes that were not part of working farms, with the exception of the village of Jericho. Chittenden County was one of the fastest-growing areas in the United States. Now the outskirts of Burlington seem to almost reach the very foot of the mountain.

14.7   This is the turn onto Pleasant Valley Road at the edge of the village.

Route 15 curves to the left, with the turn to Underhill Center appearing as a road straight ahead; there is a gas station/minimart to the left. The indications that you are approaching this turn are: 1) Mount Mansfield, which has been directly ahead of you, is now to the right, 2) you've just entered a 35 MPH speed zone, and 3) the yellow diamond-shaped sign shows a left-curving arrow with a black line to the right.

This alternate route takes you on the Pleasant Valley Road to Underhill Center and then follows the base of Mount Mansfield to Jeffersonville. Route 15 also takes you to Jeffersonville, but it's not exciting or scenic and is only .4 mile shorter. The Pleasant Valley Road is not a fast bypass, but a premium road for both touring and scenic vistas.

ALTERNATE ROUTE:
Pleasant Valley Road Underhill to Jeffersonville

14.7   You will be riding past the Underhill Elementary and the Underhill High School, both on the right. Mount Mansfield is now directly ahead of you as you travel to Underhill Center along the Pleasant Valley Road, one of the more beautiful roads in Vermont and a local favorite.

17.3 In the village of Underhill Center you have to come to a complete stop next to the general store. Continue out of the village, past the school on the left, toward the foot of Mount Mansfield.

18.5 From here to Jeffersonville you'll be skirting around the highest mountain in Vermont. As you drive through the woods you'll catch occasional glimpses of the mountain. The road is nice and twisty, going up and down small hills and past interesting houses; then you break out of the woods on a rise and see the beautiful farming valley ahead and the mountain rising above you.

24.0 At the end of Pleasant Valley the road comes to a T. The road to the left is the Lower Valley Road that goes to Route 15 in Cambridge. **Turn right** and climb over the foot of the mountain.

28.2 The road junctions at Route 108 in Jeffersonville. The Smugglers Notch Inn is on the left and the Second Congregational United Church of Christ is directly ahead. This is downtown Jeffersonville. *If you turn left, you'll see Route 15 directly ahead .2 mile and can rejoin it at 27.7 miles. If you turn right you'll travel on Route 108 up the mountain, through Smugglers Notch, and down into Stowe and Route 100.*

15.3 If you missed the turn to Underhill Center and the alternate route, you can take the road on the right, at the small green in the village of Underhill Flats. Once you leave the village, the highway is rather boring until you reach Cambridge.

For a few miles the highway is posted for moose, and the extensive beaver pond at the base of Metcalf Hill provides an ideal habitat for these and other creatures.

24.7 On the left is the junction of Route 104 that *goes over to Fairfax and St. Albans (twenty-two miles) following the Lamoille River.*

25.3 The village of Cambridge is in the town of Cambridge. On the right is Cambridge Village Market and just past it you'll find Lower Valley Road that goes to the Pleasant Valley Road. As you leave the village and cross the Lamoille River, be prepared for a ninety-degree turn right at the end of the bridge.

27.7 The intersection of Route 108 is in Jeffersonville. On the left is a restaurant and Jana's Cupboard Delicatessen & Bakery. Stop and pick up lunch or just coffee and pastries. If you're out driving or just riding around enjoying the day, this is the place to decide where to go from here. It's also an excellent place to regroup if you're part of a tour.

Alternate Routes: Route 108 over Smugglers Notch to Stowe and Route 100; Route 108 to Enosburg Falls and Route 105; and Route 109 to Route 118 to Route 242 to Jay. Route 15 will intersect Routes 100, 12, and 16 before ending at Route 2.

ROUTE 15W:
West Danville to Jeffersonville

For people coming from New Hampshire or eastern Vermont, Route 15 is the easiest way to reach the north-central part of the state. It connects the St. Johnsbury area with Hardwick, Morrisville, and Johnson; used in combination with other roads, it's the quickest way to Stowe, St. Albans, or Montreal. This highway connects with so many others that it is ideal as part of a day tour of the Northeast Kingdom.

0.0   The eastern end of Route 15 begins in West Danville at Route 2 and Joe's Pond, which is named after a famous Indian scout who lived here and fought with the Green Mountain Boys against the British at the Battle of Bennington. Joe aided General Jacob Bayley in the creation of the Bayley-Hazen military road and was highly regarded by George Washington. His contributions to the Republic of Vermont were recognized, and he was awarded a pension, a rare honor.

3.5   The Walden General Store is on the right with the parking/picnic area on the left. The brook cascades down over the rocks at the far end of the picnic area.

5.4   Here you get your first good view of the mountains ahead.

5.5   The junction of Route 125 is on the left next to the Walden fire station. *Route 125 goes through Cabot and junctions at Route 2 in Marshfield.*

Descending from Walden you have a spectacular panoramic view of Vermont's northern mountains. Spruce Mountain in Plainfield, the cone-shaped peak on the left, is part of the Vermont Piedmont; the northern Green Mountains are to the right; the Worcester Range, Presidential Range, and Lowell Mountains lie in between.

7.8   On the left is a road that will take you to Cabot.

10.3   The junction of Route 16N is on the right a couple of miles east of Hardwick. *Route 16 goes to Barton and ends on the north shore of Lake Willoughby at Route 5A.*

12.4   The only motel in Hardwick is on the right at the edge of the village.

12.7   Route 15W merges with Route 14N at the blinking light in downtown Hardwick. **Turn right** to continue on Routes 15W and 14N. *If you continue straight you'll be heading toward Barre and Montpelier.* You drive through the commercial portion of Hardwick, past the car dealerships and other services.

Fallen on hard times since the granite industry moved to Barre, Hardwick used to be the largest granite center in the world in the 1870s. The stone was quarried on top of the mountain in Woodbury and transported, first by sled with mules and oxen and later by railroad, down the grade where Route 14 now runs, to the finishing sheds on the Lamoille River.

At the end of July this village plays host to the Old-Time Fiddler's Contest.

13.8   Here is the division of Routes 14N and 15W. **Continue straight on Route 15W.** *Route 14 turns right and goes north to Newport.* From here to the next town, the small family farm becomes the predominate feature of the upper Lamoille River Valley.

16.7   On the left, the Fisher Bridge, now a Vermont historical site, was built in 1908 and is the last railroad covered bridge still in use in Vermont and the only one in the United States with its original cupola, designed to allow the smoke to escape as the steam engine passed through.

18.9   Wolcott was named after one of the lesser-known signers of the Declaration of Independence, Oliver Wolcott.

23.4   When you reach the Mountain View Campground you get your first glimpse of Elmore Mountain.

Mount Mansfield and Sterling Mountain are the rugged peaks you see as you approach Morrisville.

24.8   Route 15A on the left leads into Morrisville and junctions at Route 12 only a couple of hundred yards from Route 100S. If you plan to go to Stowe, take this road rather than the intersection of Routes 15 and 100.

26.5 At the traffic light Route 100 merges with Route 15. **Continue straight on Routes 100N and 15W.** *Route 100S goes into Morrisville and the northern end of Route 12, then to Stowe.* The large filling station on the far left has a wide selection of coffees.

26.7 The Charlemont Restaurant and the Sunset Motel are on the right.

You can see Morristown on the left and two of the mountains of the Sterling Range—Morse (3,380 feet) and White Face (3,715 feet). The names and listings of Vermont's mountains can be confusing. The Sterling Range is a series of peaks that are part of the Green Mountain Range—Spruce, Madonna, Morse, Sterling, and White Face—lying between Mount Mansfield and the Lamoille Valley.

28.3 At the blinking light Route 100N turns to the right and **Route 15W continues straight.** The highway is relatively straight and open as it follows the Lamoille River northeast to Johnson. Just prior to entering the village of Johnson the road twists and turns as it descends down a small gulf.

32.8 There's a corner store on the right at the junction of Route 100C in the village of Johnson.

Just past the junction is the Johnson Woolen Mills Factory Outlet. The Johnson Woolen Mills were once world famous, especially for their red-plaid hunting jackets. This is also the home of Johnson College, a state school.

The summer events held in Johnson include the PRCA annual rodeo, the Lamoille County Field Days, and the locally popular Johnson Mud Races. For the more culturally inclined, the Burklyn Ballet Theater has performances staged by American and European masters from early July to early August.

41.3 There's a motel on the left as you approach the village of Jeffersonville.

41.8 The intersection of Route 108 is on the edge of the village of Jeffersonville adjacent to the Bell-Gates Lumber Company. *Route 108N (on the right) leads to Enosburg Falls, while Route 108S (on the left) goes into the village and up the mountain, through Smugglers Notch, and down into Stowe.*

42.1 On the left is a second access to the village and Route 108. On the right is Jana's Cupboard where I ended Route 15E from Burlington.

Jeffersonville is a village in the town of Cambridge. The naming of the village and the pass through the mountains (Smugglers Notch) came in response to the smuggling activities of Vermonters after the unpopular enactment of the Embargo Act of 1807. Many Vermonters opposed President Jefferson's policies, and the smuggling of cattle and supplies to British Canada continued until the British attacked Plattsburgh in 1814, when popular opinion quickly reversed itself. Thus, this village was named as a statement of political defiance—a Yankee in-joke.

ROUTE 109:
Jeffersonville

This route is short and sweet with plenty of curves, valleys, and mountain views. The drawback is that there are few places to pass, and if you get stuck behind a school bus or a farm tractor, you may find yourself following them for miles. This highway will take you to Route 118, where you can go south to Route 100 or north to Route 242 going over Jay Peak.

0.0 Start at the intersection of Routes 15 and 108 in Jefferson-ville. If you are on Route 15, turn onto Route 108N. If you are on Route 108 coming from the village of Jeffersonville, the lumberyard is on the left; continue straight. You'll immediately cross the bridge over the Lamoille River.

0.2 There is a great pull-off to the right with picnic tables along the river. If you've picked up lunch at Dana's Cupboard, this is a good place to stop and enjoy it.

0.4 The junction of 109N is on the right. *Route 108 continues north to Enosburg Falls (nineteen miles) and Route 105.*
Turn right.
The Lamoille River is now on the right. The road twists and turns with ups and downs as it follows the river. Residential houses and old farmsteads are situated along this great touring road—a fun drive and extremely scenic. The road leaves the river, and when the highway crosses the next one, you'll be following the North Branch Lamoille River.

In the small village of Waterville, the river cascades over the rocks on the left.

8.5   You now see great cascades on the North Branch Lamoille River as the river rushes down from higher in the mountains. This is a excellent stream for trout fishing.

11.0   In Belvidere Center, Tallman's [general] store is on the left. You continue to climb in elevation to reach the upper plateau.

14.3   Ahead you may be able to see a light-gray hill sitting on the side of Belvidere Mountain (3,360 feet). This light-gray material is the tailings, or waste, from the Vermont Asbestos Company's mine. (To dispel a misconception, only the short-fiber and crushed/powdered forms of asbestos are dangerous. The long, fibrous crystals that were mined here have not caused asbestosis.)

At one time this quarry produced over 60 percent of all asbestos mined in the United States. The mine is also a famous mineral collecting site, world known for its rare green uvarovite garnets. Aragonite, magnetite, green diopside, and vesuvianite are other crystals I've collected here. Besides the rare green garnets, a collector can find hessonite (orange grossular) and red (pyro-almandine) garnets.

The Vermont state gemstone is hessonite garnet, and it was a faceted gem from this location that helped convince the legislature to pass a resolution making it so.

15.0   Route 109 ends at Route 118 in the Averys Gore Wildlife Management Area, and the vast marshlands ahead, as well as the North Branch of the Lamoille River, are fed from Long Pond.

Route 118S

15.0   Turn right to go to Route 100.

16.0   Long Pond on the left is prime moose habitat, and there's plenty of other wildlife here in the Averys Gore Wildlife Management Area. In another mile Route 118 crosses the Long Trail. As you continue south you'll see a beautiful panorama of the Worcester and Presidential Ranges.

21.6   Route 118 junctions at Route 100. *You can go north to Newport or turn right and follow Route 100 to Morrisville and Stowe. Route 109 combined with Routes 118, 100, and 108 make an exceptionally nice day tour.*

Route 118N

15.0 Turn left to go to **Montgomery Center and Route 242,** another pleasant road with a gradually widening valley and open farmland.

23.0 The junction of Route 242 is on the right in the village of Montgomery Center. *You can take this superb mountain road or continue north on Route 118 to Route 105 in East Berkshire. Route 58 also junctions on the right, and this gravel road goes through Hazen Notch to Route 100 in Lowell.*

Route 242 is one of the highways favored by motorcyclists. Taking this road over the shoulder of Jay Peak, riders generally go north on Route 101, then west on Route 105, before returning to Jeffersonville on Route 108 south. Those touring in RVs will have a more enjoyable time continuing north on Route 118 to Route 105; Route 58 is beautiful, but I don't recommend it for motorcycles or RVs.

ROUTE 114:
Lyndonville to the Forty-Fifth Parallel

This road is for those who wish to escape the crowds. North of the village of Island Pond, Route 114 goes through Warren's Gore (population, 2), adjacent to Averys Gore (population, 0), Averill (population, 7), and the township of Norton (population, 169). You'll get few scenic views, and this highway is not the best way to get to Quebec City. However, if you're looking for a road you haven't been on before or just want to get away from it all for a few hours, this may be just what you want.

0.0 The junction of Route 114 is on the right across from a motel on the northern outskirts of Lyndonville. The road quickly becomes an old-fashioned, narrow Vermont-state highway with grasses and wildflowers growing through the pavement cracks on the nonexistent shoulders. You can see Burke Mountain directly ahead.

3.2   You follow the East Branch Passumpsic River, past small residential homes, cornfields, and woods.

3.9   There's a convenient turnoff on the right.

4.1   Entering the town of East Burke you'll see Bailey's Country Store. This small pleasant village is in contrast to the commercial ski villages of southern Vermont. As you leave the village, the turn to Burke Mountain ski area is on the right.

4.8   The highway immediately opens up as you pass the playing field and cemetery. The twisting road follows the brown rust-colored brook, and posted yellow signs warn of moose. There are a few scattered dwellings, no open vistas, and hardly any traffic for mile after mile. Route 114 travels through the townships of East Haven and Newark. Densely populated in comparison to other townships in the Northeast Kingdom, these two towns have over seventy-five acres per person.

20.7   The road comes to a T as it merges with Route 105. **Continue right.**

21.8   You enter into Island Pond on Derby Street. This village in the town of Brighton is so named because of the twenty-two-acre island in the middle of the six-hundred-acre pond. I'm certain that more people have heard of Rudy Vallee than of this village where he was born.

22.7   As you approach the center of the village, there's a motel on the right with the lake behind it, and on the opposite side of the street you'll find the restored hotel.

22.8   The separation of Routes 114 and 105 is downtown. Route 105 continues to the right. **Turn left onto Pherrins Street.** If you take a hard right it will lead you to the village beach.

The wonderful depot building, now a division office of the Canadian National Railway, reflects on the days when this town was the headquarters of the Grand Trunk Railroad. Island Pond is the commercial center for hundreds of square miles of northeastern Vermont. You'd better fill the gas tank and get something to eat if you're continuing north.

25.5   The junction of Route 111 is on the left. *Route 111 leads to Derby Center and connects with Routes 105 and 5. This is the best route*

Two bull moose, their antlers still buds covered with velvet, browse alongside Route 9 in Searsburg.

to take if you plan on entering Canada. If you're on a day tour, it's your last chance to circle back toward western or central Vermont.

Route 114 now heads north through a vast wilderness.

27.5 The highway sign may say Narrow Bridge, but you're about to go through a narrow underpass. There's a nice turnoff on the right just beyond the underpass. Highway signs warn of moose. Almost any low-lying area in the Northeast Kingdom will be cedar swamp, an environment where moose thrive, which the highway follows from here to Norton Pond.

This highway follows the western edge of the Northeastern Highlands. In this region the soil is not very deep and quite acidic. Bedrock is solid granite, formed as part of the upwelling of magma that produced the White Mountains of New Hampshire. The shallow soil and the granite bedrock hold the runoff from rain and snow in shallow depressions. Without drainage these shallow wetlands become more and more acidic and result in bogs and cedar swamps. On the hillsides softwoods predominate; therefore, it's interesting that the highway is lined by deciduous trees such as maple and birch.

30.8 You're in Warren Gore when you get your first glimpse of Norton Pond. A gore is a parcel of land that technically is part of a nonadjacent township. This seven-thousand-plus acre of land, with a population of two, is technically part of the town of Warren in central Vermont.

33.0 This is the only good view of the pond from the highway.

38.1 The Norton Country Store is on the left as you enter the village of Norton. The buildings are somewhat scattered, and this does not feel like a village, but rather as somewhat of an outpost. Of the 178 people who live in the township of Norton, 169 of them reside in the villages of Norton and Averill.

Norton is above the forty-fifth parallel and directly on the U.S.–Canadian border. You are now halfway between the equator and the North Pole.

38.8 The junction of Route 147, into Canada, is on the left. This border crossing is primarily used by Canadian tourists going to the beaches of Maine and Americans going to the Canadian Maritimes. It's off the beaten track, and commercial traffic is rare here.

41.3 The highway continues east, weaving back and forth across the forty-fifth parallel. The road passes under the electric lines that bring Canadian hydroelectric power from James Bay into the United States. The woods are a mix of deciduous and softwoods, tending toward scrub.

42.6 On the right is Little Averill Road, which follows the edge of Great Averill Pond to Little Averill Pond.

45.1 This is one of the few scenic views in this area.

46.8 Wallace Pond is in the town of Canaan. If names like Island Pond and Beecher Falls sound familiar, it might be because you've read the novels of Frank Mosher. This area is the setting for *Northern Borders* and *A Stranger in the Kingdom*.

47.2 You'll find a motel and cabins on the right. There are numerous summer cottages around this pond, and the U.S.– Canadian border runs through the center of this small body of water.

51.2 The junction of Route 141 to the Canadian border is on the left.

52.2 In the village of Canaan you'll find a four-way intersection.

On the left Route 253 goes to Beecher Falls and the point of entry into Canada. This border crossing is closed to commercial traffic. Route 114 continues straight for a few hundred yards, crossing the Connecticut River to Route 3 in West Stewartstown, New Hampshire. Route 102S begins on the right.

ROUTE 102S:
Canaan to Route 2

Route 102S and Route 3 in New Hampshire are the only roads in the area that take you south.

0.0   The four corners in the village of Canaan are the northernmost end of Route 102. Route 3 in New Hampshire follows the eastern side of the Connecticut River valley, while Route 102 goes south on the western side.

0.8   Leaving the village behind, the land feels different from what you've been traveling through. There are more farms, a mix of soft and hardwoods, the land is rolling, and the road twists and turns as it follows the edge of the valley. This is the Northern Highlands, but the river has deposited soil along its banks for thousands of years, and the ecosystem is quite different from the land just a couple of miles west.

5.4   Occasionally an open stretch allows views of the mountains ahead. This highway follows the early dirt tracks, built in the days when roads followed the contours of the land.

7.9   The first view of the Connecticut River comes as you approach the junction of New Hampshire Route 26. *Route 26 intersects Route 3 in Colebrook, New Hampshire, and continues southeast, cutting across northern New Hampshire to junction at Route 2 in Bethel, Maine. This is the road to take if you're going to either northern Maine or its coast.* The river is rather shallow this far north. The mountain rising up on the right is Mount Monadnock.

12.3   The Columbia covered bridge connects Route 102 with Route 3. Bridges of this type used to span the river from Canaan to Brattleboro, but now few remain. As you continue down the Connecticut River Valley, you get glimpses of the White Mountains in New Hampshire.

20.9   The junction of Route 105 is in Bloomfield. There's a gas station, convenience store, and restaurant in the building at this junction. *On the left the bridge crosses the river to North Stratford. Route 105W leads to Island Pond, Newport, and eventually St. Albans. As the main east-west highway across the northern part of Vermont, it connects with numerous north-south routes, including Routes 14, 100, 7, and 2.*

Continue straight, go under the narrow underpass, and follow the Connecticut River south. The highway still varies from sections that are straight and languid to those filled with sharp corners that twist along the edge of the valley. You have the sensation of always traveling downhill mile after mile. Occasionally there are breaks in the trees to the left, where you can see the river and the White Mountains of New Hampshire where Mount Washington is the prominent peak.

This part of Vermont is wilderness. The land to the right (west) has no villages or settlements and, except for access to Maidstone State Park, no roads. Geologically this is part of the White Mountains, solid granite that has been scraped and gouged by the four great glaciations of the past. The ecosystem in most of the Northern Highlands is the Northern Boreal Forest. Only in the Connecticut River Valley does the flora resemble other habitats in the state.

36.5   The village of Guildhall is where Route 102 makes a wide turn around the large, empty green and the Essex County Courthouse. Essex County isn't even close to the town or village of Essex and is another example of how confusing place names can be in Vermont. Guildhall has the recognition of being the only town bearing that name in the United States.

From here to Route 2, the highway is generally straight and flat, with small farms and few scenic views.

42.1   Looking south (left) the White Mountains and Mount Washington are clearly visible.

43.6   Route 102 ends at Route 2 by the steel bridge leading over the river into Lancaster, New Hampshire.

Continue straight on Route 2W. *Turning left will take you on Route 2E through the White Mountains and into Maine.*

ROUTE 16N:
In the Northeast Kingdom

lthough Route 16 intersects Route 15 east of the village of Hardwick, the most scenic way to reach it is by traveling over the hills through the village of Greensboro. Route 16 is less than thirty miles in length and mainly used to connect the village of Barton with Hardwick. On this route you'll be traveling in the Northeast Kingdom, an area roughly defined as being east of Route 100 and north of Route 15. Senator George Aiken is credited with coining this phrase for this region, and all agree that this rural, independent corner of the state holds the last vestiges of the traditional Vermont lifestyle.

To Route 16 Through Greensboro

0.0   The blinking stoplight marks the merging of Routes 14 and 15 in the village of Hardwick. **Continue straight through the light into downtown.**

During the middle of the 1800s, this town was the Granite Capital of the World. The quarries were actually in Woodbury, and the teams of oxen or mules, and later the railroad, would haul the stone blocks to the finishing sheds in town. When Barre began to eclipse Hardwick in granite production during the 1880s, most of the companies and workers just moved to central Vermont. As late as 1895 there were still seventeen firms quarrying, polishing, and working marble and granite in the village.

0.1   In downtown Hardwick a cafe is on the left. *If you continue straight on Route 15E, you'll reach the junction of Route 16 (2.3 miles) and finally the junction of Route 15 (12.6 miles) at Route 2 in West Danville.*
Turn left and cross the bridge. Proceed one block (.1 mile) to the intersection; the beautiful red-brick library is on the left, and the stone municipal building/police department is on the right.
Turn right and continue down Maple Street. The street turns to the left, you cross the railroad tracks, and then go up the hill.

1.7   After you crest the hill, this road, Center Road, continues through farmland, with vistas of rolling mountains on the right. This road is relatively straight but undulates as it travels over the rolling landscape.

As you enter Greensboro and coast down the hill into town, you'll see Caspian Lake on the left. This 790-acre lake is very cold and exceptionally clean—you can drink the water directly from the lake—which makes it ideal for lake trout.

The population of this quiet mountain resort town increases substantially during the summer months. Chief Justice William Rehnquist and author Sig Longren are two of the town's better-known residents, but John Gunther and Wallace Stegner used to summer in this village and Laura H. Wild, Ann Stoddard, and Silas Mason were born here.

6.6   Willey's Store, on the right at the bottom of the hill, is sort of an icon—the modern general store carrying groceries, hardware, clothing, household utensils, and more. This is the village center, and the access to the public beach is to the left, next to the Miller's Thumb. **Continue right around Willey's Store for one block, then turn right onto the Garvin Hill Road at the post office.** Garvin Hill Road becomes the Bend Road as it takes you through the woods and gradually decreases in altitude. Just before you reach Greensboro Bend and the intersection with Route 16, the road twists and turns down a steep hill passing the church on the left.

9.3   The junction of the Bend Road with Route 16 is at the bottom of the hill. Directly ahead is the Stannard Mountain Road leading into Greensboro Bend.

Caution: There is usually sand at this junction.
Turn left onto Route 16N.

Route 16N

0.0   The junction of Route 16 at Route 15 is 2.3 miles east of the village of Hardwick. For those in a hurry it's actually quicker to ride from Hardwick to the beginning of Route 16 rather than going over the hill to Greensboro, and if you're coming from points west, this is the obvious choice.

As you turn onto Route 16 you cross a bridge over the Haynesville Brook, but the brook the highway follows north is the upper reaches of the Lamoille River. The soil of this region and the short growing season make dairy farming the only viable agricultural option. The land seems sparse, even in the summer, compared to southern or western Vermont.

4.7   On the left is the junction of the Bend Road coming from Greensboro, while on the right is the Stannard Mountain Road, which leads you through Greensboro Bend and the village of Stannard.

Spruce, balsam, and tamarack trees become more prominent as you travel north among the rolling hills of the northern piedmont. You'll see more cedar swamps and beaver ponds along the highway. This is the southern edge of the Northern Boreal Forest habitat.

10.4   Horse Pond is on the left. This is moose country so be extra cautious around dusk.

After passing Horse Pond you'll see an area of cattails on the left, and you may notice a granite historic site marker for Runaway Pond. In 1810, when the flow of water was critically important for the powering of any type of mill, a group of men decided to change the outlet of Long Pond so its waters would flow down toward Clark's Pond and the Barton River. They succeeded in constructing the ditch to direct the new stream, but when they breached the banks of this pond, the ground turned out to be quicksand and Long Pond began to move. In fifteen minutes two square miles of water rushed northward, a tidal wave sixty-feet high rushed through the villages of Glover and Barton. The pond never refilled, and this swampy area has been known as Runaway Pond ever since.

12.5   Clark's Pond is on the left.

15.8   The junction of Route 122 is on the right next to the cemetery. Route 122 leads east to Lyndonville and the Bread and Puppet Museum is located a short distance down this road.

17.2   In the village of Glover, Currier's Market and Country Store is on the left.

Glover is best known for the Bread and Puppet Theater. Peter Schumann brought his radical religious-political puppet theater from New York City to Vermont in 1970. Finding fertile ground in the creative anarchy of Plainfield's Goddard College community, the Bread and Puppet Theater became world famous with its giant puppets and neo-Medieval imagery. In 1974 the greatly expanded theater troupe moved to their base in Glover. Every year the Bread and Puppet Summer Pageant is held in this village, and for that weekend, people from Vermont, from all over the United States, and even from Europe converge on Glover for a spectacle that can't be replicated by television or the printed page.

19.3   Here's an access onto I-91 (Exit 25).

20.3   The village of Barton (population, 908) is in the town of

Barton. The architecture facing the green will take you back to the turn of the last century. *If you continue straight on Route 5N you'll come to the village of Orleans, also in the town of Barton.*

At the green take a hard U-turn right onto combined Routes 5S and 16N. After a couple of hundred yards, the routes divide, with Route 5S heading south to Lyndonville and along Crystal Lake. **Turn left** on Route 16, cross the railroad tracks, and climb the hill.

20.9   Crystal Lake, visible on the right as you continue to climb the mountain, is 778 acres in size and much prized for its rainbow trout.

23.9   Once again you crest a mountain ridge and begin to descend into the next valley.

27.5   The north shore of Lake Willoughby is the place to stop, park, and take a break or a swim. From the north shore you have a great view of this glacial lake looking south, with Mount Pisgah (2,751 feet) to the left and Mount Hor (2,500 feet) to the right.

This lake is extremely popular with Vermont scuba divers. Since Lake Willoughby is a thousand feet above sea level, a depth gauge doesn't accurately indicate how deep a diver is. As a result, this location is used as a training ground for adjusting the navy decompression tables and depth-gauge readings. The underwater terrain is magnificent, as the cliffs and boulder- strewn hillsides continue into the lake's depths.

This lake is also known for its record-sized lake trout. If you stop into any store in the area, you'll probably see photos of the huge fish people have caught here.

27.6   Route 16 ends at the junction of Route 5A. Be careful here, especially on a summer day. For safety I usually stay to the right of the traffic island (as if I were going south on Route 5A), and then turn left to continue north on 5A. You can consider taking a short drive along the shore of the lake and the cliffs of Mount Pisgah to the south shore and back. *Turning left on Route 5A leads north to Routes 58, 111, and 105. Route 5A south meets Route 5 in West Burke.*

ROUTE 58W:
Lake Willoughby to the Green Mountains

The eastern end of Route 103 junctions at Route 5A, only 1.3 miles north of the junction of Route 16 at Lake Willoughby. This road climbs over the mountain ridges and intersects the north-south routes that follow the valleys northward. This road has interesting villages, beautiful farmland, and magnificent mountain views.

0.0   The junction of Route 58 is on the left; **turn left** and follow it west.

The view from the crest of the first ridge is magnificent. Looking back you can see the gap between Mount Pisgah and Mount Hor in which Lake Willoughby rests. Ahead, the predominate mountain is Jay Peak.

2.6   The Evansville Trading Post, on the right in Evansville, is a good stop to get gasoline or diesel, to return your bottles and cans, to rent a video, or to buy this week's groceries. You can also select a handgun, rifle, shotgun, and a full range of hunting gear. A great selection of boots, moccasins, plaid coats, duck pants, tackle, rods, reels, and other outdoor accessories is stocked here. Perhaps you just need a nut and bolt, a screwdriver, or other hardware. I'm sure you can find it here. Need a car battery? How about a handmade gift to send back home? This is a real trading post, the kind of store that is almost extinct in the lower forty-eight states.

Evansville is in the town of Brownington, and with only 705 people in the township, it averages out to 26.5 acres for every man, woman, and child.

In late August the Abnaki Indians hold their international, intertribal powwow in Evansville, and many of the events are open to the public.

6.5   The village of Orleans, with a population of 806, is in the town of Barton.

As you leave downtown Orleans, the Ethan Allen Furniture factory is on the left.

7.0   On the western side of the village Route 5S is on the left, immediately followed by the Exit 26 access ramps onto I-91; Routes 5N and 58W briefly merge.

7.5 **After going under the I-91 bridges, turn left onto Route 58W.** *Route 5N continues straight. Route 5N will take you to the junction of Routes 14 and 5 in Coventry and then into the city of Newport.* Climb the hill and wind your way over to Irasburg.

10.8 Irasburg is one of three Vermont towns named after Ira Allen, one of the leaders of Vermont's independence movement, founder of UVM, and early land speculator. Route 58W briefly merges with Route 14N at the green. **Turn right.**

11.0 Route 58W divides from Route 14N outside of Irasburg. **Turn left.** As you cross the valley you pass a round barn, one of the few left in Vermont and one of only a couple still used for their original purpose. You then climb another ridge.

15.3 Once again, upon cresting a ridge you're presented with a spectacular panoramic view of the northern Green Mountains. Jay Peak is the prominent peak ahead, and the notch off to the right is the distinctive glacial gap along Route 105 between Newport Center and North Troy. The view stretches north into Canada.

20.2 The village of Lowell is where Route 58 intersects Route 100. Although Route 58 continues straight, it turns to gravel outside of the village. This portion of Route 58 is part of the Bayley-Hazen Military Road, built in 1779 by Jacob Bayley as a strategic military road to Canada. It travels through Hazen Notch and the Hazen Notch State Park to Route 118 in Montgomery Center. This is a beautiful scenic ride.

ROUTES 105 AND 111:
East from Newport to the Connecticut River

This is the most scenic of the three eastern routes to the Connecticut River, and combined with Route 102, the only way to loop south to the White Mountains of New Hampshire. It's also one of two routes to St. Johnsbury. This shows you a different part of Vermont, the Northern Boreal Forest. Although you can travel on Route 105E all the way to Bloomfield, Route 111 is much more scenic and offers more possibilities for the photographer.

0.0   The mileage begins on West Main Street at the bridge on the southern end of Lake Memphremagog in downtown Newport. Cross over the bridge, on East Main Street, and **continue on combined Routes 5 and 105.**

After crossing the bridge you'll find Waterfront Plaza with a Grand Union on the left. On the right is public Gardner Park, where the Clyde River empties into the lake. Consider picking up lunch at the Grand Union deli and eating it on the shore of the lake behind the parking lot. It's not fancy, but it's the best access to the lake you'll find.

0.5   At the blinking light you have the option of continuing straight or turning right onto Route 191. *If you turn onto Route 191 you will travel for one block to Western Avenue (where you can turn left at the light and travel another block to link up with Route 5) and continue straight on Route 191 for about 2.3 miles to I-91. Turn left onto I-91 north and travel for one exit (2.4 miles), and turn back onto Route 5 (4.7 miles total). This would be a good idea at the end of a business work day or if traffic was especially heavy even though Route 5N is shorter.*

Continue straight on combined Routes 5 and 105. This is a busy commercial street with local service industries. After about 1.5 miles you'll encounter motels and restaurants, including the Miss Newport Diner, servicing this busy interstate access. Make sure you tank up with gas here before going to Canada or east into the Northeast Kingdom.

3.2   The I-91 exit has a couple of large service stations that offer another chance to pick up something to eat along your trek into the remote northeastern corner of Vermont.

4.5   In the village of Derby Center the road forms a reverse Y with Route 5N continuing straight. There's a corner market and a gas station on the right, a restaurant across the street, and the Border Motel, overlooking an elk farm, just ahead on Route 5N.

Turn right onto Routes 5A and 105E.

5.0   In the village you quickly reach the junction of Route 111 where you **turn left.**

This is a fast-moving country road that twists and rolls through farmland. The deciduous trees provide brilliant foliage in the fall.

Route 105E also goes to Island Pond (we're just taking a more scenic highway), while Route 5A goes south to Lake Willoughby and Route 16.

10.7   In Morgan you get glimpses of part of Seymour Lake from your vantage point above the lake.

12.9   On the shores of Seymour Lake is the village of Morgan Center. Like many of these northern lakes, this one offers remarkable fishing. The seventeen hundred-plus-acre lake is home to brook, brown, and lake trout plus landlocked salmon.

19.5   **Route 111 ends. Turn right onto Route 114S** and continue toward Island Pond. *Route 114N leads to Norton and the port of entry into Canada before continuing along the Vermont-Canadian border to the town of Canaan.*

22.2   The center of Island Pond village has a confusing junction with Routes 105W and 114S on the right. If you go straight you will end up at the municipal beach on the shores of Island Pond.

Turn left toward the stone railroad depot to go on Route 105E. As you climb up the overpass and cross the railroad tracks, you get a nice view of the lake to the right, including the twenty-two-acre island for which it was named.

This used to be the headquarters of the Grand Trunk Railway, but now is a division of the Canadian National Railway. The village remains the commercial center for hundreds of square miles of the northeast Vermont.

The highway runs through the heart of the Northeast Kingdom and Vermont's boreal forest, where thousands of acres of bogs and dozens of small ponds and lakes in these remote woods create an ideal habitat for moose and other wildlife. You'll see plenty of road signs warning you of moose because there are more moose than people in this very rural area. Route 105E travels through the township of Ferdinand, a township of 33,792 acres and a population of 23 people. The townships and gores to the north—Warners Grant, Warren Gore, Averys Gore, Lewis, Averill, and Norton—with total of approximately 100,000 acres and a population of 178 people are even more remote, especially considering that 169 live in the villages of Norton and Averill. Most of this land is owned by the lumber companies and pulp mills. There is considerable lumber and logging truck traffic on this highway, and log trucks have the legal right-of-way.

38.2   Route 105E ends at the intersection of Route 102N-S in

Bloomfield. The only gas station and restaurant in the area are located at this junction. *Continuing straight will take you over the bridge that crosses the Connecticut River and onto Route 3 in New Hampshire. Turning right on Route 102S leads to Route 2; to the left Route 102N goes north to Quebec.*

ROUTE 105W:

Newport to St. Albans

R oute 105, the primary east-west route across the northern part of the state, is in many places within five miles of the U.S.–Canadian border. This is one of the best foliage routes in the fall and contains some of the fastest, most open stretches of touring road in the state. It also connects several highways and enables one to plan several day tours in northeastern Vermont.

0.0   The end of Route 100 junctions with Route 105 on the western outskirts of Newport. Coming from Newport, Route 100S continues straight at the bottom of the hill; Route 105W turns right. Coming from Routes 14N and 100N turn left to continue on Route 105 without going into Newport.

Hilliker's store is on the left, and directly ahead you see the northern end of the Green Mountains to the west.

1.9   From the village of Newport Center you have spectacular views of the mountains. To the left is the prominent mountain of Jay Peak. Route 105W will go over the western shoulder of that mountain. Numerous large farms ringed in by the mountains are visible from this vantage point.

The effects of the last great glaciation (Wisconsin) is evident in the shaping of the mountains to the right (northwest). This entire bowl was once a great inland sea as the last glacier receded. At one point, water from the Atlantic Ocean was able to fill this depression and the entire Lake Champlain Valley. The weight of the glacier was so great that the earth's crust sagged, allowing the ocean to enter from the St. Lawrence Valley. After the glacier fully retreated, the land rose again cutting off access to the ocean.

To Big Falls (1.4 miles)

This is the place to take a break from a long day of riding. I recommend a picnic on the rocks overlooking the gorge and, weather permitting, a swim in one of the upper pools. If you're just touring northern Vermont, a few pictures of Big Falls are a must.

As you begin the long descent into North Troy, look for River Falls Road on the left.

Caution: This is a hidden, reverse Y, and a sharp left turn onto a gravel road.

Continue along the road, through a farm, and back into the woods. As the road climbs up the hill and into the woods, look for a turnoff into the pines on the right at 8.6 miles where you'll find a beautiful series of pools, waterfalls, and cascades in a gorge on the Missisquoi River. Big Falls is one of the highest waterfalls in the state.

7.2   On Route 105W you continue descending the hill and cross the Missisquoi River into the village. The Missisquoi River is the watershed for the eastern as well as the western side of the northern Green Mountains. One branch of the river actually begins in Hazen Notch, but instead of flowing down the western side of the notch, these waters flow east, then north into Canada, rounding the northern end of the Green Mountains before beginning the westward journey to Lake Champlain.

8.0   In the village of North Troy, on the right, is the junction of Route 243N that leads into Canada. The village of North Troy abuts the border of the United States and Canada. **Continue straight on Route 105W.**

8.2   At this junction going right will lead you to Route 243N. This is the beginning of Route 101S. **Turn left** to follow combined Routes 101S and 105W.

10.2   This is where Routes 101S and 105W divide.

Route 101S leads to Route 242W, a fantastic drive, and to Route 100. At this point you can consider taking Route 101E to Route 242E, then Route 118S to Route 109 to Jeffersonville (a beautiful trip). From Jeffersonville you can go to Stowe or Burlington.

Turn right on Route 105W. From the junction you begin to climb into the mountains and the deciduous forest. This twelve-mile stretch of major foliage-touring highway runs over the most northern gap and the last peaks in the Green Mountains. This relatively wide road has some great curves as it twists up through the gap and down the western side. Route 105 has no towns, villages, or even homes until you reach Stevens Mill and the junction of Route 105A.

22.7   This is the junction of Route 105A that goes north for two miles to the Canadian border and the village of East Richford. Here Route 105W again meets the Missisquoi River and follows it with the twists, curves, ups and downs typical of a river road. The Missisquoi River has brown, brook, and rainbow trout here in its upper reaches. You might even hook a landlocked salmon.

25.7   Here is the village of Richford.

26.2   This is the junction of Route 139N; **turning right on Route 139 leads to downtown Richford and into Quebec, Canada.**
   Turn left and continue on Route 105W along the Missisquoi Valley. The road remains fairly straight as it travels along this broad valley. The Green Mountains can be seen off to the left.

30.7   In East Berkshire the junction of Route 118S is on the left. Many people doing a day trip take a loop around Jay Peak. *Route 118S on the left leads to Route 242 in Montgomery Center; Route 242 is a great drive over Jay Peak and junctions with Route 101; Route 101 can take you north back to Route 105 or south to Route 100. Route 118S also will take you to Route 109 leading to Jeffersonville, and Route 100 in Eden.*
   Continue straight on Route 105W.

36.2   You are in the village of Enosburg Falls. Susan Mills, founder of Mills College in California, and Larry Gardner of the Boston Red Sox are two of the famous natives of this village.

36.6   The junction of Route 108N is on the right. Just past the shopping area straight ahead, you'll find the junction of Route 108S leading to Jeffersonville, Route 15, and continuing over Smugglers Notch into Stowe and Route 100.

39.1   On the right is the junction of *Route 236 that leads to Lake Carmi State Park, and it junctions with Route 120 in the village of East Franklin. You can take Route 236 north to Route 120, travel around Lake Carmi, and then south back to Route 105.*

41.1   The junction of Route 120 is on the right.

43.3   The junction of Route 78W is on the right in Sheldon Junction. *Route 78 is the best route to take if you're planning to go to 1) Montreal, Canada, (2) northern New York, or (3) the Champlain Islands.*

44.9   You are now in the village of Sheldon. Crossing over the Missisquoi River you have a panoramic view of Jay Peak, the Cold Hollow Mountains, and other peaks of the Green Mountains off to the left.

This was the site of the first Fenian Raid in 1866. The large group of several thousand Irishmen, members of the Irish Revolutionary Brotherhood (Fenians), planned on invading Canada and creating an Irish Free State. The group came from Boston to St. Albans by train and then began advancing on Canada. Although some made it to Canada, most made it only as far as here before being dispersed peacefully by federal troops. There is a Vermont historic site marker on the bridge crossing the Missisquoi River.

The road rolls over and meanders through the low hills and farmlands as you continue west.

52.2   The junction of Route 104 is on the left. *Route 104 bypasses St. Albans and leads to Fairfax to end at Route 15 in Cambridge (18.5 miles).* In .3 mile farther you ride across a bridge crossing over I-89.

52.9   As you go down the hill you'll see, ahead to the west, magnificent views of Lake Champlain, the upper Champlain Valley, and New York state toward Plattsburgh.

53.5   Route 105 ends at Route 7 on the northern edge of the city of St. Albans. *Route 7N leads to Swanton and Canada; Route 7S goes through downtown St. Albans and south to Burlington.*

ROUTE 104:
Cambridge to St. Albans

I n the 1950s there were more than five hundred working farms in the Lamoille Valley; now there are only eighty-seven. The small family farm is struggling in Vermont, and one of the new approaches to keep them alive is to offer farm vacations and tours. The Boyden dairy farm, located at the junction of Routes 104 and 15, is one of these working family farms open to the public.

0.0   The junction of Routes 104W and 15 is on the eastern edge of the village of Cambridge. From Cambridge to Fairfax the highway follows this agricultural valley along the Lamoille River. Fields of corn raised on the fertile bottomlands along the river support the herds of dairy cattle that are the primary occupation of this area.

6.4   On the left is the junction of Route 128 that leads over through Westford to Essex and junctions with Route 15 in Essex Center.

6.8   When you cross the Lamoille River you enter into the village of Fairfax. The road turns to the left by the post office and continues up the hill, leaving the river valley behind. From here Route 104 curves and rolls over the uneven landscape. This is still farm country, but not as fertile as the bottomlands you've just traveled through.

7.0   The junction of Route 104A is on the left. *Route 104A goes back to the Lamoille River and follows it east to Route 7 in the town of Georgia.*

9.5   The Maple Grove campground is on the right.

As you approach North Fairfax, you'll see what looks like a white golf ball on the crest of a hill ahead. This is the U.S. military radar complex on Believe Hill outside of St. Albans. You'll enter another of those listed, but nonexistent villages, North Fairfax, then make a turn to the west and pass the St. Albans reservoir. From here you'll begin the descent into the Champlain Valley.

14.7   A minimart is on the left, while ahead is a magnificent vista of Lake Champlain and the upper Champlain Valley. Continuing down the hill, under the I-89 bridges, the highway then curves to the north and follows the base of the mountain, Believe Hill, to the right. This mountain is on the Hinesburg Fault, which runs from Bristol in the south to Canada in the north. Along this fault line, the older metamorphic rocks of the Green Mountains have been pushed westward up and over the younger sedimentary rock of the Champlain Valley.

16.9   The radar complex on the crest of the hill to the right is the one you saw as you were approaching North Fairfax while on the other side of the mountain. It's my understanding that this military installation is part of NORAD and was used in support of the Plattsburgh Air Base to the west.

17.9 An access onto I-89 (Exit 19) is on the right. *To go to St. Albans and Route 7, turn left* on the St. Albans State Highway.

Continue straight on Route 104, skirting around the eastern edge of the city of St. Albans.

18.6 The intersection of Route 36 has a blinking traffic light. *Turning left on Route 36W, Fairfield Street, brings you to St. Albans and Route 7.*

As you approach the end of Route 104, you'll get spectacular views of the upper Lake Champlain and broad Champlain Valley. Looking west across to New York state, you can see the ending of the Adirondack Mountains and the broad sweep of the land far into Canada. Farm silos dot the landscape, as this is the most fertile land in the state, as well as having a slightly longer growing season due to the lake effect.

At the turn of the century, St. Albans had the largest dairy creamery in the world. The Franklin County Creamery had the capacity of twenty-five thousand pounds of milk a day, according to an advertisement in Walton's Vermont Register and Business Directory of 1895. The lush pastures of the upper Champlain Valley encouraged the growth of Vermont's dairy industry, but it was St. Albans as a railroad center that enabled the creamery to become the largest in the world.

20.4 The end of Route 104 is at the junction of Route 105. *Ahead Route 105E leads to Enosburg Falls, while to the left, Route 105W takes you to Route 7 on the northern city limits of St. Albans.*

ROUTE 78W:
Sheldon Junction to Swanton

This is the best route to take if you're riding west across northern Vermont on Route 105 and are planning to go to: 1) Montreal, Canada, (2) northern New York, or (3) the Champlain Islands.

0.0 The junction of Route 78 and the Country Motel are on the right in Sheldon Junction.

2.8 The village of East Highgate is along a beautiful stretch of the Missisquoi River. In the village the S-turn is tight, so be cautious.

6.7 In Highgate Center the junction of Route 207N is on the right, and the junction of Route 207S is a block farther on the left. *Route 207N leads to Canada through the farmland of Highgate; Route 207S leads to the north side of St. Albans.*

Six thousand years ago native people had built permanent settlements along the Missisquoi River between Highgate and Swanton. During that era the shoreline of the lake was farther westward, so these Woodland peoples were living in an area rich in game and fish; later Woodland-period sites (850 B.P.) provide us with evidence of early cultivation of maize and grain. During the mid-eighteenth century, when white settlers were beginning to venture into this area, the Abnaki Indians had a large village on the Missisquoi Bay. Today most of Vermont's Abnaki Indians still reside in Swanton and Highgate.

10.0 You are entering into Swanton when you go under the I-89 bridges. Swanton has a population of about 5,600 and is only 155 feet above sea level.

Swanton is known for its red "marble" and lime works. From the late 1700s until about thirty years ago, the limestone of this area was crushed, roasted, and turned into the finest quicklime in the United States. Quicklime is the primary ingredient in plaster, cement, and whitewash, but is also used to neutralize acid soil, as an medicinal antacid, and as a water softener. It's used in the production of glass, leather tanning, and sugar refining and as a filler in paint and paper. The beautiful red and tan "marble" of the region is actually a dolomite and was mined for use as tile and for facades.

10.9 The Swanton green is directly ahead where Route 78 meets Route 7. *Turn right to continue on Route 78W or Route 7N or turn left to go south on Route 7 to St. Albans.*

11.0 At the north end of the green in Swanton you'll see Route 7N continuing on the right and Route 78W continuing on the left.

Turn left at the end of the green and you'll cross the Missisquoi River after .2 mile. The junction of Route 36S is on the left, .1 mile beyond the bridge. There is a large grain elevator at the junction, but despite the signs, it's not clear that this is the northern end of Route 36. *Route 36 follows the lake south to the city of St. Albans.*

You quickly leave the village of Swanton and find yourself traveling along the Missisquoi River going west to Lake Champlain.

13.5 You don't travel very far east before you enter the Missisquoi National Wildlife Refuge, the only national wildlife refuge in Vermont.

You are on the delta of the Missisquoi River as Route 78 follows along the main channel of the river. This area is a refuge for migratory birds in the spring and fall, as well as the northern nesting area for a number of species. Shad Island, at the mouth of the Missisquoi, is the site of one of the largest blue heron rookeries in the northeast. This refuge is also the nesting grounds of the American bittern, the common snipe, wood ducks, pintails, mallards, the common goldeneye, the hooded merganser, blue-winged and green-winged teal, the northern harrier, and numerous songbirds. You might spot any number of raptors in this area, including the osprey. Of course, there are also otter, muskrat, beaver, skunk, fox, deer, and probably moose in this area.

You'll find numerous pull-offs on the right along the river used for canoe and boat launching, fishing, and just taking a break. This is a popular fishing area for northern and walleyed pike, large and smallmouth bass, perch, and pickerel.

17.2 This bridge takes you across Lake Champlain from West Swanton to East Alburg. The township of Alburg is a peninsula with Lake Champlain on three sides and its northern boundary being the United States–Canadian border.

22.0 Route 78W junctions at Route 2 in Alburg Center. *If you turn right Route 2 will lead you across the bridge at Rouses Point and into New York. Turning right will lead you south on Route 2E through the islands to Milton and the Burlington area.*

Maps

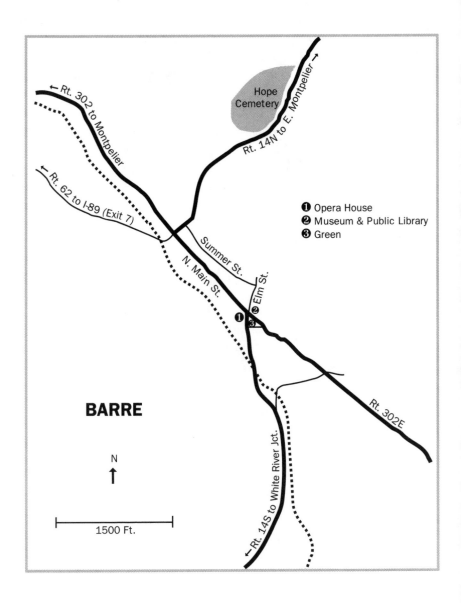

← Rt. 302 to Montpelier

← Rt. 62 to I-89 (Exit 7)

Rt. 14N to E. Montpelier →

Hope Cemetery

Summer St.

N. Main St.

Elm St.

❶ Opera House
❷ Museum & Public Library
❸ Green

❶❷❸

Rt. 302E

BARRE

N
↑

Rt. 14S to White River Jct.

1500 Ft.

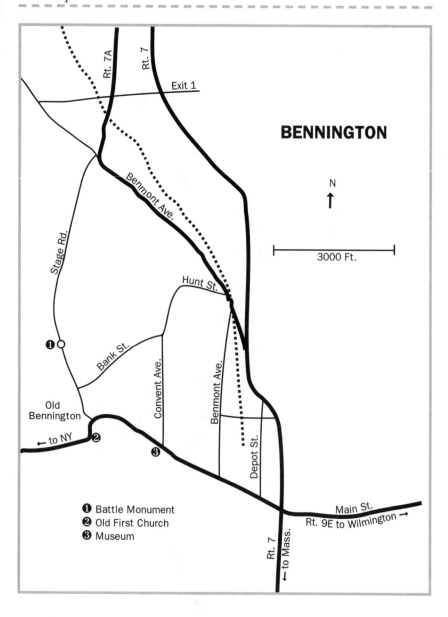

BENNINGTON

N

3000 Ft.

Rt. 7A
Rt. 7
Exit 1
Benmont Ave.
Stage Rd.
Hunt St.
Bank St.
Convent Ave.
Benmont Ave.
Depot St.
Old Bennington
← to NY
Main St.
Rt. 9E to Wilmington →
Rt. 7
← to Mass.

❶ Battle Monument
❷ Old First Church
❸ Museum

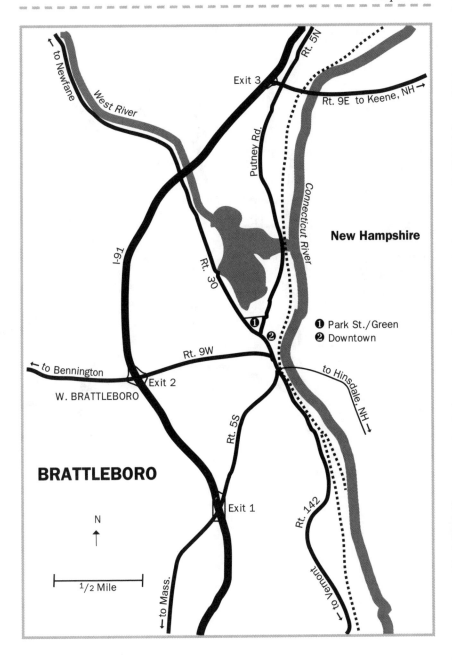

to Newfane

West River

to Keene, NH →

Rt. 5N

Exit 3

Rt. 9E

Putney Rd.

Connecticut River

New Hampshire

I-91

Rt. 30

❶ Park St./Green
❷ Downtown

❶
❷

← to Bennington

Rt. 9W

Exit 2

to Hinsdale, NH →

W. BRATTLEBORO

Rt. 5S

BRATTLEBORO

N

Exit 1

Rt. 142

½ Mile

to Mass. ←

to Vermont ←

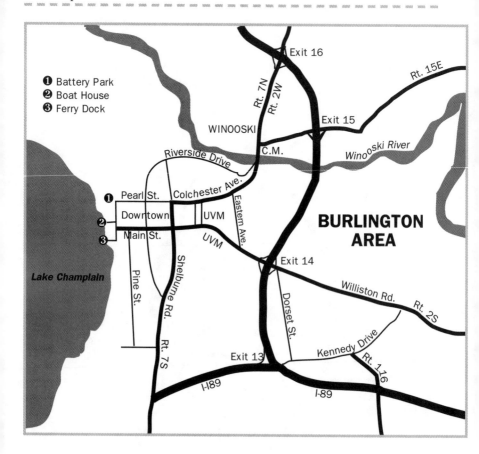

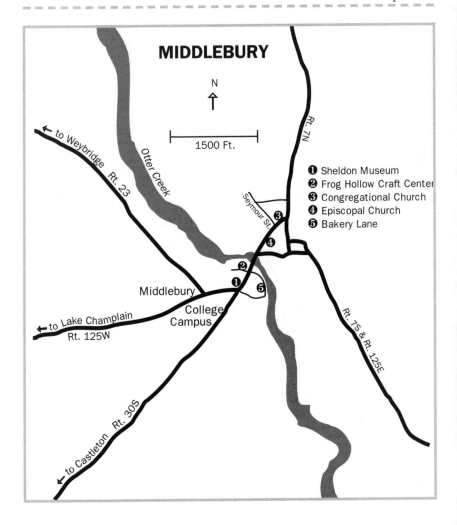

MIDDLEBURY

N

1500 Ft.

to Weybridge Rt. 23

Otter Creek

Seymour St.

Rt. 7N

❶ Sheldon Museum
❷ Frog Hollow Craft Center
❸ Congregational Church
❹ Episcopal Church
❺ Bakery Lane

Middlebury
College
Campus

to Lake Champlain
Rt. 125W

to Castleton Rt. 30S

Rt. 7S & Rt. 125E

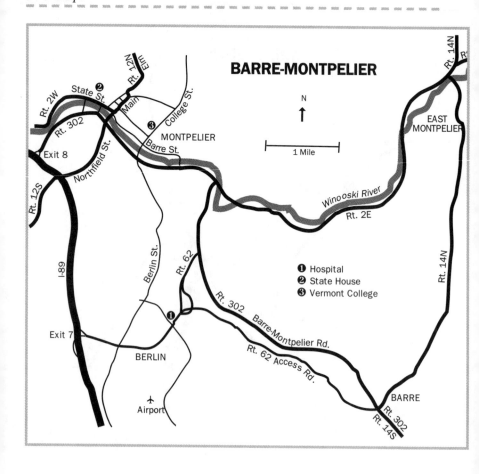

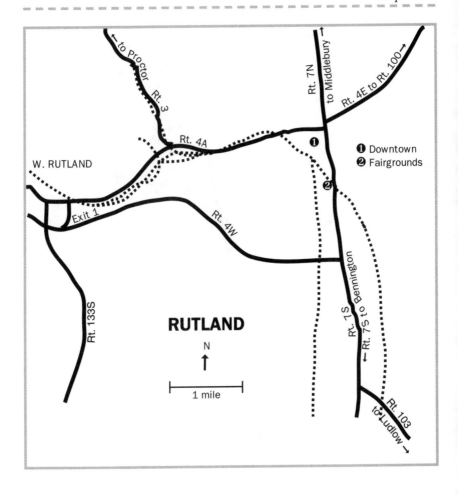

RUTLAND

N

↑

|—— 1 mile ——|

❶ Downtown
❷ Fairgrounds

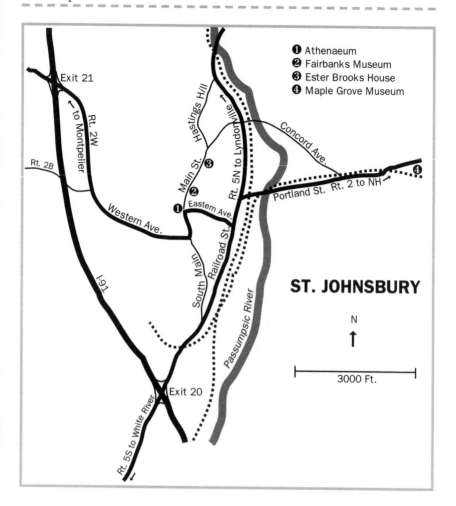

❶ Athenaeum
❷ Fairbanks Museum
❸ Ester Brooks House
❹ Maple Grove Museum

Exit 21

Rt. 2W to Montpelier

Rt. 2B

Hastings Hill

Main St.

Rt. 5N to Lyndonville

Concord Ave.

Western Ave.

Eastern Ave.

Portland St. Rt. 2 to NH

South Main

Railroad St.

Passumpsic River

I-91

Exit 20

Rt. 5S to White River

ST. JOHNSBURY

N
↑

3000 Ft.

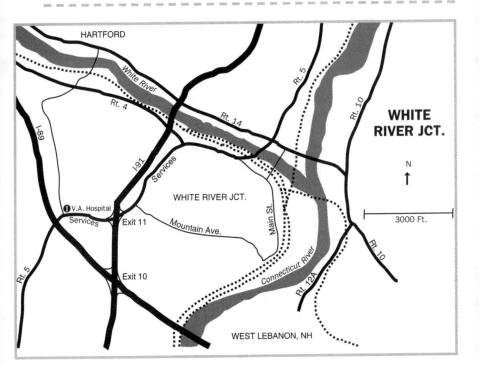

HARTFORD

White River

Rt. 4

Rt. 14

Rt. 5

Rt. 10

WHITE RIVER JCT.

N

3000 Ft.

I-89

I-91

Services

WHITE RIVER JCT.

ⓘ V.A. Hospital

Services

Exit 11

Mountain Ave.

Main St.

Connecticut River

Rt. 10

Rt. 5

Exit 10

Rt. 12A

WEST LEBANON, NH

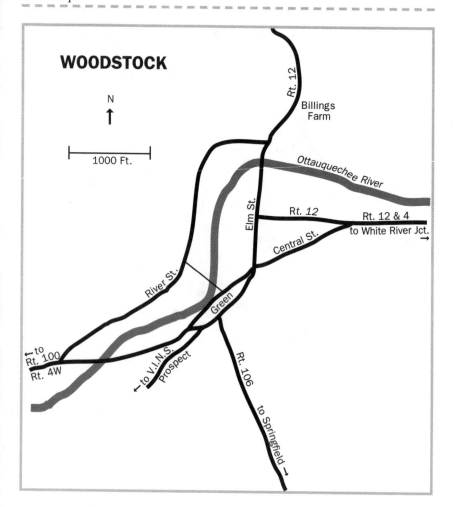

WOODSTOCK

N

1000 Ft.

Rt. 12

Billings
Farm

Ottauquechee River

Elm St.

Rt. 12

Rt. 12 & 4

to White River Jct.

Central St.

River St.

Green

←to
Rt. 100

Rt. 4W

to V.I.N.S.

Prospect

Rt. 106

to Springfield

Appendix

Available Information

Vermont Attractions Map and Guide (free)
The Vermont Attractions Association
PO Box 1284, Montpelier, VT 05601

Vermont Official State Map (free)
The Vermont Travel Division
134 State Street, Montpelier, VT 05602

Vermont Guide to Fishing Map (free)
Vermont Fish & Wildlife Department
103 South Main Street
Waterbury, VT 05671-0501

Antiquing in Vermont (free, SASE #10)
Jim Harley
RR1 Box 155, Reading, VT 05609

Guide to Vermont Historic Sites (free)
VT Division for Historic Preservation
135 State St, Montpelier, VT 05633

Vermont Campgrounds (free)
The Vermont Travel Division
134 State Street, Montpelier, VT 05602
(Lists both private and state campgrounds)

Vermont State Parks: Fee Schedule and Camping Reservation
Application
Vermont Agency of Natural Resources
Department of Forest, Parks, and Recreation
103 South Main St., Waterbury, VT 05671-0603

Bicycle Vermont Map and Guide ($2.95)
Backcountry Publications
PO Box 175, Woodstock, VT 05091

Lake Champlain Ferries
Lake Champlain Transportation Company
King Street Dock, Burlington, VT 05401
(schedules and fees)
Vermont Project Directory (free)
The Nature Conservancy
27 State Street, Montpelier, VT 05602
(listing of preserves open to the public)

Back Road Bike Tours: A Guide to Day Trips in Central Vermont (free)
Central Vermont Chamber of Commerce
P.O. Box 336, Barre, VT 05641

Vermont Country Inns and B&Bs (free)
Vermont Chamber of Commerce
P.O. Box 37, Montpelier, VT 05601

There are guides, flyers, and brochures for just about everything Vermont has to offer. Most of these can be obtained at the Vermont Welcome Centers, the local and regional Chamber of Commerce offices, or the Vermont Travel Division.

Some Vermont Chamber of Commerce Offices

Brattleboro Area Chamber of Commerce
180 Main Street
Brattleboro, VT 05301

Mt. Snow Valley Region Chamber of Commerce
Main Street, Page House
P.O. Box 3
Wilmington, VT 05363

Bennington Area Chamber of Commerce
Veterans Memorial Drive
Bennington, VT 05201

Manchester & the Mountains Chamber of Commerce
RR2, Box 3451
2 Main Street
Manchester Center, VT 05255

Great Falls Regional Chamber of Commerce
55 Village Square
P.O. Box 554
Bellows Falls, VT 05101

Chester Chamber of Commerce
P.O. Box 623
Chester, VT 05143

Springfield Chamber of Commerce
14 Clinton Street
Springfield, VT 05156

Ludlow Area Chamber of Commerce
P.O. Box 333
Okemo Marketplace Clock Tower
Ludlow, VT 05149

Upper Valley Chamber of Commerce
P.O. Box 697
15 Main Street, Suite 311
White River Junction, VT 05001

Woodstock Area Chamber of Commerce
4 Central Street
P.O. Box 486
Woodstock, VT 05091

Rutland Region Chamber of Commerce
256 North Main Street
Rutland, VT 05701

Addison County Chamber of Commerce
2 Court Street
Middlebury, VT 05753

Central Vermont Chamber of Commerce
P.O. Box 336
Beaulieu Place, Stewart Road
Barre, VT 05641

Sugarbush Chamber of Commerce
Rt. 100, Village Square
P.O. Box 173
Waitsfield, VT 05673

Stowe Area Association
Main Street
P.O. Box 1320
Stowe, VT 05672

Northeast Kingdom Chamber of Commerce
30 Western Avenue
St. Johnsbury, VT 05819

Lake Champlain Regional Chamber of Commerce
60 Main Street, Suite 100
Burlington, VT 05401-8418

There are also smaller offices located throughout the state: Arlington; Barton; Brandon; Bristol; East Burke; Cavendish; Danville; Dorset; Fair Haven; Hardwick; Island Pond; Jay; Killington; North Hero; Lake Willoughby; Morrisville; Londonderry; Lyndonville; Northfield; Poultney; Randolph; Rochester; Jeffersonville; St. Albans; Swanton; Vergennes; Montpelier; Newport; Waterbury; Wells River; and Weston.

Bibliography

200 Years of Soot and Sweat: The History and Archeology of Vermont's Iron, Charcoal, and Lime Industries, Victor R. Rolando, Vermont Archeological Society, 1992

A Second Walk Through Montpelier, Montpelier Heritage Group, Montpelier, VT, 1976

Days of Old: The History of the Wiley's and Other Early Settlers of Saxons River, Vermont 1783–1850, compiled by Ruth M. Buxton, A.G. Press, Bellows Falls, 1980

Full Duty, Vermonters in the Civil War, Howard Coffin, The Countryman Press, Inc., Woodstock, VT, 1993

Gazetteer of Vermont Heritage, The National Survey, Chester, VT, 1976

Historic Vermont: A Guide to its Historic Sites and its Roadside Markers, ed. Earle W. Newton, The Historic Stites Commission, State of Vermont, Montpelier, ?

History of Stowe to 1869, Mrs. M. N. Wilkins, Mrs. A.M. Hemenway–Stowe Historical Society, Stowe, VT, 1987

History of the Town of Grafton 1754-1975 and Sidelights On Grafton History, Grafton Historical Society, Grafton Historical Society, Grafton, n.d.

History of the Town of Rockingham, Including the Villages of Bellows Falls, Saxtons River, Rockingham, Cambridgeport, and Bartonsville 1907–1957, Mrs. Frances Stockwell Lovell and Mr. Leverett C. Lovell, published by the Town, Bellows Falls, VT, 1958

Journal of Vermont Archaeology Vol. 1, 1994, Vt. Archaeological Society, 1994

Lake Champlain Key to Liberty, Ralph Nading Hill, The Countryman Press, Woodstock, VT, 1985

Mineral Collecting in Vermont, Raymond W. Grant, Vermont Geological Survey, Department of Water Resources, Montpelier, VT, 1968

Norwich University: The One Hundredth Anniversary of Its Founding 1819–1919, Edit: Centennial Committee, Norwich University, Northfield, 1920

Roadside Geology of Vermont and New Hampshire, Bradford B. Van Diver, Mountain Press Publishing Co., Missoula, 1987

The Century Book of Facts, Edit: Henry W. Ruoff M.A. D.C.L., The Kings-Richardson Co. Springfield, MA, 1903

The Connecticut River Valley in Southern Vermont and New Hampshire, Lyman S. Hayes, The Tuttle Co., Marble City Press, Rutland, 1929

The Nature of Vermont: Introduction and Guide to a New England Environment, Charles W. Johnson, University Press of New England, Hanover, NH, 1980

The Vermont Quiz Book, Frank Bryan and Melissa Lee Gryan, The New England Press, Shelburne, VT, 1986

Vermont Historic Architecture, A Second Celebration, photos by Sanders H. Milens, compiled by Paul A. Bruhn, Preservation Trust of Vermont, 1985

Vermont Mines and Mineral Localities, Philip Morrill and Robert G. Chaffee, Dartmouth College Museum, Hanover NH, 1964

Vermont Wildlife Viewing Guide, Cindy Kilgore Brown, Falcon Press Publishing, Helena, MT, 1994

The Vermont Weather Book, David M. Ludlum, Vermont Historical Society, Montpelier, Vt., 1985

Vermont's Granite Railroads, The Montpelier & Wells River and the Barre & Chelsea, Robert C. Jones, Whitney J. Maxfield, William G. Gove, Pruett Publishing Co., Boulder, CO, 1985

Walton's Vermont Register and Business Directory for 1895, Home Publishing Co., Burlington, VT, 1895 [ed. Yes, eighteen ninety five]

What Style Is It? : A Guide to American Architecture, John C. Poppeliers, S. Allen Chambers, Jr., Nancy B. Schwartz, Preservation Press, 1983

Index

More good reading from Down East Books

If you enjoyed *Touring Vermont's Scenic Roads*, you'll want to know about these other Down East titles:

VERMONT: *A View From Above*, by Charles Feil. Aerial photographer Charles Feil captures Vermont's beauty from a unique perspective in this collection of one hundred color photographs of the Green Mountain State as seen from the air. Feil combines superb photographic and piloting skills with a keen eye for the artistic as he takes us over rolling green farmlands, through steep mountain passes, and above picturesque villages in a scenic tribute to every part of the state in all seasons. 0-89272-458-7

***Maine's Most Scenic Roads*,** by John Gibson. Much of Maine's beautiful scenery is off the state's heavily traveled highways. Here is a selection of twenty-five of Maine's most scenic, pleasurable, and spectacular drives in all areas of the state. Some are loop routes, while others are point-to-point. Each can be worked into a larger itinerary. Thorough directions and easy-to-follow maps ensure that you can relax and enjoy the view. 0-89272-422-6

***The Park Loop Road: A Guide to Acadia National Park's Scenic Byway*,** by Robert A. Thayer. From the steep coastal headlands to the rounded mountaintops rising above fragrant balsam forests, Maine's Mount Desert Island and Acadia National Park offer a remarkable diversity of natural and human history. This book guides the visitor along Acadia's famous twenty-one-mile Park Loop Road, providing a rich visual tour of the region's scenic beauty, natural preservation, and cultural significance. 0-89272-443-9

***The Coast of Maine: An Informal History & Guide*,** by Louise Dickinson Rich. In her own comfortable, witty, and vivid way, Louise Dickinson Rich takes the reader on an armchair tour of Maine's coast in a volume that is as informative, inspiring, and delightful today as when it was first published more than thirty years ago. 0-89272-342-4

Check your local bookstore, or order from Down East Books at 800-685-7962. Visa and MasterCard accepted.